Aesthetic Testimony

Aesthetic Testimony

An Optimistic Approach

JON ROBSON

Great Clarendon Street, Oxford, OX2 6DP,
United Kingdom

Oxford University Press is a department of the University of Oxford.
It furthers the University's objective of excellence in research, scholarship,
and education by publishing worldwide. Oxford is a registered trade mark of
Oxford University Press in the UK and in certain other countries

© Jon Robson 2022

The moral rights of the author have been asserted

First Edition published in 2022

Impression: 1

All rights reserved. No part of this publication may be reproduced, stored in
a retrieval system, or transmitted, in any form or by any means, without the
prior permission in writing of Oxford University Press, or as expressly permitted
by law, by licence or under terms agreed with the appropriate reprographics
rights organization. Enquiries concerning reproduction outside the scope of the
above should be sent to the Rights Department, Oxford University Press, at the
address above

You must not circulate this work in any other form
and you must impose this same condition on any acquirer

Published in the United States of America by Oxford University Press
198 Madison Avenue, New York, NY 10016, United States of America

British Library Cataloguing in Publication Data

Data available

Library of Congress Control Number: 2022941542

ISBN 978–0–19–286295–2

DOI: 10.1093/oso/9780192862952.001.0001

Printed and bound in the UK by
Clays Ltd, Elcograf S.p.A.

Links to third party websites are provided by Oxford in good faith and
for information only. Oxford disclaims any responsibility for the materials
contained in any third party website referenced in this work.

For Ann and Henry (but not Sara) Robson

Acknowledgements

My primary debt in the creation of this work is to Aaron Meskin who has provided far more support (both intellectual and otherwise) over the years than I've had any right to expect. Any novel contributions in what follows are merely 'footnotes to Meskin'. Rob Hopkins has also been exceptionally kind with his assistance at various stages of this project (especially given how much of it has been focused on arguing that his views are mistaken).

Many other people have contributed, through their helpful advice and feedback, to this book being less bad (and more written) than it would otherwise have been. These include Dani Adams, Sarah Adams, James Andow, Carl Baker, Tom Baker, Tom Crawley, Greg Currie, Trenton Q. Cyril, David Davies, Matt Duncombe, Maria Forsberg, Sasha Garwood, Allan Hazlett, Michael Hannon, Louise Hanson, Zach Hoskins, Andrew Huddleston, Anna Ichino, Mark Jago, Ali Kay, Matthew Kieran, Marcus Lee, Shen-yi Liao, Hans Maes, Penelope Mackie, Irene Martínez Marín, Annelies Monseré, Margaret Moore, Thi Nguyen, Jem Page, Emily Paul, Elisabeth Schellekens Dammann, Karen Simecek, Neil Sinclair, Ema Sullivan-Bissett, Rebecca Wallbank, Daniel Whiting, Nick Wiltshire, Chris Woodard, and, of course, the various excellent people who I forgot to include in this list (you were always my favourites). I am also exceptionally grateful for the helpful comments on an earlier draft by two anonymous readers from the Press and for Peter Momtchiloff's work as editor. Finally, I benefited greatly from comments from audiences at the ASA, BSA, and ESA, as well as audiences at talks in Aberdeen, Antwerp, Auburn, Leeds, Kent, Nottingham, Sheffield, Southampton, St Andrews, Uppsala, Wroclaw, and York.

I have drawn, with kind permission, on the following previously published works: Chapter 3 includes material from 'A Social Epistemology of Aesthetics.' *Synthese*, 191 (2013): 2513–28, and 'Against Aesthetic Exceptionalism' in H. Bradley, P. Noordhof, and E. Sullivan-Bissett *Art and the Nature of Belief*, Oxford University Press, 2017. Chapter 4 includes material from 'Aesthetic Testimony and the Norms of Belief Formation.' *European Journal of Philosophy*, 23 (2015): 750–63. Chapter 6 includes material from 'Norms of Belief and Norms of Assertion in Aesthetics.' *Philosophers' Imprint*, 15 (2015): 1–19.

Contents

Introduction 1
  0.1 Testimony: Aesthetic and Otherwise 1
  0.2 Testimony 2
  0.3 The History of the Debate 5
  0.4 The Purpose of This Work 9
  0.5 Overview 10

1. Optimism and Pessimism 13
  1.1 Optimism, Pessimism, and Aesthetic Judgement 13
  1.2 The Scope of the Aesthetic 13
  1.3 The Scope of Aesthetic Judgement 16
  1.4 What are Optimism and Pessimism? 18
  1.5 The Two Asymmetry Theses 20
  1.6 Optimistic Pessimists and Pessimistic Optimists 23
  1.7 Some Varieties of Pessimism 28
  1.8 Some Varieties of Optimism 30

2. Constitutive Pessimism 32
  2.1 A Royal Road to Pessimism? 32
  2.2 Pessimism by Stipulation 34
  2.3 Was Sibley a (Constitutive) Pessimist? 36
  2.4 Non-Cognitivism and Aesthetic Judgement 38
  2.5 Scruton, Todd, and Aesthetic Expressivism 42
  2.6 Lopes on Aesthetic Appreciation 46
  2.7 Appreciation Revisited 50

3. The Presumption of Optimism 54
  3.1 The Burden of Proof 54
  3.2 Pessimism and Folk Belief 55
  3.3 Pessimism and Folk Practice 57
  3.4 A Presumption of Optimism? 60
  3.5 Pessimists of the World Unite 64
  3.6 Constitutive Considerations 68
  3.7 Objections and Replies 71
  3.8 Beyond BP 73
  3.9 Constitutive Optimism? 78

x CONTENTS

4. Pessimism and the Appeal to Cases — 79
   - 4.1 Pessimism and Cases — 79
   - 4.2 Pessimistic Intuitions — 79
   - 4.3 Rejecting Pessimistic Intuitions — 82
   - 4.4 Accommodating Pessimistic Intuitions — 84
   - 4.5 Unusability Pessimism and Non-Epistemic Norms — 86
   - 4.6 Contextualism and Expertise — 88
   - 4.7 Contextualist Optimism — 94
   - 4.8 Some Further Cases — 96

5. Optimism and the Appeal to Cases — 99
   - 5.1 Pessimistic Intuitions and Optimistic Intuitions — 99
   - 5.2 Optimism and the Variety of Aesthetic Judgements — 99
   - 5.3 Rejecting Optimistic Intuitions — 101
   - 5.4 Accommodating Optimistic Intuitions — 103
   - 5.5 Optimistic Practices — 105
   - 5.6 The Unusability Account — 108
   - 5.7 Weighing Things up — 111
   - 5.8 Defending my Account — 113

6. Pessimism, Assertion, and Signalling — 119
   - 6.1 Aesthetics and Assertion — 119
   - 6.2 Norms of Assertion — 120
   - 6.3 The Argument from Assertion — 123
   - 6.4 The Appreciative Signalling Account — 124
   - 6.5 Some Initial Objections — 128
   - 6.6 A Further Worry — 130
   - 6.7 Analogues to the Aesthetic Signalling Account — 132

7. The Debate Concerning Assertion — 137
   - 7.1 The State of the Dialectic — 137
   - 7.2 Epistemic Explanations and Pragmatic Explanations — 138
   - 7.3 A Wider Range of Cases — 141
   - 7.4 A Gustatory Analogy — 144
   - 7.5 Summing up — 148
   - 7.6 A Third Contender — 149
   - 7.7 Where to Now? — 152

Bibliography — 155
Index — 165

Introduction

0.1. Testimony: Aesthetic and Otherwise

Philosophers haven't always held testimony in the highest regard. This is especially so if we focus, as I will in this work, on what Rob Hopkins (2011: 138) terms 'pure testimony' where a subject is asked to form the belief 'that *p* on the basis that her informant T claims that *p*, and independently of any evidence that T offers for that claim'. Extended discussions of testimony have been something of a rarity in the history of philosophy and, when testimony *is* mentioned, it is often to denigrate it in comparison to other sources of judgement. For example, while Augustine (2010: 66) admits that 'when speaking casually' we can legitimately allow that testimony provides us with knowledge, he is keen to stress that 'when we speak properly' we must deny that it does any such thing (ibid. 67). And John Locke (1689/1849: 49) famously insists that the 'floating of other men's opinions in our brains, makes us not one jot the more knowing, though they happen to be true. What in them was science, is in us but opiniatrity.'[1] There were, of course, some exceptions to this general trend—most notably Thomas Reid who argued at length that a reliance on testimony was crucial and that the 'wise and beneficent Author of Nature' intended 'that we should receive the greatest and most important of our knowledge by the information of others' (1983: 93)—but, for the most part, testimony was either denigrated or ignored.

Things have, however, shifted dramatically in recent years. First there has, particularly following the publication of C. A. J. Coady's (1992) influential monograph, been an explosion of philosophical interest in the nature and epistemology of testimony. Second, while there remain numerous controversies between recent writers on testimony—concerning, for example, the precise scope of genuine instances of testimony and the exact conditions under which we can acquire testimonial knowledge—there is a near consensus that testimony serves as 'a vital and ubiquitous source of knowledge' (Lackey 2006a: 432).[2] Or, rather, a consensus that testimony concerning *most* matters serves this role. It is, however, frequently claimed that there are some exceptions to this general trend, domains where there

---

[1] Though for doubts about whether this accurately represents Locke's considered view see Shieber (2009).

[2] So much so that Meskin (2006: 110) claims that the view 'that testimony may, at least under certain circumstances, provide justification and knowledge is as close to beyond dispute as philosophical matters get'.

Aesthetic Testimony: An Optimistic Approach. Jon Robson, Oxford University Press. © Jon Robson 2022.
DOI: 10.1093/oso/9780192862952.003.0001

is something peculiarly problematic about reliance on testimony. These domains include ethics (Hills 2009), gustatory taste (Sweeney 2007), mathematics (Williams 1972), religion (Jay 2016), and philosophy itself (Ranalli 2020). I will briefly touch on some of these positions in later chapters, but my primary focus will be on a single area, aesthetics. In particular, this work will discuss the view which has become known as 'pessimism concerning aesthetic testimony' (hereafter 'pessimism')—according to which we can't legitimately form aesthetic judgements on the basis of testimony. My primary aim in this book will be to argue that pessimism is mistaken and that we should accept the opposing view—optimism concerning aesthetic testimony (hereafter 'optimism')—according to which testimony *can* serve as a legitimate source of aesthetic judgement.[3]

This introduction is primarily intended to provide some useful background concerning the nature and scope of the aesthetic testimony debate. In §0.2, I introduce some of the key positions in general debates surrounding the nature and epistemology of testimony. §0.3 discusses the history of pessimism and differentiates the pessimist's view from the oft-discussed claim that legitimate aesthetic judgements can't be based on inferences from the non-aesthetic properties of a work. In §0.4 I consider some motivations for pursuing the particular debate I have narrowed in on. §0.5 offers a brief overview of my arguments in the remainder of this work.

0.2. Testimony

As already mentioned, the philosophical literature on testimony has been growing rapidly in the last few decades and this literature is replete with extended discussions of both the nature and epistemology of testimony. This work is not primarily intended as a contribution to these general debates but, rather, to provide an account of how testimony functions in one specific area, aesthetics. Still, such a discussion would be impossible to conduct without saying a little about testimony in general. In this section I will briefly focus on two questions which have been at the forefront of recent discussions of testimony. First, what precisely is included within the domain of testimony? Second, under what conditions can we acquire testimonial knowledge?

What is testimony? Coady (1992: 42) offers three individually necessary and jointly sufficient conditions for an instance of S testifying that *p*. First, that 'S's stating that *p* is evidence that *p* and is offered as evidence that *p*'. Second, 'S has the relevant competence, authority, or credentials to state truly that *p*'. And, finally, that 'S's statement that *p* is relevant to some disputed or unresolved

---

[3] The terms 'optimism' and 'pessimism' were first used by Hopkins (2007) as names for the moral analogues of these positions.

question (which may or may not be p) and is directed to those who are in need of evidence on the matter'. There is much that could be (and, indeed, has been) said concerning this proposed definition.[4] (Why, for example, limit testimony to cases which are disputed or unresolved?) For my purposes, though, the most concerning aspect of this account is the way in which it appears to rule out certain defective instances of testimony merely by fiat. There cannot be testimony from those who lack relevant competence etc. and, more generally, there cannot be any genuine instance of testimony that p which fails to count as providing some degree of evidence for p. These features certainly make Coady's account seem somewhat anomalous when proposed as a general definition of testimony (rather than, say, as a definition of successful instance of testimony). And, more troublingly for my purposes, it makes it controversial whether there are even genuine instances of aesthetic testimony. The optimist will allow that there are, but many pessimists will deny this.[5] Given this, it seems desirable to have an account of the nature of testimony which doesn't presuppose anything about its epistemic credentials.

Fortunately, there is no shortage of such definitions. Graham (1997: 227), for example, presents an adapted version of Coady's account according to which

G1. S's stating that p is offered as evidence that p

G2. S intends that his audience believe that he has the relevant competence, authority or credentials to state truly that p

G3. S's statement that p is believed by S to be relevant to some question that he believes is disputed or unresolved (which may or may not be p) and is directed at those whom he believes to be in need of evidence on the matter.

Lackey (2006b: 188) claims that 'S testifies that p by making an act of communication a if and only if S reasonably intends to convey the information that p (in part) in virtue of a's communicable content'.[6] And Sosa (1991: 219) presents a minimal account according to which one testifies 'that p if and only if one states one's belief that p'.[7] Each proposed definition of testimony is tasked not only with providing a plausible general account of testimony but also with offering verdicts concerning various problem cases. Can non-verbal responses (such as nodding one's head) count as testimony? What about a soliloquy which is overheard by

---

[4] For some criticisms of Coady's proposal see e.g. Lackey (2006b: 179–81) and Graham (1997: 227–31).

[5] Many but not all. As we will see in later chapters, some pessimists concede that there are those who are competent to offer aesthetic testimony (and indeed that such testimony can provide us with knowledge) but still deny that it is legitimate to form aesthetic judgements on the basis of testimony.

[6] Lackey's original definition uses 'testifies$_s$' to differentiate what she calls 'Speaker Testimony' from what she calls 'Hearer Testimony'. I will not be concerned with this distinction here.

[7] In a similar spirit Elizabeth Fricker (1995: 396) claims that testimony is the domain of 'tellings in general'.

eavesdroppers? What about what Roy Sorensen (2007) terms 'bald-faced lies' (that is, putative lies which are completely undisguised)?

For the purposes of this work, I won't be arguing for any particular account of testimony, nor will I be taking sides on the vast majority of disputed cases. Rather, I will aim to focus on cases of testimony which we should expect to uncontroversially come out as genuine on any prominent account.[8] I will, however, briefly highlight two points about the examples of testimony I will be focusing on. First, I will focus exclusively on cases where someone's testimony that 'P' is intended to support the claim that P (rather than those where it is intended to provide rather less direct support for some further claim). Second, I will focus exclusively on what we can learn based on the *content* of this testimony. The pessimist need not deny, for example, that I can legitimately believe that you have a beautiful singing voice based on your melodiously testifying to this fact. However, this is only because the manner in which your testimony is delivered—rather than the content of the testimony itself—does the epistemic work here.

A second question is under what conditions we can acquire testimonial knowledge. For the most part the history of this debate has been dominated by two views, reductionism and non-reductionism. The non-reductionist view, which is frequently traced back to Reid, is typically taken to be committed to something like the following pair of claims. First, that testimony is akin to perception in being a fundamental source of warrant. Second, that we have some kind of 'default entitlement' to accept testimony. That is to say that I am, in the absence of defeaters, warranted in forming the belief that P on the basis of your testimony that P (even in the absence of any other positive reason to believe P). Reductionists, whose view is often traced back to Hume, deny both of these claims. They hold that testimonial warrant isn't *sui generis* but, rather, that any warrant I have for believing your claim that P must ultimately be accounted for by appeal to sources other than testimony (by, for example, an inductive inference based on your previous track record of reliable testimony).[9] Further, they reject the default entitlement claim and argue that I need to have some, sufficiently weighty, positive reason(s) to legitimately accept a piece of testimony. Discussion of these two competing views has tended to dominate the literature on the epistemology of testimony (with the non-reductionist view proving the most influential) but a number of other candidate views have recently entered the field.[10] These include hybrid views (which combine elements of reductionism with elements of

---

[8] Excluding those (such as Coady's) which build epistemic demands into the definition of testimony.

[9] Importantly this epistemic claim does not entail—as some critics of reductionism (such as Coady (1992: 143)) seem to suggest—the manifestly implausible psychological claim that I actually perform an inference of this kind every time I (legitimately) accept a piece of testimony. Rather, all that is required is (roughly) that I am in possession of some evidence which would support this inference.

[10] Fricker (1994) presents one of the few contemporary versions of reductionism. Prominent non-reductionists include Coady (1992) and Burge (1993).

non-reductionism) and interpersonal views (which stress the importance of factors, such as trust, which only arise because testimonial exchanges occur between persons).[11]

As with debates surrounding the nature of testimony, I will aim to remain largely silent on the general question of how we acquire testimonial knowledge. While my own sympathies lie with the Reidian non-reductionist tradition, I will not be arguing for this view (since doing so would require an exceedingly lengthy diversion away from my main line of argument). Thankfully, no such argument is needed since my arguments against the pessimist are intended to be largely neutral between the various competing contemporary accounts of the epistemology of testimony.

There is, however, a related issue on which I *will* have something to say in what follows. As we will see in later chapters, many pessimists have proposed that the account we offer of the conditions for testimonial knowledge (or legitimate judgement) in the aesthetic case should differ from that which we endorse in (most) non-aesthetic cases.[12] I will argue in subsequent chapters (especially Chapter 3) that this position is mistaken and that there is no fundamental difference between the requirements for knowledge in cases of aesthetic testimony and those in cases of non-aesthetic testimony. The conditions required for acquiring aesthetic knowledge via testimony are just the conditions—whatever these may be—for acquiring *any* knowledge via testimony. One consequence of this will be that there is no need to offer any specifically *aesthetic* account of the nature of testimonial knowledge. What I offer in this work, then, is not such an account but, inter alia, an account of the ways in which I believe pessimists (and others) have mistakenly supposed that there is something exceptional when it comes to the epistemology of aesthetic testimony.

0.3. The History of the Debate

The locus classicus for discussion of the supposedly exceptional nature of aesthetic testimony is Kant's third Critique and, in particular, his famous claim that

> If a man...does not find a building, a prospect, or a poem beautiful, a hundred voices all highly praising it will not force his innermost agreement...he clearly sees that the agreement of others gives no valid proof of the judgment about beauty...that a thing has pleased others could never serve as the basis for an aesthetical judgment. (1790/2005: 94)

---

[11] See e.g. Lackey (2008) and Faulkner (2011), respectively.
[12] Indeed, as we will also see, some pessimists take this claim to be constitutive of being a pessimist. I will, however, argue in §1.6 that this position is mistaken and that a genuine pessimist could reject this claim (and a genuine optimist endorse it).

As with much of Kant's work this claim has been subject to a range of radically different interpretations.[13] It is clear that Kant is dismissive of the idea of using testimony to ground an aesthetic judgement, but it is far more controversial precisely what his concern is. On one interpretation, Kant is claiming that there would be something illegitimate (either epistemically or otherwise) about forming aesthetic judgements on the basis of testimony. On another, he is claiming that it is literally impossible to form such judgements in this way. I will briefly return to these exegetical issues in Chapter 2, but my main concern isn't with the details of Kant's own view but, rather, with the ways in which his comments have influenced subsequent discussions of the role of testimony within aesthetics.

The most striking feature of historical discussions of aesthetic testimony after Kant is their absence. Kant's own discussion of testimony is frustratingly brief and he quickly moves on from claiming that testimony cannot serve as a source of (legitimate) aesthetic judgement to rejecting the use of inference—at least where such an inference is 'determined by an a priori proof, in accordance with determinate rules' (1790/2005: 94)—in forming aesthetic judgements.[14] It is this latter point which enjoys far more detailed examination within Kant's Critique and the role (or lack of same) for inferences in forming aesthetic judgements has been a mainstay of subsequent discussion. In particular, Kant (1790/2005: 95) famously argues that we should reject an appeal to any 'principle of taste' in aesthetics. That is, an appeal to 'a principle under the condition of which we could subsume the concept of an object and thus infer by means of a syllogism that the object is beautiful' (ibid.). For Kant and his contemporaries—such as Alison (1790/2019) and Knight (1805/2018)—the focus was on the question of whether we could identify some feature(s) of an object—such as Hutcheson's (1726/2004) famous 'uniformity amidst variety'—from which we could validly deduce that the object in question *must* be beautiful (or possess some other aesthetic property).[15]

Turning to the rather more recent history of aesthetics, the debate surrounding the legitimacy of inferences based on principles of this kind proved to be one of the central pillars in twentieth-century aesthetics.[16] While it would be difficult to find anyone in these debates defending the specific claim which Kant appears to be attacking—that we can make deductively valid inferences from a work's possessing a particular non-aesthetic property to its being beautiful—there have been some notable defences of rather weaker versions of this thesis. For example,

---

[13] For a discussion of some of these interpretations see Gorodeisky (2010).
[14] Kant himself clearly holds these two sources of judgement to be importantly distinct since he notes (ibid.) that the latter is even more problematic than the former (though, again, his reasons for claiming this are far from clear).
[15] As Shelley (1998: 30) discusses, earlier writers (such as Hume) use 'principle of taste' in an importantly different sense.
[16] Some key contributions to this debate (in addition to those cited below) include Isenberg (1949), Kennick (1958), Sibley (1959), Hungerland (1968), Dickie (1987). For a more recent exegetical take on the debate see Bergqvist (2010).

Monroe Beardsley (1962) claims that there are certain features which always serve to make a work better (and other features which always tend to make it worse).[17] He argues that this would allow us to infer of a work, from the fact that it possesses one of these properties, that it is aesthetically better (or worse) than it would have been otherwise. Others rejected even these diluted appeals to critical principles. Mary Mothersill (1961: 75), for example, maintains that there 'is *no* characteristic which is amenable to independent explanation and which by its presence enhances the aesthetic value' of a work (or of any sub-class of works).

I do not propose to offer any thoughts about the legitimacy of inferences based on critical reasons here. Rather, my aim is merely to highlight two things. First, this debate has very little connection to controversy surrounding testimony in aesthetics.[18] As mentioned above, it is very rare for contemporary philosophers working in the epistemology of testimony to regard testimonial warrant as inferential in nature (and even those who do so take the inferences in question to concern, for example, the track record of the testifier).[19] Second, the debate over principles of taste enjoyed a long period of prominence (roughly coinciding with the second half of the twentieth century) during which the issue of the role of aesthetic testimony was largely neglected. Indeed, discussions of aesthetic testimony didn't become commonplace until the start of the twenty-first century, with the emergence of a trio of influential papers—Hopkins (2000), Budd (2003), and Meskin (2004)—which took the debate surrounding aesthetic testimony as their central focus (prior to this there wasn't, so far as I am aware, a single work which primarily focused on the debate surrounding aesthetic testimony).[20]

This is not, of course, to claim that intervening period was entirely devoid of discussions of aesthetic testimony, and readers who are even passingly familiar with some of the key debates in twentieth-century aesthetics will doubtless be poised to cite some examples. However, as I will discuss at length in Chapter 2, it is by no means clear that some influential aestheticians—most prominently Frank Sibley—who are often taken to endorse pessimism really did anything of the sort.

So far as I am aware, the first significant and unambiguous investigation of aesthetic testimony in the twentieth century arose out of Tormey's discussion of critical judgement (which he takes (1973: 35) to be synonymous with 'aesthetic

---

[17] Beardsley (1962) goes on to claim that this applies not only to individual features but also to 'pairs and clusters of features', some of which 'contribute value, to speak, on their own while others do so only in combination'.
[18] One exception here is that there are, as we will see later, certain general principles in aesthetics which are often taken to rule out both judgements based on inferences from critical principles and those based on testimony.
[19] It is important to stress that—as highlighted by e.g. Mothersill (1961: 77-8)—we could deny that critical reasons give us any licence (whether inferential or otherwise) to accept the critic's judgement without thereby denying that there is any value to the enterprise of critical reason giving.
[20] Although it does occupy a significant percentage of the discussion in Zangwill (1990).

judgement').²¹ Tormey followed earlier discussions in taking (something like) direct experience to be a necessary condition for (legitimate) aesthetic judgement, claiming (1973: 39) that 'in *art*, unlike the law, we do not admit judgments in the absence of direct or immediate experience of the object of the judgment'.²² Where he differs from many of his predecessors, though, is in taking care to explicitly note (1973: 38) that cases of reliance on testimony are intended to be excluded from the realm of critical judgement. Still, his discussion of testimony is rather brief and leaves a number of important points underexplored (it isn't clear, for example, whether he takes reliance on testimony to be distinct from reliance on inference tout court or merely from inferences based on various non-aesthetic properties of the works themselves).²³

Another well-known exception to this general trend of neglect occurs during Richard Wollheim's discussion of the Acquaintance Principle (*AP*) according to which 'judgements of aesthetic value, unlike judgements of moral knowledge, must be based on first-hand experience of their objects' (1980: 233).²⁴ This general principle is quickly followed by the more specific claim that such judgements are not, 'except within very narrow limits, transmissible from one person to another' (ibid.). That is, a denial that such judgements can be (legitimately) formed on the basis of testimony. However, Wollheim's brief remarks on testimony here are rather gnomic and there is famously no account of what these 'very narrow' limits might be.²⁵

Philip Pettit (1983) offers a rather more detailed examination of the role of testimony in aesthetics. He begins with the claim that—in contrast to ordinary matters where both 'perception and testimony may count as titles to the full knowledge of the truth which that sentence expresses' (1983: 25)—perception is the only route to 'full knowledge' in aesthetics. He then goes on (ibid. 28–33) to argue at length that we can explain the impermissibility of aesthetic testimony

---

²¹ I welcome the inevitable counterexamples from those with a more comprehensive knowledge of the history of aesthetics.
²² I say 'something like' since Tormey (1973: 35) allows that aesthetic judgements can also be based on an encounter with 'adequate surrogates' for the work themselves. As subsequent discussion (such as Livingston (2003)) has made clear, though, it is no easy matter to specify what precisely qualifies as an adequate surrogate here. As is the case with Kant, it isn't entirely clear whether Tormey is laying out conditions for making a genuinely aesthetic judgement or merely for such judgements being legitimate.
²³ When he first introduces a case of reliance on the testimony of 'an art historian and critic for whom I have great respect' (and with whom I have frequently agreed in the past) on some aesthetic matter, he suggests that it might 'seem on purely inductive grounds that I have excellent reasons' to share this judgement (Tormey 1973: 38). Yet, he also explicitly distinguishes between 'inference and [testimonial] authority' as distinct 'avenues of evidence' (1973: 39).
²⁴ While *AP* is now closely associated with Wollheim, he clearly doesn't take himself to have originated this principle—as some of the references above illustrate—but, rather, sees it as 'a well-entrenched principle in aesthetics' (1980: 233).
²⁵ Lopes (2014b: 173–4) has recently denied that this remark even concerns testimony. For reasons to reject this interpretation see Wallbank and Robson (2022).

while still endorsing realism in aesthetics.[26] While Pettit differs from his predecessors in giving extended consideration to the role of testimony, he shares their tendency to treat the truth of pessimism (and of more general principles such as *AP*) as a datum to be explained rather than as a controversial thesis to be argued for. In recent years things have, thankfully, shifted in this respect and—owing to influential work by e.g. Budd (2003), Meskin (2004), and Brian Laetz (2008)—optimism is now generally regarded as a live option. Still, most contemporary discussions still regard pessimism (or, at best, some of the rather pessimistic variants of optimism I will discuss in the next chapter) as the default position in these debates. In this book, I will argue that this is a mistake and that we should endorse an unflinchingly optimistic stance concerning aesthetic testimony. When it comes to aesthetic testimony, the glass is (at least) half full.

0.4. The Purpose of This Work

My main aim in this book is to defend a version of optimism according to which testimony in aesthetics doesn't differ in any fundamental way from testimony in other domains. In some respects, this may seem like a rather strange project, and it would be bizarre indeed to imagine someone writing a parallel book arguing for the (presumably true) claims that testimony concerning narwhals or nitrogen is fundamentally the same as testimony about other matters. The main disanalogy between these cases is, of course, that the aesthetic claim has been so frequently denied. A large part of my purpose is, therefore, a negative one, arguing that the numerous philosophers who have taken there to be something importantly anomalous about the aesthetic case—and those who have defended broader principles such as *AP*—are mistaken. Further, I hope to say something illuminating about why these mistaken positions have seemed so attractive to so many.[27] My purpose is not entirely negative, though, and my defence of optimism will also require our adopting some controversial positive theses—concerning, for example, the nature of aesthetic assertion and the psychology of aesthetic judgement formation.

Finally, I fondly hope that this work will serve as a 'ground-clearing' exercise when it comes to further investigations into social epistemology within aesthetics. Epistemology in general has benefited a great deal in recent decades from a 'social turn' towards considering 'epistemic properties of individuals that arise from their relations to others, as well as epistemic properties of groups or social

---

[26] The account Pettit offers fails to explain the illegitimacy of aesthetic testimony for reasons highlighted in Budd (2003).
[27] I suspect that there will also be lessons to learn from this when it comes to combating those who argue for an analogue of pessimism in e.g. the moral case. I will not, however, pursue that project directly.

systems' (Goldman 2010: 1). This has led to a considerable increase in our understanding of the nature of testimony, of disagreement, of pathologies of social epistemology (such as echo chambers), and much more besides.[28] These developments have, however, been slow to make inroads within aesthetics. One reason for this is, doubtless, the thought that aesthetic judgement is a peculiarly anti-social matter.[29] We seem, as Nguyen (2020a: 1127) puts things, to 'want appreciators to arrive at their aesthetic judgments through their own cognitive efforts'. Once we realize, though, how ubiquitous and essential our reliance on testimony is, this barrier to the integration of social epistemology within aesthetics will be lifted. These, at least, are my aims.[30] In the next section, I will explain in a little more detail how I plan on realizing them.

0.5. Overview

The claim that testimony cannot serve as a legitimate source of aesthetic judgement is problematically under-specified in a number of respects. In particular, it is unclear both how broad the scope of the aesthetic is intended to be, which of the manifold senses of 'judgement' is being employed here, and what precisely is meant by 'legitimate'. The main purpose of Chapter 1 will be to get clear on precisely what claim the pessimist is making (and the optimist denying). After clarifying some key aspects of the pessimist's claim, I then go on to distinguish between two competing contemporary versions of pessimism. The first, unavailability pessimism, claims that we cannot achieve aesthetic knowledge on the basis of testimony. The second, unusability pessimism, allows that aesthetic judgements formed on the basis of testimony can sometimes attain the status of knowledge but maintains that there is some additional (non-epistemic) norm which still renders such judgements illegitimate. Finally, I introduce my own preferred optimistic view.

In Chapter 2 I focus on some prominent defences of pessimism which take this view to be entailed by the very nature of aesthetic judgement, with the result that it is impossible (rather than impermissible) to form aesthetic judgements on the basis of testimony. In particular, I focus in detail on attempts to motivate this 'constitutive pessimists' view by appeal to expressivist accounts of the nature of aesthetic judgement as well as to accounts which link such judgements very closely to some form of appreciation. I argue that each of these defences either proves unconvincing or else renders the constitutive pessimist's view (virtually)

---

[28] See e.g. Lackey (2008), Christensen (2009), and Nguyen (2020b).
[29] For scepticism concerning the epistemic role of disagreement in aesthetics see Hopkins (2001).
[30] One further, though rather niche, aim of this book is to give a satisfactory explanation to my sister of how I can be so confident that the *Twilight* novels are terrible despite never having read them. A large part of me probably cares more about that aim than any of the others.

trivial. I conclude, then, that we must look beyond constitutive motivations if we are going to find a compelling reason to endorse pessimism.

Chapter 3 begins with a discussion of the pessimist who maintains that it is not necessary for them to support their view by appeal to argument, since it is the natural default position with respect to aesthetic testimony. I argue that this view is mistaken and that there should, on the contrary, be a presumption of optimism. I begin by surveying, and rejecting, some candidate motivations for taking pessimism to be the default view. In particular, I focus on attempts to motivate pessimism by appeal to the claim that, in contrast to other areas where testimony is uncontroversially acceptable, we typically *don't* form aesthetic judgements on the basis of testimony. I argue that this claim is mistaken and that we frequently do form aesthetic judgements in this way. I then go on to motivate a presumption in favour of optimism by appeal both to this descriptive fact and to the difficulties which the pessimist encounters in taking the role of testimony in aesthetics to be so markedly different from the role of testimony in (most) other domains. Finally, I argue that there is not only reason to accept a presumption in favour of optimism but also good grounds for endorsing a constitutive version of optimism (according to which the optimistic view of aesthetic testimony is entailed by the very nature of aesthetic judgement).

One common motivation for pessimism comes via an appeal to intuitions concerning various cases. The pessimist will describe some situation where they claim that (i) an individual forms an aesthetic judgement on the basis of testimony, (ii) the standard conditions for testimonial knowledge (in non-aesthetic cases) are met, and (iii) the individual's aesthetic judgement is intuitively illegitimate. In Chapter 4 I offer two lines of argument against using such appeals to motivate pessimism. First, I briefly highlight some reasons for being sceptical as to whether these 'pessimistic intuitions' really carry much epistemic weight. Second, I argue that (even granting the force of these intuitions) it is possible to construct an optimistic view which can incorporate many of these intuitions. In order to demonstrate this, I spend the majority of the chapter outlining an account of this kind (one which draws on some insights from contextualist theories in epistemology).

In Chapter 5 I argue that a large portion of the apparent intuitive appeal of pessimism comes from a tendency to focus on a very narrow range of cases, and that consideration of a wider range of cases quickly unearths a great deal of intuitive support for optimism. This includes appeal to intuitions about certain kinds of aesthetic judgement (such as those concerning lost works) as well as to various aspects of our aesthetic practice which are best explained by an appeal to optimism. I then move on to ask which view of the epistemology of aesthetic testimony is best able to account for the full range of cases (combining discussion of the cases outlined in this chapter with those discussed in Chapter 4). I argue that standard versions of optimism fare better here than either unavailability or unusability versions of pessimism, but that even these perform less well than my own preferred optimistic view.

Chapters 6 and 7 consider an argument for pessimism based on the impermissibility of assertions such as 'the painting is exquisitely beautiful, but I've never seen it' or 'the melody is graceful but I've never heard it'. A natural explanation here is that these assertions are illegitimate because we cannot *know* the aesthetic claims which they express in the absence of direct experience and so, a fortiori, cannot know them on the basis of testimony.

In Chapter 6 I argue that pessimistic explanations of this kind aren't the only option and that, on the contrary, the optimist can offer an independently plausible (and non-ad hoc) account of this infelicity. The explanation I offer draws on a comparison with accounts of aesthetic creation according to which one key role of aesthetic creativity is to signal to our conspecifics that we possess various advantageous qualities. I argue that an account of this kind can be expanded to other areas of aesthetic practice including, crucially, critical discourse. I propose that it is, ultimately, the misleading signals that the relevant assertions produce within critical discourse, rather than their violation of a knowledge norm, which makes them problematic. I then defend my account from some immediate objections.

In Chapter 7 I compare the plausibility of the account I offered in the previous chapter with that of the pessimist's preferred account. I argue that—as with the debate in Chapters 4 and 5—the pessimist's position gains some initial attraction by focusing on a selective range of cases but discussion of a full range of cases ultimately favours the optimist. I also briefly consider, and reject, some alternative explanations which a pessimist might offer for the impermissibility of the relevant assertions.

1
Optimism and Pessimism

1.1. Optimism, Pessimism, and Aesthetic Judgement

In the introduction, I briefly presented pessimism as the claim that aesthetic judgements cannot legitimately be formed on the basis of testimony and optimism as the denial of this claim. These positions are, however, underspecified in various important respects. Most obviously, it is unclear both how broad the scope of the aesthetic is intended to be here, what precisely is meant by 'judgement', and what the (il)legitimacy in question amounts to. The primary aim of this chapter will be to clarify what claim the pessimist is making (and the optimist denying) with respect to aesthetic testimony.

I begin, in §1.2, by considering various controversies concerning the 'aesthetic' part of 'aesthetic judgement' and declare myself (for present purposes at least) neutral with respect to such debates. In §1.3 I take a less ecumenical stance and outline my own preferred understanding of the 'judgement' part of 'aesthetic judgement'. In §1.4–§1.6, I consider some further questions about how best to understand the debate between the optimist and the pessimist. The upshot of these sections is twofold. First, that a genuine pessimist can allow that *some* aesthetic judgements are legitimately formed on the basis of testimony. Second, that even such a limited pessimism must still maintain that there is some significant, though defeasible, difficulty with forming our aesthetic judgements in this manner. §1.7 outlines some competing contemporary versions of pessimism in order to arrive at a better sense of what the pessimist's claim of illegitimacy amounts to. Finally, in §1.8, I survey some extant optimistic positions before briefly introducing some key aspects of my preferred form of optimism.

1.2. The Scope of the Aesthetic

What is it for a particular judgement to be an *aesthetic* judgement? To answer this question, we will need to turn our attention to some of the ongoing debates concerning the scope of the aesthetic. These debates have—to run the risk of comical understatement—failed to achieve any consensus as to the precise delineation between the aesthetic and the non-aesthetic.

First, there are debates concerning which objects are capable of instantiating aesthetic properties. For example, some, such as Monroe Beardsley (1981: 46), have maintained that '[t]he aesthetic object is a perceptual object' (that is, an 'object some of whose qualities, at least, are open to direct sensory awareness' (1981: 31).[1] Whereas opponents have argued that some objects which aren't (straightforwardly) perceptible—such as certain works of conceptual art (Costello 2007), people's characters (Novitz 1991), mathematical theories (Breitenbach 2015), and God (Robson 2011)—are capable of instantiating aesthetic properties.

Further, even within the domain of the perceptual, there are debates over which non-art objects can instantiate such properties. There is, of course, a long tradition (see e.g. Aristotle (1997: 14–15), Hume (1757/1875: 85), and Kant (1790/2005: 48–50)) of ascribing aesthetic properties to (the more scenic elements of) the natural world.[2] Discussion of the putative aesthetic properties of non-artworks has, however, become the focus of an intense degree of philosophical attention in recent years, leading some philosophers to ascribe aesthetic properties to a vast range of objects including 'unscenic' nature (Saito 1998), food and drink (Korsmeyer 2002), and even bodily sensations such as itches (Irvin 2008). On the other hand, sceptics regarding this expansion—such as Brian Soucek (2009)—have argued that this tendency towards broadening the scope of the aesthetic would, if taken to its natural conclusion, undermines any meaningful distinction between the aesthetic and the non-aesthetic.

Other debates regarding the scope of the aesthetic concern which *properties* are genuinely aesthetic. Consider, for example, Frank Sibley's famous distinction between aesthetic concepts and aesthetic verdicts. Many philosophers of art have tended to focus their discussion of the aesthetic on Sibleyan aesthetic concepts (gracefulness, gaudiness garishness, and the like), sometimes combined with a denial that what Sibley (1965: 136) terms aesthetic 'verdicts'—that is, 'purely evaluative judgments' as to 'whether things are aesthetically good or bad, excellent or mediocre, superior to others or inferior, and so on'—are really aesthetic at all.[3] Other views of the aesthetic include, inter alia, properties which are the subject of both judgements and verdicts in Sibley's sense. Indeed, as Berys Gaut (1998: 183) highlights, 'aesthetic value' is sometimes used in a way which is synonymous with 'the value of an object *qua* work of art, that is its artistic value'. While Gaut (1998) and others have defended the utility of this this wider

---

[1] Others have argued that we should restrict the scope of the aesthetic to certain sensory modalities. For instance, Roger Scruton (1979: 114) has argued that the so-called 'lower senses' (such as smell and taste) aren't able to provide us with genuinely aesthetic experiences. For arguments against this view see e.g. Baker (2016).

[2] For an overview of the history of the aesthetic study of the natural world see the first chapter of Carlson (2000).

[3] For some discussions of the nature and relevance of Sibleyan aesthetic concepts see the various essays in Brady and Levinson (2001).

understanding of the aesthetic, opponents (such as Zangwill 2002) have criticized it for being overly permissive.[4]

Nor is there even a consensus that all aesthetic properties need to be evaluative properties. Indeed, Sibley's own (1959: 421) representative list of aesthetic concepts includes some such as *sombre* and *tragic* which either aren't themselves evaluative or, at the very least, fail to wear their evaluative nature on their sleeves.

Of course, this brief (and by no means exhaustive) survey hardly does justice to the various subtle and complex positions within these debates. However, my aim is not to propound a full account of these controversies, and still less to resolve any of them, but merely to use them to illustrate that delineating the exact (or even approximate) scope of the aesthetic is no easy matter. Fortunately, though, I need not attempt to do so here. For each candidate sense of 'aesthetic' there is a corresponding form of pessimism. One form of pessimism will maintain that we are unable to legitimately form Sibleyan aesthetic judgements on the basis of testimony, another that we are unable to form aesthetic verdicts, and yet another that we cannot form either. Similarly, one form of pessimism will restrict its scope to sensibilia whereas another will extend it to include the putatively aesthetic properties of mathematical theories.[5] My aim in later chapters will be to convince you that *all* of these forms of pessimism should be rejected. Given this, there will (for my purposes at least) be no need to reach any conclusions regarding how best to delineate the scope of the aesthetic.

Despite this ecumenical stance, it will still be necessary (in order to keep subsequent discussions to a manageable length) to make some decisions as to which objects, and which properties, will form the focus of my investigation in later chapters. In terms of my choice of objects, I will aim to be fairly conservative, focusing primarily on those objects which have been (almost) unanimously accepted as proper objects of aesthetic evaluation. In terms of the range of properties discussed, I will be focusing primarily on straightforward cases of *evaluative* aesthetic properties.[6] Within the scope of such evaluative properties, though, my focus will be rather broad. Previous discussions of aesthetic testimony have featured detailed discussions of cases involving both judgements and verdicts in

---

[4] Importantly, many of those who are critical of the wider notion of the aesthetic are still happy to allow that (some of) the properties Gaut lists are relevant to the assessment of art. For a debate concerning the tenability of this category of non-aesthetic artistic value see Lopes (2011) and Hanson (2013).

[5] For comparison, consider the various debates concerning the Acquaintance Principle and the scope of the aesthetic in Hanson (2015), Konigsberg (2012), and Robson (2013).

[6] I do not mean to suggest that these are the only genuinely aesthetic properties (nor the only ones concerning which someone might wish to advocate for some form of pessimism). Indeed, Roger Scruton's (1976) paradigm example of an aesthetic attribution in his defence of pessimism concerns describing a work as 'sad'—an attribution which doesn't carry any apparent evaluative force. Of course, appearances here may be deceptive and some may be inclined to maintain—as e.g. Levinson (2001: 80) and Young (2017: 9) suggest with respect to properties such as *dark* and *tragic*—that *sad*, in its aesthetic sense, is actually a thick evaluative concept.

Sibley's sense.[7] And, more generally, these debates feature frequent reference to both 'thick' and 'thin' evaluative concepts.[8] Given this, restricting myself to an exclusive focus on either thick or thin aesthetic judgements would risk overlooking some important aspects of the aesthetic testimony debate as it has thus far been conducted. This broad focus is, however, liable to prove controversial. Meskin (2004: 69), for example, is explicit that his defence of optimism is only intended to apply to thin '"verdictive aesthetic properties" (e.g. aesthetic or artistic goodness) rather than [thick] "substantive aesthetic properties" such as fragility or elegance'.[9] By contrast, several pessimists have indicated (in conversation) that their pessimism is intended to apply primarily, perhaps even exclusively, to thick aesthetic evaluations. Fortunately, I do not think that very much hangs on this issue for my purposes. Although my arguments will frequently be framed in terms of one particular kind of aesthetic evaluation, this dependence is, for the most part, merely superficial (and a sceptical reader could easily substitute an example involving other kinds of evaluation).

Before moving on from debates about the scope of the aesthetic, though, it's worth highlighting one way in which these debates themselves might tell in favour of optimism. One lesson which we might be tempted to draw from such widespread disagreement is that there *is* no single precise divide between those judgements which are aesthetic and those which are not. Rather, what we have is a range of different uses of 'aesthetic', most of which appear to allow—alongside paradigm aesthetic and paradigm non-aesthetic judgements—a variety of borderline, inconclusive, or otherwise problematic cases. If something like this picture is right, though, then the pessimist's position—with its sharp contrast between aesthetic and non-aesthetic in testimonial matters—becomes harder to motivate. Still, I don't intend to place much argumentative weight on this speculative suggestion, since the lesson I suggest here is far from being the only moral which could be drawn from observing the continued debates concerning the scope of the aesthetic.[10]

1.3. The Scope of Aesthetic Judgement

When it comes to the 'judgement' part of 'aesthetic judgement', even a brief examination of the literature demonstrates that this term has been used in a plethora of

---

[7] For some representative examples of the former see Budd (2003: 387–91), Laetz (2008: 355), and Whiting (2015: 91). For examples of the latter see Gorodeisky (2010: 53), Hopkins (2011: 138), and Hazlett (2017: 49).
[8] For a useful overview of the distinction between thick and thin evaluative properties see the essays in Kirchin (2013).
[9] The terminology Meskin employs is from Zangwill (1995).
[10] I will, however, return to a variation on this theme in Chapter 7.

different ways in aesthetics.[11] Consider, for example, the relationship between judgement and belief. 'Aesthetic judgement' has sometimes been used as a synonym for 'aesthetic belief' (Hopkins 2006), sometimes in a way which makes belief a necessary (but not sufficient) condition for such judgements (Tormey 1973), and sometimes contrasted with belief (Todd 2004).

One potential response to this confusion would be to maintain, as I have with the 'aesthetic' part of 'aesthetic judgement' above, that optimism is true (and thus pessimism false) for any candidate understanding of 'judgement'. In this case, though, such a sweeping claim would be mistaken, since there are some senses of 'judgement' according to which we cannot legitimately form aesthetic judgements on the basis of testimony. However, I will argue in the next chapter that this is not the boon to my opponents which it may initially appear. For the time being, though, I will merely stipulate that my preferred sense of 'judgement' is the one often employed in debates within metaethics, such that judgements are something like:

> a set of mental states, the contents of which can be expressed by a declarative sentence. If Pepe judges that his inbox is not his postbox, his judgement is a mental state with content expressible by the indicative sentence 'My inbox is not my postbox'. (Lillehammer 2002: 1–2)

I say 'something like' since this account, as it stands, would include a rather wider range of mental states—including imaginings and suppositions—as judgements than I intend to allow. A complete account would need to add some additional constraints such that a judgement is not just expressed by a declarative sentence but 'by sincere assertoric use of [such] a sentence' (Sinclair 2006: 253) or that a judgment correlates with the mental state of 'someone who competently, sincerely and without delusion about their own state of mind utters' (Ridge 2009: 198) some claim. In what follows, I will aim to accommodate such insights by adopting a working definition of 'aesthetic judgements' according to which this phrase refers to the set of mental states which correspond to competent sincere aesthetic assertions.

Although I have presented my preferred understanding of 'judgement', I don't mean to suggest that this is the single correct usage of 'judgement' nor even that it is the only usage appropriate within aesthetics. Rather, my aim is the significantly more modest one of proposing that this account provides us with the best understanding of 'judgement' when it comes to conducting the debate over aesthetic testimony. This is primarily because it allows us to conceptualize this debate in a

---

[11] And within philosophy more generally (see e.g. Shah and Velleman 2005: 503).

way which doesn't immediately prejudice the debate in favour of any particular view.

My reasons for holding this should become clearer in the next chapter. For now, though, it's worth briefly highlighting one additional advantage of this account: that it allows us to conduct the aesthetic testimony debate while remaining neutral regarding some important controversies in meta-aesthetics. The account is, of course, compatible with taking aesthetic judgements to be beliefs in a straightforward cognitive sense (which, for the record, is how I think we should regard them) but it does not commit us to treating them as such. Rather, it is intended—as I will explore further in the next chapter—to be neutral between a range of meta-aesthetic accounts of the mental correlates of aesthetic assertion. Most relevantly, it is compatible with the position of those, such as Scruton (1976), Blackburn (1998), and Todd (2004: 290) who maintain that we should understand these mental correlates in expressivist terms. In most of this work I will, for ease of exposition only, largely talk as if aesthetic judgements are beliefs in a straightforwardly cognitivist sense. I will, however, pause at times to consider cases where adopting a different meta-aesthetic account may make a difference to the arguments I will offer.

Some may worry, though, that my preferred usage of 'judgement' is question-begging. After all, I have already conceded that there are some senses of 'judgement' according to which pessimism will be the correct view of aesthetic testimony. Given this, shouldn't my opponent merely adopt one of these understandings of 'judgement' in formulating their claims regarding the proper conditions for aesthetic judgement? In the next chapter, I will aim to demonstrate that they should not. In particular, I will argue that any understanding of 'judgement' which renders the corresponding form of pessimism true would either be trivial or else fail to meet some key desiderata for a pessimist account. For now, though, let's work with the account of judgement I have outlined and ask where this leaves us with respect to the debate over aesthetic testimony.[12]

1.4. What are Optimism and Pessimism?

The aim of the previous sections was to clarify what I will mean when ascribing certain views regarding aesthetic judgement to optimists or pessimists. Even with these clarifications in place, though, more needs to be said to explicate the claim which the pessimist is making (and the optimist denying). In this section, I will offer a more precise account of the controversy between these two camps.

---

[12] Those not interested in the details of these claims can safely skip to §1.6.

To begin, it is important to note that some of those who maintain that it is never legitimate to form aesthetic judgements on the basis of testimony will not qualify as pessimists in the sense which is relevant to the present investigation. Consider, for example, the kind of global sceptic who denies that *any* judgement, aesthetic or otherwise, is ever legitimate. A sceptic of this stripe would, *a fortiori*, deny that we can legitimately form aesthetic judgements on the basis of testimony. Something similar would also apply to a more specific kind of sceptic who denies—perhaps owing to the kinds of consideration outlined in Irvin (2014), Lopes (2014a), and Meskin (n.d.)—that any of our *aesthetic* judgements are ever legitimate.[13] Finally, someone who specifically denied the legitimacy of all *testimonial* judgements (aesthetic or otherwise) would also fail to count as a pessimist. While I believe that each of these broader sceptical views is mistaken, it is no part of my purpose in this work to argue against them. My pessimist opponent intends to draw some important *contrast* with first-hand aesthetic judgements as well as judgements formed via testimony in (most) non-aesthetic domains.[14] Given this, my earlier rough characterization of pessimism—as the claim that it is illegitimate to form aesthetic judgements on the basis of testimony—stands in need of some amendment.

A natural suggestion for such an amendment would be to take the pessimist's position to be a combination of this initial statement with the further claim that first-hand aesthetic judgements, and testimonial judgements concerning non-aesthetic matters, are sometimes (indeed often) legitimate. It is far from clear, though, that the pessimist should accept that it is *never* legitimate to form aesthetic judgements on the basis of testimony. While the pessimist's position is often stated in these stark terms (see e.g. Hopkins 2011: 139, Lord 2016: 1, McKinnon 2017: 177, Nguyen 2017: 20, Robson 2015b: 750), there is good reason to think that the pessimist might wish to avoid commitment to such an extreme stance. In particular, a position of this kind is worryingly precarious since it can be refuted by adducing even a single instance of a legitimate testimonial judgement in aesthetics. Of course, it is always open to the pessimist to insist that this isn't a genuine difficulty since there really are no such instances. However, as a matter of descriptive fact, views of this extreme kind tend to be the exception rather than the rule.[15] Instead, it is customary for pessimists to concede that there are some (perhaps very rare) instances in which we may legitimately form aesthetic judgements via testimony. Wollheim (1980: 233), for example, claims that aesthetic judgements cannot be transmitted from person to person 'except within very narrow limits' (though he is famously silent as to what those narrow limits

---

[13] Of course, the authors cited don't themselves endorse a conclusion of this kind.
[14] For discussion of this see e.g. Meskin (2006: 112–13), Alcaraz León (2008: 292), Pettit (1983: 25), Whiting (2015: 91), and Andow (2014: 211).
[15] Though some pessimists such as Scruton (1976), Goldman (2006), and Todd (2004) appear open to endorsing the more extreme claim.

might be) and Hopkins (2011: 154) states that the additional norms of belief he proposes in aesthetics, norms which he regards as rendering aesthetic judgements formed on the basis of testimony illegitimate, do not hold 'come what may' but, rather, lapse under certain conditions. Nor is allowing this kind of exception the only way in which pessimists have shied away from the extreme version of their claim. Indeed, some pessimists take the position they are defending to be a considerably weaker one. Alan Hazlett (2017: 49), for example, maintains merely that 'there seems to be some kind of asymmetry, at least in some cases,…between aesthetic testimony and non-aesthetic testimony' and James Andow (2014: 211) that it 'seems more difficult to gain knowledge of aesthetic properties based solely upon testimony than it is in the case of other types of property'. Given all of this, it begins to seem rather implausible to maintain that any genuine pessimist must maintain that it is *never* legitimate to form aesthetic judgements on the basis of testimony. We should, therefore, endeavour to make our official characterization of pessimism sufficiently broad to include these views as well as the more extreme forms of pessimism.

As a first step, I propose that we take the pessimist to be someone who seeks to establish two comparative claims. First, some version of what Brian Laetz (2008: 355) terms 'the asymmetry thesis' according to which 'aesthetic testimony is [somehow] inferior to nonaesthetic testimony'.[16] Second, the claim that aesthetic judgements formed on the basis of testimony are somehow inferior to aesthetic judgements formed on the basis of first-hand experience (let us call these the 'first asymmetry thesis' and the 'second asymmetry thesis', respectively). As things stand, though, both asymmetry theses are in need of fleshing out.

1.5. The Two Asymmetry Theses

The most pressing difficulty regarding the two asymmetry theses as just presented is that first-hand aesthetic judgements and second-hand non-aesthetic judgements are hardly uniform categories. The former include both the judgement that the brush strokes of some complex artwork instantiate a particular kind of gracefulness and the judgement that a natural vista is spectacular. The latter concern matters as diverse as morality, the shapes and colours of medium-sized objects, conspiracy theories concerning the moon landing, complex scientific facts, the existence of mermaids, and the contents of other people's mental states. Paying proper attention to this diversity becomes particularly pressing when we consider the epistemic contrasts between these different kinds of judgement. For example,

---

[16] Laetz's original formulation talks about the judgements in question being 'epistemically' inferior but, for reasons I will highlight below, I do not wish to commit the pessimist to an epistemic understanding of their claim.

even setting aside other putative problem cases such as morality, it is typically much easier to attain testimonial knowledge about some non-aesthetic matters (such as the approximate time or the location of the nearest station) than others (such as the truth of some disputed scientific claim). And, again, similar complexities arise when it comes to the different kinds of first-hand aesthetic judgement. Given these complications, it is not immediately clear precisely what contrast is being employed in either asymmetry thesis.

Beginning with the second asymmetry thesis, we might try to address these worries by insisting on comparing like with like. That is, we should take the second asymmetry thesis to be the claim that, all else being equal, a first-hand aesthetic judgement that, say, Michelangelo's *Pietà* is beautiful will be more secure than a parallel judgement formed on the basis of testimony. Still 'the all else being equal' aspect of this claim stands in need of further explication. Both first-hand judgements and testimonial judgements can be better and worse in a variety of respects. How secure the former are will depend on factors such as the quality of our perceptual apparatus and our distance from the object judged. The quality of the latter will depend on factors such as the competence and honesty of the testifier. It is not clear, then, precisely what would count as comparing like to like in such cases.

What about the first asymmetry thesis? As already indicated, aesthetics is not the only putative problem case when it comes to testimonial judgements and scepticism has been expressed concerning testimony in domains as diverse as morality (Hopkins 2007, Hills 2009), mathematics (Williams 1972), and gustatory taste (Sweeney 2007). Predictably, pessimists concerning aesthetic matters have often proven sympathetic to endorsing parallel claims in (some of) these other domains.[17] As such, the first asymmetry thesis cannot be taken to depend on a contrast between testimony in aesthetics and testimony in *all* other domains.[18] It is, however, no easy matter to specify precisely which domains are relevant in drawing this contrast. In order to sidestep such worries, I will focus on a contrast between aesthetic testimony and testimony in what I will term 'mundane' areas. I will make no attempt to delineate the precise extension of the mundane but will merely stipulate that I intended for it to pick out those domains where (absent very general sceptical considerations) testimonial judgement is taken to be uncontroversially acceptable. This will likely include testimony regarding such simple matters as the colour of medium-sized objects and the time at railway stations as well as far more complex cases concerning historical weather patterns in distant countries and the intricacies of legal precedents.

---

[17] E.g. Hills (2009, 2017, forthcoming), Hopkins (2007, 2001), Hazlett (2017), and Mogensen (2015) all adopt parallel pessimistic positions concerning moral and aesthetic testimony.
[18] Contra Laetz (2008: 356) who explicitly intends the asymmetry principle to which he appeals to include a contrast between aesthetic and moral testimony.

However, judgements about morality, mathematics, and, of course, aesthetics, will be excluded.

Yet, even once we have established the relevant contrast as between aesthetic and mundane testimony, it is not entirely clear which pairs of cases we should be comparing. It is clear that (as discussed in e.g. Buud 2003: 387) it is much easier to find reliable testimony concerning the colour of a nearby car parked in plain sight than about the quality of the latest exhibition at MoMA. This does little to help establish the pessimist's case, though, since the optimist can merely retort that this is an unsurprising consequence of the relative paucity of aesthetic experts (at least when it comes to the aesthetics of complex artworks). Further, this difference, is no less pertinent when it comes to assessing the likelihood of someone arriving at legitimate first-hand belief in these areas or when we compare certain instances of mundane testimony to others. Again, then, it seems advisable to try and compare like to like. That is, we should focus on a comparison between pairs of cases, one aesthetic and one mundane, where it is equally difficult to arrive at legitimate first-hand judgement. Regarding such cases, the first asymmetry thesis will be the claim that, all else being equal, it is easier to arrive at legitimate testimonial judgement in the mundane case. As with the second asymmetry thesis, though, the 'all else being equal' clause hides some important complications. For example, even restricting our attention to pairs of cases where it is equally easy to establish legitimate first-hand judgement, there are important differences in the reliability of testimony concerning mundane matters. The most obvious cause of these differences is the fact that there are some mundane matters concerning which individuals are rather more prone to dishonesty than others. Similarly, there are going to be important differences regarding how (dis)honest people are generally disposed to be when it comes to testifying concerning different aesthetic cases.

We have seen, then, that the pessimist is committed to accepting some version of the two asymmetry theses but that it is no easy matter to spell out the exact versions of these claims they should endorse. I will not, however, attempt to offer a perfectly precise account of how either asymmetry thesis should be explicated. My reason for this is—as I will explain in more detail later—that I don't take the debate in question to be one which properly allows for this degree of precision. Instead of offering such an account, then, I will merely highlight two general elements which I believe that any suitably pessimistic versions of these theses must incorporate.

First, the pessimist must allow that aesthetic testimony performs badly in the kinds of 'like for like' comparison I just mentioned. That is, any genuine pessimist must hold that (in principle at least) there is some legitimate way of spelling out the 'all else being equal' clauses I appealed to such that aesthetic judgements formed on the basis of testimony lose out to both first-hand aesthetic judgements and mundane testimonial judgements. I do not mean to suggest by this that the pessimist must maintain that aesthetic testimony would lose out in *all* such comparisons. Indeed, given that there are cases of both first-hand aesthetic judgement and mundane testimonial judgements which seem to be (almost) entirely lacking in warrant, such a claim would be manifestly implausible. What I do maintain, though, is that any genuine pessimist will be committed to accepting some version of these comparative claims when these are interpreted as generics rather than universal generalizations.

The second element is that the pessimist is not merely committed to accepting that these asymmetries exist but also to rejecting a particular method for explaining them. To begin to see why, consider the position of someone who holds that there is some general difficulty with arriving at legitimate aesthetic judgements (whether testimonial or otherwise) as well as some general difficulty in forming legitimate testimonial judgements (regardless of subject matter). Further, let us assume that they don't take these difficulties, whatever they may be, to be sufficiently acute to justify some form of blanket scepticism concerning either testimonial or aesthetic judgements. Forming legitimate judgements of these kinds is, they maintain, difficult but not impossible. Someone who held such a position could easily accept the letter of the first asymmetry thesis but maintain that the comparative weakness of aesthetic testimony is to be accounted for by reference to a general concern regarding aesthetic judgements. Similarly, when it comes to the second asymmetry thesis, they could take this to be fully explained by whatever broader concern they have regarding testimonial judgement. Yet, such an individual would not qualify as a genuine pessimist. Rather, the pessimist must maintain that the problem with aesthetic testimony is one which cannot be fully explained by appealing to general worries about either testimony or aesthetic judgement (nor by merely combining the two). Rather, they must take the truth of the two asymmetry theses to be explained, at least in part, by some concern(s) specific to aesthetic testimony.

1.6. Optimistic Pessimists and Pessimistic Optimists

In the previous section, I argued that the pessimist must accept versions of the two asymmetry theses which incorporate the two features I have outlined. Let's formulate our revised asymmetry theses as follows:

- *First asymmetry thesis:* all else being equal, aesthetic judgements formed on the basis of testimony are somehow inferior to mundane judgements formed on the basis of testimony.
- *Second asymmetry thesis:* all else being equal, aesthetic judgements formed on the basis of testimony are somehow inferior to aesthetic judgements formed on the basis of first-hand experience.

Further, we have seen that the pessimist must maintain the problem with aesthetic testimony is one which cannot be fully explained either by appeal to general worries about testimony or by appeal to general worries about aesthetic judgement (nor by merely combining the two).

Yet, merely highlighting some necessary conditions for being a pessimist falls crucially short of providing a full account of their position. Indeed, there is good reason to deny that accepting these theses is jointly sufficient for being a pessimist since some self-described optimists are willing to endorse both of them. Meskin (2006: 109), for example, appears to accept the first asymmetry thesis and goes so far as to label acceptance of something like the second as a 'master constraint' on any successful account of aesthetic testimony (2006: 123). More needs to be said, therefore, in order to precisely distinguish between the two key positions in the aesthetic testimony debate. Clearly someone who claimed that, as a matter of principle, aesthetic judgement can never legitimately be transmitted via testimony (without making similar claims regarding either non-aesthetic testimony or first-hand aesthetic judgement) would count as a pessimist and someone who completely rejected both asymmetry theses would be an optimist. Less extreme cases are, however, rather more difficult to classify, and it is not obvious how we should distinguish between pessimistic views with optimistic qualifications and optimistic views with pessimistic qualifications.

Hopkins (2007: 613, 2011: 139–42) attempts to draw the relevant distinction by suggesting that it is only the pessimist who will hold that there is some specific principle or norm active in the aesthetic case which does not govern more mundane instances of testimony. This norm will (sometimes) disallow aesthetic judgements formed on the basis of testimony while permitting those formed on the basis of first-hand experience. The optimist, by contrast, will claim that the additional problems (if any) which arise in relation to aesthetic testimony can be accounted for entirely by appeal to the greater prevalence of factors—dishonesty, lack of expertise, and the like—which sometimes prevent testimonial judgements from being legitimately transmitted even in mundane cases. So, for example, Hopkins himself would be a pessimist on this account since he maintains that there is some additional norm of aesthetic judgement (though he remains agnostic as to the precise nature of this norm) that justifies our acceptance of the two asymmetry theses.[19] By contrast, while Meskin also accepts both asymmetry theses he explains these (2006: 120–3) by reference to a localized difficulty in identifying suitable informants in the aesthetic case. That is, he explains the putative problem with aesthetic testimony by appeal to the kind of factor which can also undermine testimonial warrant in mundane cases but maintains that these

---

[19] Hopkins (2011) considers two candidate norms. The first of these is a non-epistemic version of *AP* and the second is a principle according to which 'having the right to an aesthetic belief requires one to grasp the aesthetic grounds for it' (2011: 149).

factors are more pronounced in the aesthetic case (for reasons that don't similarly threaten the legitimacy of first-hand aesthetic judgements).[20]

However, while Hopkins's proposed distinction initially seems promising, it leads to some problematically counterintuitive results in certain cases. It would, for example, classify as an optimist someone who maintained that (owing perhaps to extreme dishonesty concerning aesthetic matters) no legitimate aesthetic judgements have ever been formed on the basis of testimony. At the other extreme, it would classify someone who believes that testimony is almost always a legitimate source of aesthetic judgement as a pessimist, provided that they also held that there were some—perhaps vanishingly rare—cases in which some aesthetic judgements were ruled out by norms unique to the aesthetic case. Given such results, I take it that Hopkins's method of delineating the optimist/pessimist distinction begins to look rather less attractive. In defending his position, Hopkins argues that without the distinction he proposes, the debate between optimists and pessimists will encompass a 'range of positions...forming a sliding scale between thinking that testimony is never a legitimate source of belief and thinking that it is always so' (2011: 139). It is not clear, though, why we must regard such a result as especially problematic. Indeed, I am inclined to find it rather attractive. Perhaps it is true that there are no sharp boundaries between the positions of the more pessimistic optimists and those of the more optimistic pessimists. And, if this is so, there may well exist certain positions which don't unambiguously belong to one camp rather than the other.

To illustrate this point, consider the position which Hopkins himself once advocated. According to Hopkins's earlier (2000) view the correct account of testimonial warrant in most domains is non-reductionist but there are some areas, most notably aesthetics, in which the reductionist view is correct. This view would certainly seem to provide good reason for taking testimony in aesthetics to be epistemically compromised when compared to testimony in mundane areas. After all, it is typically judged by most of those involved in debates over the epistemology of testimony that non-reductionist accounts will (ceteris paribus) license a great deal more testimonial knowledge in an area than will the reductionist. However, while such a position doesn't appear particularly optimistic it may still fail to comfortably qualify as a form of pessimism. Acquiring testimonial knowledge may be a more difficult task on a reductionist model but it is not obvious that it is an impossible, nor even a particularly daunting, one.[21] This will mean that, as Hopkins himself (2011: 141) points out, this position would entail that there was nothing illegitimate about forming aesthetic judgements on the

---

[20] I consider Meskin's view in more detail in §4.4.
[21] For an argument in support of the claim that we can have widespread reductionist testimonial knowledge see Fricker (1994).

basis of testimony given the 'availability of a sufficiently strong Humean argument'; an argument which

> reasons to the truth of the informant's claim that *p* from the type of informant and the type of topic on which he is offering a view; the past correlation, as experienced by the recipient, between testimony by such informants on such matters and the truth of their claims; and the prior probability, for the recipient, that *p*. (Hopkins 2011: 141)

It seems to me that merely having a position of the kind described on the table—alongside other difficult to classify views presented in e.g. Andow (2014), Hazlett (2015), and Nguyen (2017)—will give us reason to be suspicious of the claim that there is a clear and principled divide between optimism and pessimism. Indeed, such positions seem to fit much better with viewing the debate in question as one concerning where on the scale between extreme forms of optimism and extreme forms of pessimism we should fall.

In defending the principled account of the optimist/pessimist distinction, Hopkins (2011: 139) suggests that without a clear divide of this kind the debate between the optimist and the pessimist would become 'difficult to marshal' since we would often be unable to tell whether the truth of some position entailed the truth of optimism or pessimism (or was neutral between the two). This is certainly true, but I remain unconvinced that this provides any motivation for taking the debate between the optimist and the pessimist to be one between two clearly defined and diametrically opposed positions. Indeed, as James Andow (2018: 33) usefully highlights, the plethora of different ways in which parties to the optimism/pessimism controversy have described the views they are defending (and rejecting) makes it implausible to maintain that there is a single clearly delineated debate to be picked out here. Rather, there is a whole host of distinct but related debates concerning, for example, whether is it ever legitimate to form aesthetic judgements on the basis of testimony, whether either (or both) of the two asymmetry theses are true, whether aesthetic judgements formed on the basis of testimony violate some norm or principle unique to aesthetic judgements, how wide the (putative) gulf is between aesthetic and non-aesthetic testimony—and between first-hand and second-hand aesthetic judgement—and so forth. All of these debates strike me as worth having and each corresponds to a different way of drawing the boundary between the optimist and the pessimist which has been appealed to in the literature. Further, given these different ways of delineating the two positions, it is unsurprising that some accounts of the status of aesthetic testimony will count as optimistic according to some taxonomies and pessimistic according to others.

At this point it might be objected that, given these concessions, my proposed project of arguing that we should be optimists concerning aesthetic testimony begins to look like a complete non-starter. If I am inclined to maintain that there is no clear divide between optimistic and pessimistic positions, then how can I also propose that we would be best placed accepting the former and rejecting the latter? Such an objection is, however, misguided. It is certainly true that there are blurred boundaries between these two views, but this doesn't entail that there aren't also clear cases of optimism and of pessimism (any more than the vagueness of 'tall' rules out the existence of some individuals who are determinately tall). Crucially, the optimistic position I intend to argue for throughout this book is one which I take to be extreme enough to count as optimistic on any plausible taxonomy. This is because the view in question is one which rejects the two asymmetry theses which, I have argued, should be taken as necessary conditions for any pessimistic view.[22] If I succeed in defending this extreme form of optimism, then I will have shown that we should reject not only the more extreme forms of pessimism but also a whole range of positions towards the centre of my proposed optimism/pessimism spectrum.

In these last three sections I have been considering the intricacies of the optimism/pessimism debate. I have argued that, while there is no single way of correctly and precisely spelling out this controversy, we can identify some key necessary conditions which any genuine form of pessimism must accept. Having done so, though, I should reiterate that I agree with Hopkins when he claims that an approach of this kind makes the debate at hand 'difficult to marshal'. That is, I do not think that it would be a manageable task to present a sustained argument of the kind I have planned—one which seeks to argue for the falsity of all forms of pessimism—while having to constantly make explicit reference to all of the manifold ways in which one might be taken to be either an optimist or a pessimist. Given these difficulties, I will (for convenience's sake only) frequently return in what follows to talking as if the simplified understanding of the optimism/pessimism debate I present in the introduction was accurate. That is, I will take pessimism to be the claim that testimony cannot serve as a legitimate source of aesthetic judgement (and optimism to be the denial of this claim).[23] I should stress, though, that this does not mean that the various important complications addressed in these last three sections will be ignored in subsequent chapters. For the most part, this simplified way of talking will be harmless given the shape of the dialectic in what follows, but it is important to bear in mind that it *is* a simplification. Given this, I will be careful to highlight any points in my subsequent arguments where this simplified understanding becomes relevant to the arguments I am advancing.

---

[22] Another way of putting this is that the extreme optimist accepts two symmetry theses. First, that aesthetic judgements formed on the basis of testimony aren't inferior to mundane judgements formed on the basis of testimony. Second, that aesthetic judgements formed on the basis of testimony aren't inferior to aesthetic judgements formed on the basis of first-hand experience.

[23] I will say more about what this legitimacy claim entails in the next section.

1.7. Some Varieties of Pessimism

So, returning for now to this simplified understanding of pessimism, what does it mean to claim that we can't legitimately form aesthetic beliefs on the basis of testimony? According to the view I will term 'constitutive pessimist' we can't form legitimate aesthetic judgements on the basis of testimony because we cannot form *any* aesthetic judgements in this manner. It is, according to the constitutive pessimist, in the very nature of aesthetic judgements that they *cannot* be (not merely shouldn't be) formed on the basis of testimony (the different ways in which someone might try to explicate and defend a constitutive view will form the focus of the next chapter). In contrast to constitutive pessimism, the other two varieties of pessimism I will consider—unavailability and unusability pessimism—both agree that aesthetic judgements *can* be formed on the basis of testimony but maintain, for different reasons, that they shouldn't be.

The most natural suggestion as to why aesthetic judgements formed on the basis of testimony are illegitimate is that they fail to attain the status of knowledge. The pessimist who accepts a view of this kind has come, following Hopkins (2007), to be known as an 'unavailability pessimist'. According to the unavailability view, aesthetic knowledge just isn't available to us via testimony. Explicit defenders of such unavailability views include Philip Pettit (1983: 25), who argues that '[a]esthetic characterisations are essentially perceptual', meaning that perception is the only route to 'full knowledge...of the truths which they express', and Daniel Whiting (2015: 91), who maintains that 'testimony cannot deliver aesthetic knowledge'.

Advocates of the final kind of pessimism—such as Hopkins (2006, 2011) and Gorodeisky (2010)—disagree when it comes to the epistemic status of (some) judgements formed on the basis of aesthetic testimony. These 'unusability pessimists' are happy to concede to their optimistic opponents that aesthetic testimony can sometimes, indeed often, make knowledge available to us. They depart from the optimist, however, in maintaining that such judgements would nonetheless still be illegitimate. Unusability pessimists typically go on to explain this illegitimacy by claiming that aesthetic beliefs are governed by some additional non-epistemic norm(s)—that is, a norm which can render such beliefs illegitimate even in cases where 'the belief the recipient is offered would count as knowledge' (Hopkins 2011: 147)—which is not active in mundane areas. This norm perhaps, inter alia, prevents aesthetic beliefs from being legitimately formed on the basis of testimony.

While these last two forms of pessimism are importantly distinct, many of the arguments that I will consider in this work—both from the pessimist and from their optimistic opponent—will apply equally to both. As such, I will largely elide this important distinction when I present my arguments in later chapters, opting to frame the pessimist's view in epistemic terms. Again, though, this is merely intended as an expository convenience, and I will highlight differences between the unavailability and unusability positions when these become relevant to the points under discussion.

Having surveyed these different forms of pessimism, we are now a little closer to seeing what it means to claim that an aesthetic judgement formed on the basis of testimony isn't 'legitimate'. Still, it's worth making things a little more explicit. I will typically talk as if the pessimist is someone who maintains that we cannot legitimately form aesthetic judgements on the basis of testimony, either because we cannot form such judgements simpliciter or because doing so would violate some norm (whether epistemic or otherwise). However, I will also allow for pessimists who use talk of 'illegitimacy' rather more loosely to mean simply that judgements of this kind tend (in line with the one or both of the asymmetry theses discussed above) to be illegitimate, in one of these senses, more often than aesthetic judgements based on first-hand experience and/or testimonial judgements of mundane matters.[24]

What might help in making the pessimist's position clearer here is highlighting certain views which I won't be counting as genuine forms of pessimism. It is uncontroversial that there are certain features of (paradigm) first-hand aesthetic judgements which judgements formed on the basis of aesthetic testimony lack and, further, that some of these features are ones which we often value as part of our aesthetic practice. We will discuss some common candidates such as appreciation and understanding in later chapters, but these are far from being the only suggestions. For example, Thi Nguyen (2020a) has recently argued that a large part of what we value in forming aesthetic judgements isn't merely the result (having a, hopefully, correct judgement) but, rather, the process and experience of 'interpreting, investigating, and exploring the aesthetic object' (2020a: 1151).[25] However, doing so would clearly be precluded in cases where we form our judgement purely on the basis of testimony. Debates about which features we value in aesthetic judgement, and why, are worthwhile and fascinating in their own right, but no position in these debates will commit someone to pessimism (unless it is accompanied by the further claim that lacking such features prevents, or tends to prevent, aesthetic judgements from being legitimate in the senses already outlined). With the position of the pessimist more clearly in view, let's go on to consider that of their rivals.

---

[24] Again, I won't take pains to delineate the exact boundaries between a more optimistic pessimist and a more pessimistic optimist.

[25] I argue elsewhere (Wallbank and Robson 2022) that there are also various benefits in the other direction. That is, that forming aesthetic judgements on the basis of social factors such testimony can have important benefits not available to those who form paradigm first-hand aesthetic judgements. Again, though, I take this to be tangential to the central debate between the optimist and the pessimist.

1.8. Some Varieties of Optimism

In this final section, I will briefly highlight some relevant species of optimism before outlining my own preferred optimistic position. It might seem natural to begin by proposing constitutive, availability, and usability forms of optimism as logical complements of the pessimistic positions outlined in the previous section. Such a taxonomy would, however, be of little use since any form of optimism worthy of the name would exclude all three versions of pessimism. Rather, the most pressing difference between optimists will relate to their attitudes towards the two asymmetry theses. The most straightforward kind of optimist denies both theses, but we've already seen that some optimists have explicitly endorsed one or both of them. In what follows I will refer to optimists who reject both asymmetry theses as 'extreme optimists' and those who accept one (or both) of them as 'moderate optimists'. In later chapters I will argue at length that we should avoid moderation in optimistic things and endorse an extreme optimistic position.

As well as a commitment to extreme optimism, the optimistic position I will argue for has some further key features. First, I will be arguing for a view which accommodates some form of epistemic contextualism. Contextualism of this kind is a complex and nuanced position but the key thought is that, as Rysiew (2007) puts things, 'what is expressed by a knowledge attribution—a claim to the effect that S 'knows' that p—depends partly on something in the context of 'the attributor''. This will mean that the standard which a subject has to meet in order for us to truly say of them 'S knows that p' will depend on certain facts about *us*: facts such as the importance of the issue to us and what 'relevant alternatives' we have been discussing. In Chapter 4 I will say much more about this kind of contextualism and why I take it to be relevant to the debate between the optimist and the pessimist. In Chapter 5 I will suggest that a contextualist version of optimism has some key advantages over non-contextualist versions of optimism but that both forms of optimist still win out against pessimism.

The second additional element of my positive view is an account of the nature and value of aesthetic assertion. It is often noted—in, for example, Mothersill (1994: 160), Blackburn (1998: 110), Gorodeisky (2010: 53), Robson (2015b), and Franzén (2018)—that various assertions such as 'the painting is beautiful' sound odd (to say the least) in the mouth of someone who hasn't experienced the work for themselves. Further, it is commonplace to endeavour to explain this fact by denying that the corresponding judgement could be legitimate in the absence of such experience. This explanation would, of course, entail some form of pessimism. However, while I certainly share the intuition that many of the assertions in question are problematic, I do not believe that this pessimistic account offers the best explanation for their impermissibility. Rather, in Chapters 6 and 7, I will outline and defend an alternative optimist-friendly explanation which, I will argue, does a better job of explaining the relevant phenomena.

Having briefly outlined some of the key elements of my preferred extreme optimist view, I will spend much of the rest of this book trying to persuade you that it should be your preferred view too. That said, it is important to stress that I am far more committed to the truth of optimism than to any particular version of it. As such, my primary intention in what follows will be to convince you that you should be an optimist of some stripe. It is to that task which I now turn.

2
Constitutive Pessimism

2.1. A Royal Road to Pessimism?

My main focus in this work is the dialectic between the optimist and the pessimist concerning aesthetic testimony. I will focus extensively in later chapters on various arguments which aim to highlight some significant costs and benefits of these competing positions. Before doing so, though, it is worth considering a prominent family of views according to which this whole approach is misguided: *constitutive pessimism*. According to the constitutive pessimist, developing in-depth arguments in favour of pessimism is unnecessary—and in favour of optimism misguided—since the very nature of aesthetic judgement commits us to an acceptance of pessimism.

This chapter considers some of the most prominent versions of constitutive pessimism, each of which maintains that it is somehow *impossible* to form an aesthetic judgement on the basis of testimony. I begin, in §2.2, by considering some straightforward versions of the constitutive view which merely stipulate (either overtly or covertly) that something can only count as an aesthetic judgement if it is formed on the basis of (something like) first-hand perception. Such strategies would certainly ensure the truth of constitutive pessimism, but would only do so at the cost of rendering the pessimist's view trivial. I argue, then, that if the constitutive pessimist wants their view to provide a challenge to the approach I will be adopting here, they need to provide some more substantive motivations for endorsing their central claim.

In the remainder of the chapter, I go on to consider some candidate motivations for endorsing a substantive version of constitutive pessimism and argue that they are uniformly unpersuasive. In §2.3, I consider Sibley's discussion of aesthetic concepts and ask whether this can provide any basis for constitutive pessimism. I argue that the common interpretation of Sibley as endorsing some version of pessimism isn't supported by a close reading of his work and that none of Sibley's remarks offer support for a (substantive) version of pessimism. I then turn, in §§2.4 and 2.5, to consider the claim that pessimism is entailed by non-cognitivist accounts of aesthetic judgement. I argue, however, that there is no good reason to hold that non-cognitivism is incompatible with optimism. (Whether non-cognitivists *should* be optimists is a separate issue which I return to in later chapters.) Finally, I ask whether we can motivate a version of constitutive pessimism based on the claim that we cannot *appreciate* an object's aesthetic properties on the basis of testimony. §2.6 considers various pessimistic accounts which construe aesthetic judgement as a matter of appreciation rather than belief but argues that, once again, these only achieve plausibility at the cost of triviality. §2.7 argues against some more circuitous attempts to link appreciation to pessimism. I conclude, therefore, that we must look beyond constitutive considerations if we are to find a compelling motivation for pessimism.

Before proceeding, though, it is important to briefly address one glaring omission in the above. I mentioned in the introduction that Kant is often taken as providing the original—or at least the canonical—statement of pessimism. Further, it is not unreasonable to read Kant as a *constitutive* pessimist. Given this, it might seem surprising (to say the least) that I haven't chosen to address Kant's views at length in this chapter. My reason for refraining from doing so is, however, a rather simple one, I don't know which version of pessimism Kant himself endorsed. Although some writers—such as Meskin (2004: 68) and Laetz (2008: 356)—present Kant as an unavailability pessimist, there is reason to be sceptical of this interpretation. As Gorodeisky points out in her insightful discussion of Kant's view, he does 'not portray the judge who fails to meet' his requirements for genuine aesthetic judgement 'as failing to know...the beauty of the object' (2010: 61). Rather, he presents them as failing to 'prove' their own taste—something which, he maintains, is a requirement for any genuine aesthetic judgement (Kant 1790/2005: 92).

Given this, it is difficult to believe that Kant intended to endorse any kind of unavailability pessimism.[1] It is, however, much less clear what species of pessimism he *did* intend to endorse. Gorodeisky's own statement of the Kantian view has it that the

> Problem with aesthetic testimony is grounded in the normative conditions that uniquely constrain aesthetic judgement. Rather than epistemic conditions, these are *constitutive* conditions on what it takes to make an *aesthetic* judgement. Put differently, the problem with aesthetic testimony is explained by norms of success and failure that explain what it takes to succeed in making such a judgement in contrast to other kinds of judgement, and what it takes to fail to make one. (2010: 54)

It is not, however, entirely clear whether Gorodeisky's Kant should be taken as endorsing some form of constitutive pessimism or as advocating an unusability view. Her talk of '*constitutive* conditions on what it takes to make an *aesthetic* judgement' seems to favour the former, as does her later remark that if 'testimony alone is the ground of a judgement about the beauty of an object, the judgement

---

[1] Further considerations against construing Kant as an unavailability pessimist are discussed in Budd (2003: 387).

is not an aesthetic judgement according to Kant. It is either a theoretical judgement, or an imitation of an aesthetic judgement' (2010: 62). However, referring to these conditions as 'normative'—alongside the frequent parallels she draws with Hopkins's unusability view (Gorodeisky 2020: 53, 60, 61)—suggests the latter.[2]

What is clear, though, is that her interpretation of Kant is a highly controversial one. Indeed, even within the confines of the aesthetic testimony debate, we can see that many others—including Hopkins (2001), McGonigal (2006), and Todd (2004)—have proffered very different understandings of Kant's pessimism. In order, then, to have anything illuminating to say concerning Kant's pessimism, I would have to determine which (if any) of these interpretations best represents Kant's own view. I am, however, far from being a Kant scholar and so don't feel qualified to enter into such exegetical disputes. What I *will* do is argue, at various points throughout this work, that each of these putatively Kantian views either proves mistaken or else poses no threat to the kind of optimism I seek to defend.[3] Thus, while Kant's name may appear only sparingly in what follows, much of what I say can be taken as an effort to engage with various putatively Kantian views.

2.2. Pessimism by Stipulation

Let us begin our consideration of constitutive versions of pessimism by imagining a pessimist who makes the following pronouncement.

> There are two kinds of mental state which are sometimes called 'aesthetic judgements'. The first kind are formed on the basis of first-hand acquaintance whereas the second are formed in various other ways such as, most relevantly for our purposes, being formed on the basis of testimony. I will, however, only count states of the first kind as genuine instances of aesthetic judgements.

An account of this kind is, I suspect, one which many pessimists would find attractive. What is being claimed here, though, is not that aesthetic judgements formed on the basis of testimony are illegitimate but, rather, that we simply *cannot* form aesthetic judgements in this manner. There are, however, two importantly different dialectical moves which the last sentence of this pessimist's contention might be making.

---

[2] As I will discuss in §2.7 Gorodeisky and Marcus (2018) adopt a more unambiguously constitutive view.

[3] Someone might object that no contemporary version of pessimism accurately reflects Kant's view and that, as such, my arguments (even if successful) wouldn't undermine Kant's own position. The burden of proof would, however, be on the objector here to produce a novel interpretation of Kant which avoids the various difficulties I will raise for other versions of pessimism.

According to a first interpretation, when the pessimist talks of something's counting as a genuinely aesthetic judgement for their purposes they are merely making a stipulation according to which they will only use the phrase 'aesthetic judgement' to refer to those states formed on the basis of first-hand experience.[4] This stipulation is, of course, incomplete since there are various different mental states including, but not limited to, certain aesthetic beliefs which arise on the basis of first-hand encounters with artworks (and other objects of aesthetic evaluation), and it is not clear precisely which of these the pessimist is intending to christen as 'aesthetic judgements' (I discuss a number of candidates later in this chapter). Disregarding such complications for the time being, though, we can see that if all the pessimist intends is to make a bare stipulation about the meaning of 'aesthetic judgement' then there is little for the optimist to take issue with. The pessimist is entitled to introduce whatever stipulative definitions they like, but this does nothing to strengthen their position in the debate concerning aesthetic testimony. After all, similar stipulations could be made with respect to judgements concerning mundane matters and it would be equally legitimate to stipulate a sense of 'aesthetic judgement' which explicitly includes aesthetic beliefs formed on the basis of testimony. That is not, of course, to deny that there might be particular reasons to make some stipulations over others, and I am by no means suggesting that the pessimist's stipulations here would be entirely arbitrary. My point is merely that, whether made on the basis of compelling theoretical considerations or not, such stipulations would not, in themselves, do anything to advance the aesthetic testimony debate. It is clear, then, that bare stipulation is of no help to the pessimist who intends their position to go any way towards undermining either the truth or the significance of the kind of optimism I will be defending.

The second way of interpreting the hypothetical pessimist's pronouncement involves a usage of 'aesthetic judgement' which is not intended as merely stipulative. Rather, the claim is that there is some substantive reason for not classifying putatively aesthetic judgements formed on the basis of testimony (or on the basis of any source besides first-hand perception) as genuine instances of that kind. While there are a number of different ways in which this thought could be spelled out, the most promising suggestion is that there is something special about a particular state, a state which we can only arrive at via first-hand aesthetic experience, which makes it the *best* candidate for being the referent of the phrase 'aesthetic judgement'. To illustrate this thought a little further, consider my account in the previous chapter according to which aesthetic judgements are the mental correlates of sincere competent aesthetic assertion. A constitutive

---

[4] As discussions of AP (such as Hanson 2015 and Livingston 2003) make clear, it is not as easy as this hypothetical pessimist appears to assume to determine precisely what should be included within the scope of 'first-hand experience' here.

pessimist could propose that the requisite mental state is one that, for whatever reason, we simply cannot have access to on the basis of testimony. While this second interpretation of the constitutive pessimist's view *does* have potential to undermine the optimist's position, I will argue below that this potential remains unfulfilled.

My aim in this chapter will be to argue for two claims; (i) that some prominent versions of constitutive pessimism operate using something very like the first approach outlined and (ii) that those which veer more towards the second approach are uniformly unsuccessful. Given this, defenders of pessimism will need to look beyond constitutive accounts. It is, however, difficult to make progress on either of these tasks by merely considering these issues in the abstract, so I will now turn to consider some concrete (putative) versions of constitutive pessimism.

2.3. Was Sibley a (Constitutive) Pessimist?

To begin, let's consider one of the most famous passages from the recent history of aesthetics, Frank Sibley's (1965: 137) claim that:

> To suppose indeed that one can make aesthetic judgments without aesthetic perception...is to misunderstand aesthetic judgment. This therefore is how I shall use "aesthetic judgment" throughout. Where there is no question of aesthetic perception, I shall use some other expression like "attribution of aesthetic quality" or "aesthetic statement." Thus, rather as a color-blind man may infer that something is green without seeing...so someone may attribute balance or gaudiness to a painting, or say that it is too pale, without himself having judged it so.

On the basis of this—alongside similar passages such as Sibley (1959: 424–6) and (1974: 16)—many aestheticians have taken Sibley to be a committed pessimist (see e.g. Gorodeisky (2010: 58–9), Laetz (2008: 356), and Meskin (2006: 111)). Now, there is certainly a sense in which it is correct to label Sibley a (constitutive) pessimist since—as Livingston (2003: 268) notes—he guarantees, by stipulation, that genuine aesthetic judgement, in his sense, *must* be based on perception rather than being based on testimony, inference, and so forth.[5] It is, however, rather less clear whether Sibley is a pessimist in any substantive sense.

Again, by saying that Sibley's usage here is stipulative, I don't mean to suggest that this stipulation is either arbitrary or unhelpful. Once he has isolated what he

---

[5] Though Sibley clearly intends a wider than usual sense of perception since he takes it to include e.g. feeling 'the power of a novel, its mood, or its uncertainty of tone' (1965: 137).

means by 'aesthetic judgment' Sibley then goes on (1959, 1965) to offer an impressive and nuanced account of the nature of these states, one which has justly proven to be foundational for much later work on these issues. From the point of view of this chapter, though, our interest isn't in the general nature of Sibley's account of aesthetic judgement but merely in the extent to which we take Sibley himself to be defending a substantive version of pessimism. In my view, there is no evidence that he was intending to do anything of the kind.

Let's begin by considering the comparison which Sibley draws between the person attempting to make aesthetic judgements in the absence of perception and a colour-blind person inferring that an object is green. There are various ways in which we could interpret such comparisons (as I discuss at length in Robson 2018). For present purposes, though, we need not enter into such exegetical details.[6] The key point here is just that it is clear that Sibley takes the colour case and the aesthetic case to be parallel. We saw in the previous chapter, though, that a key requirement for any pessimist view is to defend an asymmetry between aesthetic testimony and testimony in mundane areas. Indeed, the contrast with the colour case has—given the various plausible parallels between aesthetic and colour judgement—served as something like the canonical method for illustrating the need for such an asymmetry in the literature (see e.g. Hungerland (1968), Laetz (2008: 356), Gorodeisky (2010: 55), Budd (2003: 387), Todd (2004: 279), Alcaraz León (2008: 292), Scruton (1976: 54), and Pettit (1983: 25)). This asymmetry is not, however, one which Sibley appears to endorse.

Of course, the single passage I have quoted above is far from being all that Sibley has to say on the subject of aesthetic judgement, but I cannot find anything in Sibley's other writing which commits him to endorsing any substantive version of pessimism. On the contrary, the close link he makes between aesthetic judgements and certain mundane judgements seem to recur. Consider, for example, the following passage from (Sibley 1959: 437).

> We see that a book is red by looking, just as we tell that the tea is sweet by tasting it. So too, it might be said, we just see (or fail to see) that things are delicate, balanced, and the like. This kind of comparison between the exercise of taste and the use of the five senses is indeed familiar; our use of the word 'taste' itself shows that the comparison is age-old and very natural.

It is, admittedly, true that he also highlights some crucial contrasts between the two. He claims, for example, that there is a much greater role for expertise in making aesthetic judgements than in making ordinary perceptual judgements (1959: 437–8) and that 'When someone is unable to see that the book on the table

---

[6] For a different exegetical debate concerning Sibley's epistemology see Bergqvist (2010) and Kirwin (2011).

is brown, we cannot get him to see that it is by talking; consequently it seems puzzling that we might get someone to see that the vase is graceful by talking' (ibid. 439). If anything, though, such contrasts seem to place aesthetic testimony in a better position than colour testimony. If, for example, there are genuine experts in a particular domain then this would seem (on the face of things at least) to give the rest of us good reason to defer to such experts even when their judgements conflict with our own.[7]

Given the above, it would be a mistake to take Sibley to be endorsing any (not merely stipulative) version of pessimism. This does not, of course, entail that he did (or even that he would) endorse optimism of the kind I am defending. What it does suggest, though, is that those looking for arguments to defend a substantive version of constitutive pessimism will need to look elsewhere.[8]

2.4. Non-Cognitivism and Aesthetic Judgement

In §1.3 I introduced my account of judgements as, roughly, the mental correlates of sincere assertions. I didn't take any particular stance as to what these mental correlates were but merely noted that I would (purely for the sake of convenience) mostly talk as if they were beliefs of a straightforwardly cognitivist kind. This, I suggested, would be harmless since (for my purposes at least) it will make little difference whether we accept this construal or some alternative account (such as non-cognitivism about aesthetic judgements). This stance is, however, a controversial one. Indeed, Cain Todd (2004: 290–1) has gone so far as to claim that it is question-begging to frame the debate between the optimist and the pessimist in terms of belief, since no pessimist 'ought to hold that aesthetic judgements are beliefs'.[9] Rather, Todd (2004: 290–1) maintains, they should take their pessimism to be 'entailed by a certain (expressivist) view of the nature of aesthetic judgement'.[10]

---

[7] Indeed, I argue at length elsewhere (Robson 2014b) for the rationality of this kind of deference to aesthetic experts.

[8] For those unconvinced by this, I consider, and reject, some attempts to appeal to Sibley's work to defend pessimism in Robson (2018).

[9] Todd also seems to suggest (2004: 290) that pessimists typically don't make this claim, citing Pettit (1983) as a rare exception. This descriptive claim strikes me as mistaken since e.g. Hopkins (2000, 2011), Andow (2014), and Whiting (2015) are all pessimists who take aesthetic judgements to be beliefs.

[10] Technically Todd's concern is not with pessimism as such but, rather, with what he terms the 'autonomy' of aesthetic judgement. It is not, however, entirely clear what he means by this. His discussion is largely focused on the arguments in Hopkins (2001) where this autonomy is taken to be equivalent to the following (putative) contrast. 'When one party finds herself disagreeing with several others who share a view, then (a) for ordinary empirical matters this is sometimes reason enough for her to adopt their view, but is never so in the case of beauty' (Hopkins 2001: 169). Yet, Todd himself defines autonomy as 'the idea that a judgement of taste *must* be made on the basis of a feeling of

Before discussing the substance of Todd's claim, it's worth briefly highlighting a concern relating to his framing of the debate between expressivism and its rivals. It has been argued in various places—including Blackburn (1980), Sinclair (2007), Ridge (2009), and Köhler (2017)—that embracing expressivism in some domain is compatible with endorsing many standard realist claims: claims concerning truth, mind independence, and, most relevantly for our purposes, *belief*. Combinations of this final kind are typically motivated by an appeal to some form of minimalism concerning belief, according to which 'there is nothing more to a mental state being a belief than that state being characteristically expressed by a sentence that wears propositional clothing' (Sinclair 2007: 343). That is, beliefs are just mental states expressed by sentences which perform many of the same roles as straightforward propositional claims; being susceptible to judgements of appropriateness, being capable of being embedded in various non-assertive contexts, and so forth. Indeed, the most prominent proponent of expressivism Simon Blackburn (1998: 70) explicitly provides an expressivist account of (a certain kind of) moral belief according to which 'believing that X is good or right it roughly having an appropriately favourable valuation of X'.[11]

What's at issue here is not, however, a merely verbal question about which states should be labelled 'beliefs'. Rather, Todd suggests that various aspects of the way in which the debate over aesthetic testimony has been carried out contribute to begging the question against the expressivist and, by extension, the pessimist. In particular, Todd (2004: 280, 290) suggests that the assumptions that aesthetic judgements are (i) truth apt and (ii) straightforwardly assertable prejudice the debate in favour of his opponent. Yet, properties such as being truth apt and being assertable are ones which most contemporary expressivists aim to incorporate into their accounts of judgement. It seems, then, that there is good reason to be suspicious of Todd's charge that any questions have been begged against the expressivist. Even if we are able to reject Todd's question-begging charge, though, this does nothing to undermine his central claim that a plausible version of non-cognitivism is available according to which pessimism is straightforwardly entailed by the nature of aesthetic judgement. What should we say concerning this claim?

It certainly seems that there are *some* versions of non-cognitivism which quickly lead to a rejection of optimism. For example, it is—as other commentators on the aesthetic testimony debate such as Laetz (2008: 355) and Meskin (2006: 115–16) have already noted—a short step from accepting 'a strong expressivism, stripped of all quasi-realist trappings' (Matravers 2005: 200) to embracing pessimism. However, conceding this point will offer little solace to the

---

pleasure' (2004: 278). Regardless of how we interpret 'autonomy', though, it is clear that Todd (2004: 295–6) takes it to be incompatible with the truth of optimism.

[11] I will return to consider the relationship between expressivism and belief in more detail in §3.8.

constitutive pessimist since there are well rehearsed reasons for regarding views of this kind as implausible.[12] Crude emotivism simply isn't a live option.[13]

So, let's turn our attention to more sophisticated contemporary forms of expressivism. Nearly two decades ago Todd (2004: 277) noted that such views have been surprisingly neglected within aesthetics and there has been little improvement in subsequent years. While many of those who discuss sophisticated expressivist views in ethics—including Blackburn (2010) and Gibbard (1990: 51–2)—have gestured at extensions of their views into the aesthetic realm, sustained expressivist treatments of aesthetic issues remain comparatively rare. This is not, however, the place to remedy such neglect and I don't intend either to construct a comprehensive taxonomy of possible expressivist views within aesthetics or to assess the plausibility of such views.[14] Rather, I will remain narrowly focused on the issue at hand and endeavour to show that there is no clear link between accepting expressivism concerning some area of discourse and rejecting testimony in that domain.

The absence of such a straightforward link is best illustrated by considering the views of one of the most influential contemporary defenders of moral expressivism: Allan Gibbard (1990). According to Gibbard, to form a moral judgement is 'to express one's acceptance of norms' (1990: 9).[15] These would include, for example, norms which permit, require, or forbid particular actions. However, Gibbard allows (1990: 174–88) that we can, and indeed should, sometimes legitimately form moral judgements—that is, come to accept certain norms—on the basis of testimony. Claiming that 'When conditions are right and someone else finds a norm independently credible, I must take that as favoring my own accepting the norm', and that when 'under good conditions for judgment...others find a norm independently credible. Then that must favor the norm in my own eyes' (1992: 180–1). There doesn't seem to be any barrier to extending views of this kind to the aesthetic realm. Indeed, Gibbard himself (1990: 52) himself suggests an aesthetic analogue of his view according to which 'aesthetic norms are norms for the rationality of kinds of appreciation'.

It seems clear, then, that aesthetic expressivists *need* not be pessimists. The issue cannot, therefore, be whether there are any defensible forms of expressivism which are compatible with optimism (there are) but whether there are any which are *incompatible* with it. We have already seen that Todd believes that there are

---

[12] See e.g. Geach (1965). Kivy (1980) argues that theories of this kind are even less plausible in aesthetics than in other domains.

[13] Indeed, it is not clear that it ever was. Even early non-cognitivists—such as Ayer and Stevneson—seem to occasionally anticipate the subsequent quasi-realist trappings that would be added to such views. See e.g. the 'retrospective comments' in Stevenson (1963).

[14] Though I do discuss these issues in Sinclair and Robson (forthcoming).

[15] More recently Gibbard (2003) has defended a somewhat modified version of this account. However, the differences between the two versions of Gibbard's expressivism aren't relevant for my purposes.

and he is not alone in this.[16] Roger Scruton (1976: 54), for example, claims that his expressivist 'affective' theory of aesthetic judgement 'takes as its starting-point the intuition that, in matters of aesthetic judgments, you have to see for yourself' and recognize that 'another cannot make your aesthetic judgements for you'.[17] In the next section, I will argue that this second interpretation of the incompatibility claim is also mistaken. There is no plausible version of expressivism which is—excluding mere stipulations of the kind discussed above—incompatible with optimism.

Before doing so, though, it is important to stress two important aspects of the claim I have just made. First, my claim is only targeted at *constitutive* justifications for an expressivist form of pessimism. Merely showing that pessimism is not entailed by any plausible version of expressivism does nothing to show that expressivists cannot be, nor even that they should not be, pessimists (nor that pessimists shouldn't be expressivists). The arguments I will offer in later chapters are, however, intended to show that everyone—whether cognitivist or non-cognitivist—has good reason to reject pessimism. Second, my claim here isn't merely that there doesn't happen to be any extant version of expressivism which fits the bill. Rather, I maintain that there is, at the very least, good prima-facie reason to maintain that optimism will be compatible with *any* form of expressivism sophisticated enough to account for the 'propositional clothing' which aesthetic judgements wear.

Again, a comparison with moral testimony is instructive here. Paulina Sliwa (2012: 177) has argued that 'any noncognitivist view that makes room for moral disagreement, does not have an easy explanation for a deep asymmetry between moral and nonmoral testimony'. Further, many of those engaged in more general work on the epistemology of testimony have taken the availability of legitimate testimonial judgement in some domain to be exceedingly minimal. Elizabeth Fricker (2006: 237) expresses this point rather forcefully when she suggests that what is required for legitimate testimonial uptake in some domain is typically only that it 'makes sense to think that one person can be better placed than another to make judgements', but that this 'restriction imposes little more than the very idea of judgement imposes in the first place'.

If we accept these claims about the minimal demands for the possibility of testimonial uptake, then it seems clear that a sophisticated expressivist account in

---

[16] Further evidence that a close link between non-cognitivism and pessimism is often presupposed can be gleaned from the need which several influential pessimists—such as Pettit (1983) and Wollheim (1980: 233)—have felt to demonstrate that pessimism is compatible with some version of aesthetic realism.

[17] I think it's plausible that Simon Blackburn is also sympathetic to some kind of link between aesthetic expressivism and pessimism. He claims e.g. (1998: 110) that if 'I have no experience of X, I cannot without misrepresentation answer the question "Is X beautiful/boring/fascinating...?"' I will, however, go on to argue (in Chapters 6 and 7) that we can explain this fact about assertion without resort to pessimism.

some domain will never, in itself, rule out testimony as a permissible source of judgement in that domain. Of course, the obvious question at this stage is whether we *should* accept these claims. I return to this point in §3.8. For now, though, let's focus on extant attempts to construct plausible versions of aesthetic expressivism which are incompatible with optimism.

2.5. Scruton, Todd, and Aesthetic Expressivism

Scruton provides by far the most comprehensive attempt to develop a plausible version of expressivism which is incompatible with optimism. According to Scruton (1976: 54):

> To agree in the judgement that the music is sad is not to agree in a belief, but in something more like a response or an experience; in a mental state that is—unlike belief—logically tied to the immediate circumstances of its arousal.

Further, Scruton goes on to claim (1976: 56) that 'the condition for the sincere acceptance of an aesthetic judgement' is not truth but, rather, a certain kind of experience, with the consequence that 'an aesthetic judgement can be sincerely made only by someone who experiences its object in the appropriate way' (ibid.). A view of this kind is almost certainly going to be incompatible with any kind of optimism, since the kind of experience required will, even granting Scruton's explicit acknowledgement (ibid.) that he is using 'experience' in a wider than normal sense, not be one which we can acquire on the basis of testimony alone. The question, then, becomes whether Scruton's affective view provides a defensible account of aesthetic judgement. I will argue that it does not.

The most prominent difficulty which the affective view faces concerns its ability to account for another source of aesthetic judgement: memory.[18] Even pessimists will typically be confident in assenting to a variety of aesthetic judgements on the basis that they *remember* having certain aesthetic experiences of the objects judged. It's clear, though, that such memories frequently have very little in common—from an experiential point of view—with the original aesthetic experiences. Given this, Scruton is faced with a famous dilemma.[19] If he denies the legitimacy of memory then our repertoire of licit aesthetic judgements would be limited to an implausible degree. We will not be able to properly judge that a

---

[18] By calling memory a 'source of judgement' I do not mean to commit myself to the claim that it is a generative source of judgement. However, I think there is good reason for taking it to be so (see e.g. Lackey 2005). I'm not aware of any extended discussion of the relationship between memory and aesthetic judgement, but see e.g. Cowan (2020) for the moral case.

[19] Versions of this dilemma can be found in e.g. Budd (2003: 391–2), Meskin (2006: 119–20), and Laetz (2008: 357).

familiar painting is vibrant unless we are looking at it *right now* or—to use Scruton's own (1976: 54) example—that a well-known piece of music is sad unless we are presently listening to it.[20] On the other hand, if we accept memory as legitimate then what motivation do we have for rejecting testimony? After all, the crucial missing element intended to render the latter inadmissible is absent with respect to the former also. As Budd (2003: 391–2) puts things:

> As [an] unreinforced memory of the work gets even more dim, his cognitive state will diverge less and less from the virtually blank slate of one who has no first-hand experience of the work; and a time might well come when the reliable informer no longer has any idea of the work's appearance but remembers that the work is graceful. If this happens, the crucial difference between the cognitive states of the [person who has experienced this work and the recipient of their testimony] has vanished.

Scruton himself appears willing to grasp the first horn of this dilemma and to accept that we cannot make a genuine aesthetic judgement regarding x unless we are experiencing x *right now*. He claims, for example that an aesthetic judgement is 'tied to the immediate circumstances of its arousal' (Scruton 1976: 54) and that the conditions for sincerely making such a judgement 'cannot outlive the presence of its object'. It seems, then, that Scruton is willing to allow that—with some possible exceptions in the case of particularly fresh or vivid memories—I can no more judge that a piece of music is sad on the basis of my recollection of a previous performance than on the basis of your testimony concerning that performance.

One possible interpretation of this response is that Scruton is merely introducing a stipulative use of 'aesthetic judgement' which exclusively picks out a certain kind of response or experiential state (one which is inaccessible on the basis of testimony). If this were the case, though, then his view would be perfectly compatible with my own. I am perfectly willing to concede—as I will discuss in the next section—that there are certain important experiential states which we cannot attain on the basis of testimony alone (and which are only rarely accessible via memory). It is clear, though, that Scruton intends something more than this. In particular, he makes it clear (1976: 15–17) that he takes judgements of this kind to be expressed by our ordinary uses of aesthetic language such as 'the music is sad' or 'the painting is beautiful'. That is, he intends to use 'judgement' in my sense, to

---

[20] Indeed, even this may be problematic, given our inability to experience an entire work of music at a single point in time.

pick out something like the mental correlates of our sincere aesthetic assertions.[21] This clearly places his position in direct conflict with my own.

What should we make of this view of aesthetic assertion? I won't say anything here about the overall prospects for attempts to link legitimate aesthetic assertion with a certain kind of experience (though I will return to this point in §7.6). What I will note, though, is that the specific proposal which Scruton appears to be making here strikes me as implausible in the extreme. Very many, indeed the vast majority, of the aesthetic assertions we make aren't made in the presence of the object of those assertions. So, on Scruton's account, all—or virtually all—of these assertions would be defective. Further, they would be so not merely because they express aesthetic judgements which are illegitimate or poorly grounded but, rather, because they fail to express *any* aesthetic judgement. Surely, though, if we are looking for the mental correlate of our aesthetic assertions then we shouldn't appeal to a state which is manifestly absent when the lion's share of such assertions is made. Further, it is important to emphasize that this problem isn't encountered either by the cognitivist who takes the mental states in question to be beliefs or by other expressivists such as Gibbard.

A defender of Scruton may, perhaps, suggest that we take the primary function of aesthetic assertions to be expressing experiences of the relevant kind but that we also allow that they can, in some derivative sense, come to express our dispositions to have such experiences in the appropriate circumstances. Indeed, it's not implausible to regard this as the view which Scruton himself *was* proposing. This modification would, however, fail to salvage Scruton's account. Clearly, we *can* be disposed to have various aesthetic experiences, and believe ourselves to have such dispositions, without actually having those experiences *right now*. The difficulty is how the expressivist can deny that we can also meet these conditions without ever having experienced the relevant object for ourselves. We can clearly possess the disposition itself in the absence of experience, so the only remaining question is whether we can *believe* ourselves to have such a disposition. Again, though, it should be uncontroversial that we can. Remember that our focus here is still on constitutive considerations and so we only need to show that such beliefs are possible, not that they could ever be legitimate. And I can think of no remotely plausible reason for insisting that we literally *cannot* form beliefs about our own aesthetic dispositions on the basis of testimony. Given this, it looks as if the person who remembers hearing the music and the one who has merely heard about the music would, again, be in the same position. Neither is actually having the experience, but both are disposed to have it, and both believe (for different reasons) that they are so disposed. So, we must conclude either that both have

---

[21] I am assuming here, contra Todd (2004: 279), that the expressivist is willing to accept that we make genuine aesthetic assertions. Those who are unhappy with the assumption can rephrase what follows in terms of some assertion-like activity.

made a sincere aesthetic assertion (and therefore formed an aesthetic judgement) in this extended sense or that neither has. The former would entail a straightforward rejection of Scruton's view. The latter would, again, render aesthetic judgements in the relevant sense a remarkably poor candidate for being the mental correlates of aesthetic assertion.

Is there a way for constitutive expressivist pessimists to respond to this worry? Although Todd's defence of expressivism is largely based on Scruton's view, he is well aware of the dilemma facing Scruton's position and argues that it can be overcome. Todd's begins his defence by suggesting that an assertion 'that "O is beautiful" can mean two different things, each based on different cognitive states: first-hand acquaintance, and indirect description or testimony' (2004: 295). He further, suggests (ibid.) that this distinction, along with the bifurcation of the mental correlates of assertion, is 'an inevitable consequence of expressivism about aesthetic judgement'. Finally, he maintains that, contra Budd (2003: 388), one key difference between these two states is that it is only someone who finds themselves in the former who can fully understand the aesthetic claims they are making (Todd 2004: 296). If Todd is correct here, then it looks as if aesthetic expressivists are committed to regarding the kind of mental state linked with first-hand experience as the only *genuine* kind of aesthetic judgement (since only the person making judgements of this kind really understands the aesthetic position they are endorsing). This would also explain why the expressivist would regard these states as the genuine correlates of sincere *competent* aesthetic assertion. It is debatable whether we are even capable of making an assertion if we don't understand the content asserted but, even if we are, such an assertion would clearly fail to qualify as competent.

There is much that could be said in response to Todd's arguments here. First, I take the overall expressivist position he is sketching to be rather implausible. In particular, it strikes me as clearly mistaken to think that I literally can't understand the *meaning* of a claim such as 'the painting in the next room is beautiful' unless I've seen the painting, and its beauty, for myself. A much more plausible claim in this vicinity would be that I would be unable to understand this claim if I had never had *any* experience of beauty. Yet, this weaker version of the claim provides no support for Todd's expressivism since it would allow someone with previous experiences of beauty to fully understand the judgement that the painting was beautiful without ever experiencing it for themselves.

Further, I think that Todd is mistaken in maintaining that the aesthetic expressivist is committed to anything like the position he sketches. It is here where the concern which I raised regarding Todd's presentation of his position in the previous section, which may initially have seemed a mere technical quibble, becomes extremely important. Todd claims that the expressivist cannot, as Budd (2003: 292) suggests, take the first kind of mental state he describes as corresponding to appreciation and the second kind to belief since, on the expressivist view, 'the distinction between appreciation and belief...is a false one'. This is far too quick, though, since—even leaving terminological debates about 'belief' aside—there is certainly a distinction which many expressivists will want to make here. Recall that for Gibbard (1990: 52) the judgement that something is aesthetically good will amount to something like the judgement that it is appropriate to appreciate the object in question. Judging that it is appropriate to appreciate something is, however, a vastly different activity from appreciation itself. So, on Gibbard's view, the expressivist is left with a distinction which appears structurally very similar to that which the cognitivist is accustomed to drawing between belief and appreciation. Of course, it is open to Todd (and other expressivist pessimists) to reject Gibbard's view here but the point remains that, for other expressivists, accepting something like this view is very much a live option. Given this, the expressivist isn't committed to the kind of semantic distinction which Todd proposes. Further, considering the difficulties highlighted for such an account above, they would be well advised to reject Todd's proposed semantic bifurcation.[22]

I have argued, then, that attempts to reach constitutive pessimism via appeal to non-cognitivism are unsuccessful. I return to my previous claim that the majority of the arguments which will follow in this work can be applied equally to cognitivist and non-cognitivist views of aesthetic judgement. As such, I will remain largely neutral between the two.

2.6. Lopes on Aesthetic Appreciation

A final strategy for motivating constitutive pessimism appeals to the claim that we cannot *appreciate* the aesthetic value of an object on the basis of testimony. Of course, merely accepting this view is not enough to help the constitutive pessimist since it is (as stated) perfectly compatible with the kind of optimism I am advocating. There is no inconsistency in holding both that aesthetic belief can be based on testimony and that aesthetic appreciation cannot. Indeed, I am aware of no optimist who would reject this combination of views. So, why might someone take an appeal to aesthetic appreciation to provide a challenge to the optimist?

One difficulty which this kind of constitutive pessimism might be taken to generate for the optimist is an exegetical one. Some have recently argued that this appreciative understanding of pessimism is the one which many of its most prominent defenders, such as Wollheim (1980: 233) in his *AP*, have actually endorsed. As such, we defenders of optimism have been targeting a view—pessimism concerning aesthetic belief—which, while certainly not undefended, is nowhere near as influential as many have assumed. The most developed

---

[22] I consider some further concerns for Todd's account, alongside the prospects for a different bifurcated view, in §2.7.

argument for a view of this kind is presented by Dominic McIver Lopes (2014b: 170) who claims that 'the controversy over the acquaintance principle ensues from an incorrect interpretation of it.' According to Lopes, 'aesthetic judgement' can refer to both 'experience-like states ascribing aesthetic value and non-experiential states ascribing aesthetic value' (2014b: 175). It is, Lopes maintains, the former with which *AP* (and by extension pessimism) is properly concerned but many recent participants in the debate concerning *AP* have mistakenly taken it to be concerned with the latter. The central controversy I focus on in this book is, therefore, largely the result of a misunderstanding.[23]

While I am, predictably, inclined to reject this overall picture, I am sympathetic to some aspects of Lopes's claim. In particular, it does seem eminently plausible that *some* of the apparent controversy between optimists and pessimists has been a merely verbal dispute between those who deny that testimony is a legitimate source of aesthetic appreciation and those who accept it is a legitimate source of aesthetic belief (and the ease of slipping between these two different kinds of claim is a phenomenon I will return to several times in subsequent chapters). Yet, it is clear that this strategy has its limitations since it is commonplace for optimists to concede that, as Aaron Meskin (2004: 76) phrases the point, 'there are things that testimony may never provide—aesthetic experiences and artistic appreciation.'[24] More importantly for my purposes, many contemporary pessimists (such as Hopkins (2000: 209, 2011: 138), Andow (2014: 211), Hazlett (2017: 49), and Whiting (2015: 91)) have been explicit that their claim is intended to be one concerning aesthetic *belief*.

It is clear, then, that there exists a genuine controversy concerning the relationship between testimony and aesthetic judgement (in my sense). One which, whatever its historical roots, is not presently grounded merely in a (mis)reading of earlier pessimists. Given this, even if Lopes is correct about the historical origins of this debate, the debate is still a substantive one in need of resolution. Having said this, it is also important to stress that I don't believe that Lopes's account of the debate's origin *should* be accepted. In particular, Lopes (2014b: 174) is rather too quick to interpret certain influential pessimists as endorsing something like his appreciative version of pessimism. For example, he takes Philip Pettit to be expressing a view of this kind when he makes his (1983: 15) claim that 'the state one is in when one sincerely assents to a given aesthetic characterisation is not a state to which one can have non-perceptual access'. However, much of what Pettit says elsewhere in the same paper seems to clearly favour an epistemic interpretation of his view. Consider, for example, his (1983: 25) claim that in aesthetics

---

[23] Ransom (2019: 421) terms this kind of bifurcated position—where we endorse *AP* for aesthetic judgement in one sense but reject it for a different sense—'reconciliationism'. Ransom herself endorses a (rather different) position of this kind but doesn't make parallel claims about exegetical errors.

[24] See also Budd (2003: 392) and Robson (2015a: 759).

'perception is the only title to the sort of knowledge which perception yields—let us say, to the full knowledge—of the truths which they express'.[25] Similarly, Wollheim (1980: 233) himself highlights that one interpretation of his Acquaintance Principle is 'highly likely to insist on some such experience as an epistemic condition of aesthetic evaluation'. It is clear, then, that Wollheim is happy to countenance at least one epistemic reading of *AP* and so, contra Lopes, those who propose such interpretations have not misinterpreted Wollheim.[26]

It seems, then, that there is good reason to reject Lopes's claims concerning the origins and nature of the debate concerning aesthetic testimony. Leaving such exegetical issues aside, though, what should we say concerning the success (or otherwise) of the kind of 'appreciative pessimism' Lopes proposes? The answer to this question will naturally depend a great deal on precisely how we understand 'appreciation' here, but appreciative pessimism does seem to be entailed by some of the most prominent accounts of aesthetic appreciation. Consider, for example Budd's (2003: 392) view according to which appreciation involves 'perceiving [a work's aesthetic properties] as realized in the work' or Dickie's according to which it requires our 'experiencing the qualities of a thing' in such a way as to find them 'worthy or valuable' (1974: 40). Clearly appreciation of *these* kinds cannot be acquired on the basis of testimony. However, the standard worry arises that these claims are only true because they are trivial. Of course, we cannot perceive a work's aesthetic qualities via testimony just as we cannot *perceive* its colour or its shape by such means.

Further, Lopes's own understanding of appreciation appears to have similar consequences. According to Lopes (2014b: 179) aesthetic appreciation is 'defined as a cognitive process where interpretation and clarification produce an ascription of aesthetic value'. This description is, of course, a little lacking in specificity, and Lopes (2104b: 179) suggests that we can fill in some of the details by claiming that 'aesthetic appreciation involves' what he terms 'α-judgements'—that is, 'experiential states ascribing aesthetic values' (ibid. 175). Lopes is keen to stress here that the experiential states in question do not have to be (directly) caused by the objects themselves and that the relevant experiences don't have to be *perceptual* experiences.[27] It is also clear then that a 'mere assertion, based on an α-judgement, that [a] song is catchy does not put you in a position to form your own α-judgement' (ibid.). That is, α-judgements cannot be transmitted via testimony. Again, though, this denial merely presents us with a claim—that testimony

---

[25] On a more concessive note, I find Lopes's exegetical claims much more plausible with respect to some of the other authors he discusses. In particular, I am sympathetic (for reasons already discussed in §2.3) with his (2014b: 174) claim that Sibley should not be interpreted as endorsing a version of pessimism which is in conflict with the kind of optimism I favour.

[26] I argue at length elsewhere (Wallbank and Robson 2022) that Lopes's exegetical claims also encounter difficulties with Wollheim's other interpretations of *AP*.

[27] This allows him to avoid some well-worn objections to other formulations of *AP* concerning e.g. exact duplicates (2014b: 181–2) and literary works (180–1).

concerning the aesthetic value of an object cannot by itself produce an experiential state which ascribes value to that object—which no optimist would feel any pressure to reject.

It is important to stress that this last remark should not be taken as a criticism of Lopes. Recall that Lopes himself holds (2014b: 170) that much of the controversy over *AP*, and consequently the recent debate over aesthetic testimony, rests on a mistake. Given this, I see no reason to suppose that Lopes would be at all hostile to the thought that his appreciative version of *AP* should be taken to be uncontroversially, indeed trivially, true.[28] This is not to deny that there is much that *is* substantive, and indeed immensely valuable, in his discussion of aesthetic appreciation and *AP* (Lopes 2014b: 169–84). On the contrary, there is much to be learned from his account of the inseparability of aesthetic content in depictions (and the inability of such depictions to serve as vehicles of testimony), his discussion of the nature of aesthetic value, and much more besides. Yet, none of this is relevant for our present purposes.

Of course, I cannot prove that there is no possible understanding of 'appreciation' which would make the claim that appreciation is unavailable via testimony substantive, but it is worth noting just how ubiquitous the link between appreciation and experience (perceptual or otherwise) is. We have already seen examples of this connection in the accounts offered by Budd, Dickie, and Lopes above and these are by no means isolated examples. Iseminger (1981: 389) claims that 'what one appreciates one has some kind of direct contact with. It is not enough to believe or even to know that the property being appreciated actually is exemplified. One must seem to see, hear, or otherwise notice that it is.' Similarly, Levinson (2009: 415) suggests that 'To appreciate something arguably involves, on the one hand, perceiving, cognizing, or otherwise experiencing it, where such experience may involve the imagination, and on the other hand, deriving satisfaction from it or regarding it positively.'

It might be objected, though, that appreciative optimism cannot be as trivially mistaken as I have assumed since there are some who explicitly defend it. In particular, Amir Konigsberg has argued that it is possible to transmit something like appreciation, as interpreted above, via testimony. According to Konigsberg (2012: 156), 'it is not only possible to transmit declarative aesthetic knowledge through testimony' but also to transmit 'aesthetically appreciative experiences'. It would, however, be a mistake to take Konigsberg as endorsing appreciative optimism here. His concern is not with aesthetic testimony as this is standardly understood

---

[28] It is worth noting that, while I think that Lopes is right that a shift to appreciation would render any debate concerning testimony insubstantial, I have some doubts about whether this claim is quite correct when applied to *AP* itself. In particular, this understanding of *AP* will face the challenge of dealing with many of the same (apparent) counterexamples faced by epistemic versions of the principle. For some recent discussions of the state of *AP* see e.g. Hanson (2015), Focosi (2019), and Ransom (2019).

but, rather, with 'aesthetic testimony' understood as 'aesthetic and non-aesthetic descriptions communicated from person to person' (2012: 154). This means that the claim which Konigsberg actually defends in his paper isn't a form of appreciative optimism but, rather, the claim that certain descriptions can allow us to appreciate certain works without ever experiencing them for ourselves. This conclusion is, for reasons highlighted in the introduction, tangential to the debate between optimism and pessimism.[29]

2.7. Appreciation Revisited

I hope to have shown, then, that there is little prospect for constructing a substantive version of *AP* merely by interpreting 'aesthetic judgement' as referring to some kind of aesthetic appreciation. Still, merely demonstrating that appreciative versions of *AP* are unhelpful does not show that there is no hope for any constitutive version of pessimism linked to appreciation. And, given the frequency with which the question of appreciation arises in debates between the optimist and the pessimist, it is worth considering whether it is possible to spell out a plausible non-trivial version of constitutive pessimism which makes some appeal to appreciation.

Perhaps the most prominent recent proposal for doing so comes from Gorodeisky and Marcus (2018) who, again, take 'aesthetic judgment' to refer to a kind of appreciation.[30] Their disagreement with the kind of optimism I am propounding is more than merely terminological, though, since they claim not only that states of this kind are inaccessible via testimony (which, I take it, they would agree should be accepted by all sides) but also (ibid. 134) that it is states of this kind which are the mental correlates of our aesthetic assertions.[31] There's much which could be said about the subtle and intricate position which Gorodeisky and Marcus put forward (and I *do* say more in Meskin and Robson (n.d.)) but, for present purposes, I will merely focus on one important concern for their proposal (and any proposal which takes something like appreciation to be 'aesthetic judgement' in my sense).

A key challenge for the appreciative account is that there are certain kinds of (apparently) aesthetic discourse which clearly don't require that I have appreciated

---

[29] For discussion of Konigsberg's view see Robson (2013) and Hanson (2015).

[30] At least they mostly talk as if aesthetic judgements are a certain kind or appreciative mental state. However, they sometimes (e.g. Gorodeisky and Marcus 2018: 113) seem to suggest that aesthetic judgement is something like a judgement about what it would be appropriate to appreciate. Views of this latter kind are discussed later.

[31] As with Todd above, they appear (Gorodeisky and Marcus 2018: 137) somewhat reluctant to endorse the thought that our aesthetic language involves straightforward assertions. Again, though, I believe that—given the availability of various expressivist accounts of assertion—there is no need for this reticence.

an object for myself.[32] Gorodeisky and Marcus themselves (2018: 135) discuss 'modally and epistemically' inflected cases ('it must be beautiful'), and—as I will discuss further in Chapter 7—something similar applies to conditionals ('If what they say is true it must be very beautiful'), questions ('Is it beautiful?'), and much more besides. As we saw in §2.5, it was concerns of this kind which led Todd to adopt a bifurcated account of the semantics of aesthetic assertions, and Gorodeisky and Marcus follow suit. They claim (2018: 137) that '"North by Northwest is excellent" can express either an appreciation of the film—a feeling that presents the film as excellent—or a belief that the proposition "North by Northwest is excellent" is true.'[33]

There are, however, a number of reasons to be wary of endorsing such bifurcated accounts. To begin, we should note that, as Hopkins (2001: 185) points out, we would need some compelling independent grounds 'for thinking that claims of the form "O is beautiful" in fact divide into two very different semantic types'. Such a move would, after all, make Gorodeisky and Marcus's aesthetic semantics significantly more complex than that of both the straightforward cognitivist and many of their rival expressivists (such as Gibbard).[34] Further, this highly bifurcated semantics makes it much less clear whether Gorodeisky and Marcus can successfully respond to some historically prominent concerns for expressivism and related views (such as the famous Frege-Geach problem). Finally, more needs to be said to show that such positions still leave appreciation as the best candidate for the title of 'aesthetic judgement'. Gorodeisky and Marcus's view initially seems to be that aesthetic assertions express appreciation, but they later accept (2018: 135) that a whole range of inflected/imbedded/qualified aesthetic assertions actually express belief and even that there are occasions on which simple aesthetic assertions do the same. Given this, we would need to hear more about why beliefs aren't (at least) as good a candidate as assertions to count as the mental correlates of aesthetic assertions. If they are, though, then it would follow that aesthetic judgement is no longer constitutively ruled out on the basis of testimony.[35]

---

[32] Some of the worries I discuss for a very different appreciative account of assertion in §7.6 may also be relevant here.

[33] Todd suggests (2004: 295) that such a cost is 'an inevitable consequence of expressivism about aesthetic judgement'. We have already seen, though, that this is not the case since Gibbard's expressivism avoids any such complication.

[34] Gorodeisky and Marcus (2018: 135) suggest that this isn't a particular problem for their view since 'the other candidates (be they semantic or pragmatic accounts) will be alternative explanations of a genuine distinction among aesthetic predication'. However, I believe that this is mistaken for two reasons. First, some of the explananda that they use to motivate this distinction are ones which the optimist (and even some pessimists) can simply reject. Second, suggesting (as I will in Chapter 6) that certain aesthetic assertions introduce additional pragmatic complexities just doesn't seem comparable, in terms of theoretical cost, to proposing a fundamental bifurcation in the mental correlates of our aesthetic discourse.

[35] These arguments are, of course, rather quick. These, and other, concerns for Gorodesisky and Marcus's view are explored further in Meskin and Robson (n.d.).

Another helpful suggestion for linking appreciation and pessimism can be found by reconsidering Gibbard's (1990: 52) claim that 'aesthetic norms are norms for the rationality of kinds of aesthetic appreciation'. On the basis of this thought, a pessimist might suggest the following appreciative version of their view:

Norm appreciation: It is a constitutive condition of the judgement that, say, x is beautiful, that I judge it rational (under appropriate conditions) to appreciate x as being beautiful. Where 'appreciate' here just means something like 'experiencing the qualities of a thing' in such a way as to find them 'worthy or valuable' (Dickie 1974: 40). We cannot, however, judge that it would be rational to appreciate something on the basis of testimony.

What should we make of the story offered in *Norm Appreciation*? The good news for the pessimist is that it isn't trivial true. The bad news is that it is false. It is, I maintain, possible for someone to judge that it would be rational to appreciate an object purely on the basis of testimony. (Indeed, we have already seen above that this is Gibbard's own (1990: 174–88) view when it comes to parallel cases in ethics.)

To begin to see why this is so, consider an agent (me) and an artwork (*Much Ado about Nothing*). As a matter of autobiographical fact, I have never seen the play in question, but I am well aware that it has been well thought of by generations of critics and that it is regarded by many as one of (if not the) best of Shakespeare's comedies. On the basis of this I have formed a number of beliefs concerning the play; that it is a work of great artistic value, that it is one of Shakespeare's better comedies, and, most relevantly for present purposes, that it would be rational for me to appreciate the play were I to view it for myself.[36] I have previously argued at length (in Robson 2019) that beliefs of this kind are perfectly legitimate (indeed, in my view such beliefs frequently enjoy considerably more warrant than our first-hand aesthetic judgements). For now, though, what is important is not whether a belief of this kind is legitimate but merely whether it is *possible*. And, on this issue, I can merely assert that beliefs of this general kind must surely be possible since some of their instances are actual.

Of course, the strategies discussed here are far from being the only connections which may be—or even *have* been—drawn between pessimism and aesthetic

---

[36] Admittedly, the actual situation here is a little more complicated than I would like since my reasons for accepting that the play is excellent are not merely testimonial. Rather, they also include inductive considerations (based on the various Shakespearean works I have encountered for myself) as well as various pieces of information I have encountered concerning the play itself. Let's abstract away from these complications, though, and focus on a slightly idealized version of this case where I formed this belief purely on the basis of a wealth of critical testimony.

appreciation.[37] They are, however, the only prima facie plausible methods I can think of for motivating an appreciative version of *constitutive* pessimism. We return, then, to my previous conclusion that there is no version of constitutive pessimism which presents us with a view which is both plausible and substantive. Support for a non-trivial version of pessimism cannot, therefore, be found merely by considering the nature of aesthetic judgement. In subsequent chapters I will ask whether it can be found elsewhere.

---

[37] E.g. Whiting (2015) argues from the illegitimacy of certain kinds of appreciation based on testimony to a (perhaps constitutive) version of pessimism. However, I believe that his arguments here are unsuccessful for reasons highlighted in Lord (2016).

3
The Presumption of Optimism

3.1. The Burden of Proof

In the previous chapter I considered attempts to justify pessimism by claiming that it is entailed by the very nature of aesthetic judgement, concluding that there is no reason to accept any (non-trivial) version of this view. Given this, it seems that anyone looking to motivate pessimism will need to offer cogent arguments in favour of their view as well as rebutting the best arguments available to the optimist (and in subsequent chapters I will argue that they can do neither). The pessimist may, however, object that I am underestimating the strength of their dialectical position. It is not, they may claim, incumbent on them to establish their view by appeal to argument since it is, in some respect(s), the default position with regards to aesthetic testimony. As such, the burden of proof lies with their optimistic opponents to show that we have compelling reason to move away from this default position. If I accepted this claim, then I would be faced with the task of demonstrating that the considerations I adduce in subsequent chapters are sufficient to overcome this presumption of pessimism (which, for the record, I believe they would be). Fortunately, though, such a task is not required since my hypothetical pessimist has things entirely backwards. In this chapter I will argue that it is optimism, not pessimism, which should be our default position when it comes to the debate surrounding aesthetic testimony. Indeed, I will go so far as to argue that there are strong (though not decisive) reasons to adopt a constitutive version of optimism.

What reasons might the pessimist give for claiming that there should be a presumption in favour of their view? The most promising motivation for this claim stems from the thought that pessimism is, in some respect(s), the folk view concerning aesthetic testimony and should, therefore, be accepted until we are given some compelling reason to reject it. What does it mean, though, to claim that pessimism is the folk view? Three different interpretations could be offered, each of which leads to its own version of the 'folk view' argument.

The first interpretation provides the most direct line of argument in favour of pessimism, an argument based around the claim that pessimism just *is* the view which the folk would endorse. This is not, of course, to maintain that the majority of people actually *do* endorse pessimism (since most people have, doubtless, never given the slightest consideration to the status of aesthetic testimony). Rather, the thought is that, if we were to present ordinary people with a description of the views of the optimist and pessimist, then the majority would judge the latter to be more plausible. The second interpretation is that pessimism is best reflected by folk theory. That is, that the judgements which the folk make (or would make) regarding the legitimacy or otherwise of aesthetic judgements in various circumstances, both actual and hypothetical, are best explained by an appeal to pessimism. Finally, the pessimist could offer an argument based on the thought that their view is tacitly endorsed via folk practice. That is, that some element of folk practice in aesthetics is inexplicable without—or at least best explained by—appeal to the truth of pessimism.

I will argue that these motivations for taking pessimism as our default view are uniformly unpersuasive. I begin, in §3.2, by considering the first argument. I concede to the pessimist that there *may* be some reason for taking pessimism to be the folk view in this sense but argue that this provides little support for the claim that pessimism should be our default view of aesthetic testimony. In §3.3 I consider the third argument for taking pessimism to be the default view (deferring consideration of the second argument until subsequent chapters). and show that this rests on a mistake since our folk practice in no way evinces an implicit acceptance of pessimism. Having argued against pessimism as the default view, I then go on to argue that there should be a presumption in favour of optimism. I begin, in §3.4, by demonstrating that a key aspect of our folk practice actually speaks in favour of optimism. I then go on to argue that the pessimist's view also faces a charge of arbitrariness in regarding aesthetic testimony as operating so very differently from testimony in other domains. In §3.5 I outline a strategy for rebutting the arbitrariness charge by appealing to various other domains where positions parallel to pessimism have arisen and argue that this response is unsuccessful. In §3.6 I offer my defence of a constitutive version of optimism, arguing that many pessimists will be unable to combine their accounts with the leading accounts of the nature of belief. §3.7 surveys, and ultimately rejects, some possible responses on behalf of the pessimist. In §3.8 I argue that, despite being initially framed in terms of a certain version of pessimism, the arguments in §3.6 have a surprisingly wide application to a range of pessimist views. In §3.9 I present some general thoughts on the prospects for constitutive optimism and consider how this ties in with my arguments in the rest of this work.

3.2. Pessimism and Folk Belief

The first argument for a presumption of pessimism maintains that the folk would endorse pessimism over optimism if presented with a straightforward choice between the two views. While I know of no empirical evidence to support this contention, I am inclined to agree that it is likely correct (though, if not, so much the better for me). Yet, this concession does little to bolster the pessimist's position, since there are a number of reasons to doubt whether folk judgements are reliable in this context.

First, we might suggest that folk-pessimism springs from the general tendency—exemplified in proverbs such as 'believe half of what you see and none of what you hear'—to be suspicious of the epistemic power of testimony. I am assuming, though, that—for reasons outlined in §1.4—the pessimist isn't a sceptic when it comes to testimonial judgements concerning mundane matters. Given this, they can only claim support from folk reticence regarding aesthetic testimony to the extent that this is not rooted in a general testimonial scepticism (or, indeed, in a general reluctance to ascribe aesthetic knowledge).[1] A second, related, worry is that some of the folk may only endorse pessimism because they also accept some further view which (virtually) all philosophically minded pessimists would vehemently reject. Consider, for example Meskin's (2004: 84) explanation for the supposed folk acceptance of pessimism.

> In short, I propose that at least some of [this] stems from some subjectivist or relativist tendencies in the folk conception of beauty. We need not advert to the truth of relativism to explain the phenomenon of our resistance to aesthetic testimonial uptake; a widespread belief in the truth of relativism will do just as good a job in explaining this psychological fact…, If A believes that aesthetic judgments have a hidden relativization (i.e., 'That's beautiful.' really expresses something whose form is closer to 'That appears beautiful to people like me.')

Yet, as Meskin himself is keen to stress, this explanation would only provide an etiological account for the acceptance of pessimism rather than justifying it. If we take the folk to be committed to some philosophically sophisticated form of relativism or subjectivism—such as those defended by Goldman (1995), Cappelen and Hawthorne (2009), Kölbel (2004), or MacFarlane (2009)—then this wouldn't rule out reliance on testimony.[2] On the other hand, while there are several simplistic 'folk' forms of relativism which *would* entail pessimism, these are generally (and correctly) regarded as philosophically untenable.

A third reason for suspicion appeals to the perennial difficulty of determining precisely what is at issue in the aesthetic testimony debate. The various interrelated issues which cluster around these debates have made it all too easy for interlocutors, even those who are trained philosophers, to talk past each other. Given this it would (if you'll pardon the pun) be rather optimistic of the pessimist to assume that no part of the folk attraction to pessimism results from such

---

[1] Indeed, a view that appealed only to a general scepticism concerning either testimonial or aesthetic knowledge wouldn't even qualify as a genuine pessimism in the sense I outlined in Chapter 1.
[2] For discussion of this point see Meskin and Robson (2015: 134–5). Andow (2014) develops a sophisticated form of relativism which he believes undermines optimism. For arguments against this claim see Meskin and Robson (2015: 139).

confusions. I suspect, for example, that many of those who initially seem to find pessimism appealing would turn out to be confusing concerns relating to judgement (in my sense) with those concerning appreciation. Similarly, there may be those inclined to confuse—as, again, even trained philosophers have—claims about what it is legitimate to believe on the basis of testimony with what it is legitimate to assert. And it is important to stress, once again, that the species of optimism I am defending is neutral with respect to these further debates.[3] Similarly, we need to make sure that the intuitions we are eliciting genuinely concern normative views about the beliefs we *should* form on the basis of testimony rather than predictive views about the beliefs that we *would* form.[4]

Once we have taken all these factors into consideration, I submit that it becomes increasingly difficult to see whether pessimism itself really qualifies as the intuitive folk view in this respect. It is important to stress, though, that I am not suggesting that these considerations show that the folk would endorse optimism, nor even that they would fail to endorse pessimism. The question of how people would react to these views is a largely empirical one and should be treated as such. Even if it turns out the folks would endorse pessimism, though (and do so on grounds which most philosophers wouldn't take to be immediately mistaken), this still wouldn't prove fatal to my overall line of argument. In subsequent chapters, I will go on to argue that many of the most likely motivations for adopting pessimism—for both philosophers and the folk—rest on a mistake. Given this, any benefit which this hypothetical folk support offer for pessimism would be extremely limited and, I will argue below, easily outweighed by countervailing considerations in support of granting optimism this status.

What about the second interpretation, appealing to the responses which the folk have (or would have) in response to various hypothetical cases? I believe that such arguments are, again, rather less compelling than it may initially appear and will argue for this in detail in the next two chapters. For now, though, let's go on to consider the third interpretation.

3.3. Pessimism and Folk Practice

The final argument for pessimism as the folk view is based on the thought that some aspect of our folk practice is best explained by appeal to pessimism. The two (putative) aspects which tend to be discussed here are an unwillingness to make aesthetic assertions in the absence of first-hand experience and a refusal to form

---

[3] I have addressed the former in the previous chapter while considering the latter in Chapters 6 and 7.
[4] I will argue in §3.3 that we are often mistaken regarding the latter.

aesthetic beliefs on the basis of testimony. I will return to the first of these in Chapter 6. For now, though, let's focus on the second.

The claim that we do not, as a matter of fact, form aesthetic judgements on the basis of testimony has a venerable history. Kant (1790/2005: 94) himself clearly held not only that we should not form aesthetic judgements on the basis of testimony but that, at least standardly, we *do not* do so.[5] When discussing the position of an individual faced with the combined testimony of 'a hundred voices' praising a particular work he claims that this 'will not force his innermost agreement' since 'he clearly sees that the agreement of others gives no valid proof of the judgment about beauty' (ibid.). And it is clear that here, as elsewhere in the aesthetic testimony debate, Kant's influence still looms. The pessimist is still typically regarded as explaining and vindicating our existing doxastic practice within aesthetics rather than as proselytizing for a rethinking of our extant reliance on testimony (see e.g. Nyugen 2020a: 1128).

As with the pessimist's normative claim, this descriptive claim is often qualified in various respects, and it is rare to hear a (non-constitutive) pessimist maintain that we *never* form aesthetic judgements on the basis of testimony. It is, however, still commonplace to highlight some resistance on behalf of ordinary agents to forming such judgements. Indeed, even optimists such as Meskin (2004: 68) allow that 'we do not accept aesthetic testimony to the same extent that we accept other sorts of testimony'. I will, therefore, focus on a view—which I will label 'descriptive pessimism'—according to which we (or at least most of us) are considerably more resistant to forming aesthetic beliefs on the basis of testimony than we are with respect to mundane beliefs.[6] I will label the denial of this view 'descriptive optimism'.

So, how might descriptive pessimism be used to motivate pessimism itself? One prima facie plausible suggestion is that descriptive pessimism highlights an aspect of our folk aesthetic practice which is crying out for explanation, and that the best explanation is one which appeals to our implicit recognition that there would be something problematic about forming aesthetic judgements on the basis of testimony. The optimist could, of course, question whether this phenomenon really is best explained by appeal to pessimism rather than by, say, a widespread but mistaken belief in pessimism. There is, however, no need to pursue this here. Since I aim to show that the proposed argument fails at a much earlier stage, there is simply no reason to hold that this putative folk practice even exists.

The claim that we should reject descriptive pessimism may initially strike you as implausible in the extreme. After all, the claim that we *do not* (or, at the very

---

[5] I am assuming here that Kant is talking about aesthetic judgements in my sense but this assumption is (as already discussed in the previous chapter) a controversial one.

[6] Even this qualified view is probably not entirely accurate as a statement of the relevant view—for reasons paralleling those concerning the normative view in Chapter 1—it will, however, be sufficient for my purposes in this chapter.

least, tend not to) form aesthetic beliefs on the basis of testimony seems like a piece of obvious common sense. Can't we just tell that we don't form our aesthetic judgements in this way?

I think not, and a growing body of evidence suggests that we are remarkably bad at introspectively identifying the sources of our aesthetic beliefs. Consider the following brief summaries of a trio of cases (representative of a much wider body of research):

(i) James Cutting (2003) conducted a series of experiments designed to show that mere exposure to an artwork can significantly affect preference for that work. In these experiments Cutting was able to manipulate student preferences for paintings merely by increasing the number of times they were exposed to reproductions of each work.[7]
(ii) Participants in an experiment by E. H. Hess (1965) were shown photographs which were identical save for (artificially generated) differences in the size of the subject's pupils. As predicted, the subjects with the larger pupil size were judged more attractive.
(iii) Hilke Plassmann et al. (2008) asked subjects to sample five putatively different wines while attached to an FMRI machine. In reality, however, there were only three different wines in the study, two of which were administered twice. For each of the wines administered twice subjects were told that the samples came from bottles which differed dramatically in price ($5 versus $45 and $10 versus $100). The subjects not only reported liking the 'expensive' wines more, but neurological imaging appeared to show that they actually gained more pleasure from drinking them.

In all of these cases, the subjects failed to correctly identify the sources of their aesthetic judgements—mere exposure, variations in pupil size, differences in perceived price—but this did not prevent them from coming up with a whole range of introspective 'reasons' for their judgements. For instance, subjects in variations of the Hess experiment readily point to all manner of non-existent differences between the pairs of photographs ('he's smiling more', 'she has a softer face') to account for their preferences.

Empirical evidence of this kind, combined with our persistent tendency to underestimate the extent to which we rely on testimony, generates a perfect storm

---

[7] It might reasonably be objected (as an anonymous referee for the Press notes) that this experiment, along with others discussed below, doesn't focus on judgement but on some other measure (preference, liking, etc.). As Meskin et al. (2013: 140) point out, though, there tends to be a high degree of consistency amongst various measures (including 'judgement') in experimental work of this kind. Given this the proponent of this objection owes us, at a minimum, a compelling reason to doubt such consistency in the specific cases I discuss here.

of introspective unreliability in this area.[8] It seems, then, that (even if true) the claim that it introspectively *seems* like our aesthetic beliefs aren't formed on the basis of testimony would provide scant evidence in favour of descriptive pessimism. (By contrast, the experiments which I outlined above, and others like them, have provided important and surprising insights into the ways in which our aesthetic judgements are formed.) Further, I'm not even convinced that this claim *is* true. As a matter of autobiographical fact, it doesn't seem to me as if I am particularly resistant to forming aesthetic judgements on the basis of testimony (and I suspect that I am not alone here).

3.4. A Presumption of Optimism?

In the previous section I argued that there is good reason to be suspicious of the motivations behind the descriptive pessimist's claim. In this section, I will go further and suggest that there is considerable empirical evidence against descriptive pessimism itself. Studies have shown, for example, that aesthetic judgements of various kinds are routinely formed on the basis of factors such as reviews by peers and experts (Dixon et al. 2015), contest results (Ginsburgh and Ours 2003), and the perceived popularity of a work (Salganik and Watts 2008).[9] Many of these clearly involve some significant element of testimonial transmission. Let's briefly consider one of these cases in a little more detail.

Ginsburgh and Ours examined results in Belgium's prestigious Queen Elisabeth music competition and found that musicians 'who are successful in the Queen Elisabeth competition seem to be rewarded by subsequent success' (2003: 294). It was shown, for example, that those who were ranked higher in the contest were typically regarded as better performers (and as producing better performances) by professional music critics. One possible explanation for this result, which Ginsburgh and Ours ultimately defend, is that the contest rankings themselves are playing a significant role in determining the later aesthetic beliefs of these critics. This explanation would, however, clearly be at odds with descriptive pessimism. Yet, this is hardly the only available explanation for this correlation and it could be that, as Ginsburgh and Ours themselves note, it simply arises because 'those who are better ranked in the competition are better musicians anyway' (ibid.). In response to this worry, Ginsburgh and Ours adopted a rather ingenious method for ruling out this alternative explanation. They began by noting the (surprisingly large) extent to which results in the contest itself were influenced by the, randomly determined, order in which performers appeared (with those who performed first and last tending to be more favourably received

---

[8] Additional evidence for our unreliability is discussed in e.g. Irvin (2014) and Lopes (2014a).
[9] I discuss the implications of such cases in detail in Robson (2014a).

than those in middle positions). After determining the extent to which the rankings of performers were affected by their order of performance, Ginsburgh and Ours then proceeded to produce an adjusted ranking of performers based on ordering effects alone. Having done so, they then compared this adjusted ranking to the reputation which each performer now enjoyed amongst Belgian music critics. Their results demonstrated a clear correlation between these adjusted rankings and subsequent reputation among critics, to the extent that Ginsburgh and Ours were willing to declare that 'the opinion of music critics is more influenced by the ranking than by the quality of the performers' (ibid.).

Again, this is only one example of a much wider phenomena and there is—as I discuss at length in Robson (2014a)—a range of other empirical evidence which appears to pose a significant challenge to descriptive pessimism. Of course, appeals to empirical results can be met with suspicion, and many philosophers have held that the findings of such investigations have no place—or, at most, a minor and incidental role—in discussions of issues within the philosophy of art. Wittgenstein, for example, famously remarked that:

> people still have the idea that psychology is one day going to explain all our aesthetic judgements, and they mean experimental psychology. This is very funny—very funny indeed... Aesthetic questions have nothing to do with psychological experiments, but are answered in an entirely different way.
> (1970: 19)

In a similar vein, but rather more bluntly, George Dickie (1962: 285) concludes 'that psychology is not relevant to aesthetics'. For the record, I am inclined to think that this general position is mistaken and believe that empirical work can shed a great deal of light on many traditional problems within aesthetics. However, we need not resolve such debates here since it is important to note that the claims I am making here—and others which I will support by appeal to empirical work in later chapters—do not (directly) concern the kind of conceptual or normative issues in which many philosophers of art have traditionally been interested. And, of course, it is precisely these traditional issues within aesthetics towards which the scepticism of those such as Wittgenstein and Dickie is directed. Rather, what is up for debate here is the methods by which our aesthetic judgements are, as a matter of descriptive fact, formed. This is precisely the kind of question which should be most tractable to work within the empirical sciences. I therefore contend that the evidence I have outlined should lead you to reject descriptive pessimism regardless of any qualms you may have regarding the value of empirical investigations when it comes to addressing perennial core issues within aesthetics.

Yet, it might be objected that evidence of this kind only undermines an extreme form of descriptive pessimism. It may show that we do not refrain from ever forming aesthetic beliefs on the basis of testimony, but it does nothing to establish that we form such beliefs with anything like the frequency that we form mundane testimonial beliefs. There is some truth to this objection, but it is important not to overstate its significance. While the results I have discussed are *compatible* with an attenuated form of descriptive pessimism, they don't cast such a view in an especially favourable light. The moderate descriptive pessimist would have to point to some feature(s) of the case outlined—and others discussed in e.g. Robson (2014a)—which makes it exceptional in terms of our reliance on testimony. Yet, it is difficult to see what feature could possibly play this role. And, in the absence of any response to this worry, it seems that we have good reason to accept some form of descriptive optimism.

So, what are the normative implications of accepting descriptive optimism? First, an acceptance of descriptive optimism undermines an important motivation for pessimism since the pessimist can no longer see themselves as merely providing an explanation for, and vindication of, an important element of our folk practice (our refusal to form aesthetic judgements on the basis of testimony). Second, any aesthetician who holds (as many do) that our theories in aesthetics should, wherever possible, respect our folk practice now has a clear motivation for taking optimism to be the default view of aesthetic testimony.

A further powerful motivation for a presumption of optimism is the apparent, and I believe actual, arbitrariness of the pessimist's view. Pessimists and optimists alike accept that testimony is a legitimate source of belief in virtually all domains, but the pessimist differentiates themselves by taking aesthetic beliefs to be an exception to this general picture. Of course, merely proposing that some class of judgement is exceptional is not, in itself, problematic, since there will sometimes be compelling motivations for taking some class of judgements to be exceptional in some respects.[10] However, in the absence of such a motivation, the pessimist's position strikes me as no less ad hoc than one which maintains that testimony is peculiarly unsuited to deliver knowledge concerning zebras or xylophones. The key question is, therefore, what the pessimist can say to motivate the exception they make for aesthetic cases.

The most obvious motivation for making such an exception would be a cogent argument for the truth of pessimism itself, and an argument of this kind would certainly overturn any presumptive advantage which arbitrariness considerations offer the optimist. In subsequent chapters I will go on to argue that no such argument exists but, for present purposes, our concern is merely with whether such a presumption exists rather than whether it remains undefeated. In terms of rejecting the presumption itself, then, what options are open to the pessimist?

---

[10] An influential, though controversial, example concerns the claim that some judgements are 'luminous' (see e.g. Neta and Rohrbaugh 2004).

One strategy would be to motivate the exception they propose by appealing to some wider norm of aesthetic judgement such as *AP*, insisting that a prohibition on relying on aesthetic testimony would no longer be arbitrary if it could be accounted for as part of a more general prohibition. Further, this move is clearly not ad hoc since most pessimists are independently attracted to such norms. An obvious worry, though, is that this response doesn't really dispel the arbitrariness charge but merely pushes it back a step. The question would now become what explains the putative fact that aesthetic beliefs are governed by a wider norm such as *AP* while beliefs in mundane areas are not. As Budd (2003: 387) notes, many discussions of *AP* merely take it for granted that the principle is correct. And Wollheim's own (1986: 232–7) project is explicitly one of considering how various views can best accommodate *AP* rather than questioning whether we should wish to do so.

That is not to say that arguments for *AP* cannot be offered. We could, for example, appeal to *AP* as an explanation for why it is that we cannot legitimately form aesthetic judgements on the basis of testimony. At this stage in the dialectic, though, an argument of this kind would be manifestly question-begging. A more promising proposal starts from the claim that various other sources of aesthetic judgement are problematic. Let's imagine, for example, that we've established that inferences from principles of taste, enumerative induction, and the like are all illegitimate as sources of aesthetic judgement. And, further, that—as Hopkins (2006) discusses—*AP* provides the best unifying explanation for the impermissibility of various sources of aesthetic judgement.[11] If all of this were true then we would have a clear motivation for accepting *AP* and, a fortiori, pessimism.

Still, there are two concerns with this proposal. First, offering this kind of complex argument seems to, once again, be aiming to overturn, rather than deny, the presumption in favour of optimism. Second, and more substantively, this proposal is largely a series of promissory notes. My own view is that, for reasons outlined in Robson (2013), the prospects for motivating a (non-trivial) version of *AP* are rather bleak. However, even if I am mistaken here, it is certainly fair to say that, as things stand, it is far from being an established fact that *any* of the sources of aesthetic judgement which *AP* rules out really are *verboten*. Further, even if the other sources of aesthetic judgement mentioned really are problematic, it is by no means obvious that the best explanation for this will be a principle (such as *AP*) which rules out testimony as well. Consider, for example, that the other proposed sources are typically inferential in nature whereas testimony, on most

---

[11] Hopkins himself (2006: 85) explicitly denies that he is offering an argument for *AP*. However, the considerations he raises in his discussion certainly seem to provide a strong motivation for someone who accepts his intuitions about the (im)permissible sources of aesthetic judgement (Hopkins himself includes testimony in his list of impermissible sources but this doesn't seem strictly necessary to offering an argument of the relevant kind) to endorse a principle in the region of *AP*.

contemporary accounts, is not. Overall, then, an appeal to *AP* provides scant help for the pessimist in rebutting the arbitrariness charge.[12] Is a better response available?

3.5. Pessimists of the World Unite

The pessimist's claim that testimony is not a legitimate source of aesthetic judgement requires drawing a sharp distinction between aesthetic testimony and testimony in most other domains. Yet, aesthetics is not the only area where such a divide has been proposed. On the contrary, there are a range of other domains where it has been argued that testimony is not a legitimate source of judgement. In this section, I will consider ways in which appeal to these other domains might be taken to help rebut the arbitrariness concern. For convenience's sake, I will amend my customary usage and use 'pessimism' and 'optimism' as general names for views concerning the value of testimony in some domain (using e.g. 'pessimism in aesthetics' when referring to the position I call 'pessimism' elsewhere).

The most prominent species of pessimism concerns moral judgements. As with aesthetic testimony, pessimism in this domain has a venerable history (one which, again, dates back at least as far as Kant).[13] However, more recent statements of moral pessimism aren't difficult to find. Bernard Williams (1995: 205), for example, advises that

> anyone who is tempted to take up the idea of there being a theoretical science of ethics should be discouraged by reflecting on what would be involved in taking seriously the idea that there were experts in it. It would imply, for instance, that a student who had not followed the professor's reasoning but had understood his moral conclusion might have some reason, on the strength of his professorial authority, to accept it

Similarly, Hills (2009: 97) maintains that 'you have reason neither to defer to moral experts nor to trust moral testimony', McGrath (2011: 111) that there 'is something off-putting about the idea of arriving moral views by simply deferring

---

[12] Another strategy would be to reject the claim that aesthetic judgements are *beliefs* in a straightforwardly cognitive sense. The pessimist could then maintain that aesthetic judgements are of an importantly different kind from mundane judgements, perhaps some kind of non-cognitive state, and so we have no reason to expect them to behave like beliefs (typical or otherwise). Nor would we have any reason to regard aesthetic judgements as a remotely exceptional instance of whichever kind they belong to. In my view this response is by far the most promising for a pessimist looking to reject the arbitrariness charge. Still, I will argue in §3.8 that it is less convincing than it may initially appear.

[13] For an excellent discussion of the different areas where Kant judges testimony to be (im)permissible see Gelfert (2006).

to an expert', and Crisp (2014: 129) that 'there is something morally or epistemically regrettable about relying on the moral testimony of others'.[14]

Another form of pessimism concerns judgements of gustatory taste.[15] Shaffer (2007: 77), for example, claims that 'there are no good reasons to accept much of the testimony' of gastronomic experts. Pessimism of this kind is typically supported by appeal to something like a gustatory analogue of AP, with Barry Smith (2007: 44) suggesting:

> We certainly rely on subjective experiences to know how a wine tastes. For even if we know a great deal about its objective chemical properties or vinification, we would not know what it tastes like without tasting it. The experience of tasting provides the only route to such knowledge.

Similarly, Carolyn Korsmeyer (2013: 258–9) suggests that 'both literal taste and taste for art require first-hand acquaintance with their objects. Just as one cannot decide that soup is well seasoned without actually sipping it, so one cannot conclude that music is moving without hearing it' and Kevin Sweeney (2007: 120) that 'gustatory judgement, like critical appreciation, must be based on our own sensory experience'.

These are, however, very far from being the only domains in which doubt has arisen concerning the legitimacy of reliance of testimony. Indeed, there have been defences of pessimism in domains as disparate as religion (Jay 2016), mathematics (Williams 1972), and philosophy itself (Allen 2019, Ranalli 2020).

Let's imagine, then, that the aesthetic pessimist is a pessimist across all these other domains. Would this help to rebut the arbitrariness charge? It's not clear that it would. On the contrary, if the pessimist were to claim no more than that testimony is unacceptable in each of domains then this might risk increasing the arbitrariness of their position. The domains listed above hardly form a natural grouping, and it is difficult to identify much in common between the following judgements: (i) *Guernica* is harrowing, (ii) God exists, (iii) the soup is overly seasoned, (iv) two is the only even prime number, (v) veganism is morally obligatory, (vi) universalism is the best answer to the special composition question. Further, the challenge isn't merely to point to some substantive property which all of these domains have in common but to one which isn't shared by any mundane domain.

Of course, the pessimist might respond to these concerns by suggesting some principle which explains why—disparate though they may be—all and only these domains present us with testimonial 'no go' areas. Yet, I have difficulty conceiving

---

[14] Other moral pessimists include Nickel (2001), Hopkins (2007), Crisp (2014), Fletcher (2016), and Mogensen (2017).
[15] I use 'gustatory taste' to refer to taste in the folk sense. This includes not only taste (strictly so called) but also flavour and correlative multi-sensory experiences.

of any remotely plausible principle which could fulfil this role.[16] Perhaps such a grand unifying principle isn't required, though, and the pessimist in aesthetics could still mitigate the arbitrariness charge by finding some common explanation for several prominent forms of pessimism.[17] It is, however, important not to underestimate the challenge which even this more modest project faces. First, we would need to identify some principle which would, if true, explain why testimony is impermissible in each of the domains which our pessimist appeals to. Second, we would need to provide some reason for accepting that this principle really applies to each of these domains (without overgeneralizing to some mundane judgements). To get a sense of the difficulty here, let's focus again on *AP*. It is abundantly clear that—as e.g. Wollheim (1980: 233) and Goldman (2006: 333) discuss—a straightforward moral analogue of *AP* would be an abject failure. It would, for example, be abhorrent to remain neutral as to the ethical status of the transatlantic slave trade merely because you lack personal acquaintance with it. Nor is this the only area where an analogue of *AP* is problematic. Indeed, it is not even clear what an acquaintance principle would amount to when applied to mathematical claims (or to a great many philosophical claims).[18] It is true that—as we have seen—some philosophers already find an analogue of *AP* attractive when applied to judgements of gustatory taste. Even here there are difficulties, though, since we would need some story about what makes these two areas—judgements of aesthetic and gustatory taste—uniquely susceptible to this kind of acquaintance demand. In particular, we'd need an account of why this demand applies to judgements of gustatory taste when no such restriction applies to judgements in other sensory modalities.[19]

Still, *AP* isn't the only game in town and other proposals do a much better job of providing a unifying principle for some of the disparate species of pessimism. One common recurring theme here is the importance of *understanding*, with various pessimists—such as Hills (2009, 2010, 2017), Hopkins (2007, 2011), and Williams (1972)—suggesting roughly that, while in most domains the norm of belief is either truth or knowledge, certain domains are exceptions to this general trend with the relevant norm there being understanding.[20] And understanding,

---

[16] This is not, of course, anything like an argument to the effect that there couldn't be such a principle. Even if such a principle is suggested, though, there will—as I discuss further below—be other difficulties for the pessimist in rebutting the arbitrariness charge.

[17] It would be open to a pessimist of this kind either to claim that we should reject pessimism in the domains not covered by this explanation or to maintain that there is some other explanation(s) for the impermissibility of pessimism in these other domains.

[18] The religious case is harder to classify. Christopher Jay (2016: 247) suggests that there is reason to hold that religious experience is a legitimate source of religious belief whereas testimony is not. Whether such experience amounts to direct experience of the relevant object is, however, an exceedingly complex issue which I will not enter into here.

[19] Meskin and Robson (2015) argue at length that no such explanation is forthcoming. I return to the (dis)analogies between the two kinds of taste in §7.4.

[20] For a discussion of different accounts of understanding see Grimm (2012).

the thought goes, is (in contrast to true belief and even knowledge) unavailable via testimony. Popular as understanding-based accounts are, though, they certainly aren't the only game in town. Other explanations appeal to considerations as diverse as the importance of certain emotional responses (Fletcher 2016), the value of authenticity (Mogensen 2017), and the social benefits of forming non-testimonial beliefs in these areas (Hazlett 2017).

Despite their differences, though, I maintain that all of these explanations fail, for the rather straightforward reason that they are attempting to account for a phenomenon, the truth of pessimism, which (in the aesthetic case at least) simply does not exist.[21] Rather than attempting to argue against these explanations on a case-by-case basis, then, my focus in subsequent chapters will be on arguing that they are rendered otiose by the truth of optimism. For present purposes, though, the question isn't whether such explanations are true but whether they are enough to overturn the presumption in favour of optimism. There are several reasons for judging that they are not.

To begin, there is no uncontroversial case here to use as the 'thin end of the wedge' (I focus here on the moral case, but parallel arguments could be offered concerning other forms of pessimism). Moral pessimism is just as controversial as pessimism in aesthetics, with a range of papers (Sliwa 2012, McShane 2018, Groll and Decker 2014) defending moral optimism. Even if it were true, then, that moral pessimism would render aesthetic pessimism less anomalous, the former cannot merely be assumed as common ground.

Further, even granting the truth of pessimism about moral testimony, it doesn't follow that the arbitrariness charge is removed entirely. The existence of one unexplained anomaly may reduce the theoretical cost of positing a second but it remains costly nonetheless. Of course, it will be objected at this point that the anomalies in question aren't unexplained but, rather, that they are explained by whichever account of them a particular pessimist chooses to offer. There is, however, good reason to be cautious of making such a confident pronouncement. It is, as the sheer numbers of such proposed explanations indicate, extremely controversial (even amongst pessimists) whether any proposed explanation is adequate in accounting for the proposed phenomenon in even a single domain. This worry is only compounded when we consider that—as I have already highlighted—there are important and wide-reaching differences between the aesthetic and moral domains (and even more so between these two and other areas where pessimistic accounts have been proposed). Indeed, a theme of later chapters will be that, even within a single domain such as aesthetics, the range of relevant cases is far broader and more variegated than many discussions have presupposed. Given these complexities, many of the explanations on offer, while in various ways

---

[21] I believe that pessimism is also mistaken in the other areas listed but arguing for that is outside the scope of this work.

ingenious, can begin to look somewhat more like promissory notes than fully fledged explanations of the (alleged) phenomena.

Finally, to repeat a point I made in relation to *AP* in the previous section, once proponents of these explanations *have* reached the stage of presenting and defending fully realized accounts of this kind then, in this context at least, they begin to look more like attempts to overturn the arbitrariness presumption rather than to deny its existence.

I have argued, then, that we should accept a presumption in favour of optimism. It is important to remember, though, that presumptions are fragile and defeasible things and that a pessimist could easily grant me this point while maintaining that this presumption is soundly defeated. Given this, a convinced optimist like myself should hope to have more to say in defence of optimism than merely arguing that it should be our default position. Fortunately, I have a lot more to say. In future chapters, I will evaluate a range of arguments in favour of pessimism and argue that the presumption of optimism is not defeated by any of these. On the contrary, the overall balance of evidence tells strongly in favour of optimism. In the remainder of this chapter, though, I will take a rather different tack and consider the prospects for a constitutive version of optimism.

3.6. Constitutive Considerations

In this section I begin my argument that optimism (or, rather more precisely, the denial of some of the most prominent forms of pessimism) is entailed by the very nature of aesthetic judgement. My argument here will centre on the tension between two theses. The first of these, *AB*, is the claim that aesthetic judgements are beliefs in a straightforwardly cognitivist sense. The second, *AN*, is the claim that aesthetic judgements are subject to some additional norm not active with respect to mundane judgements. The underlying thought here is a remarkably simple one. It is standardly held that states such as belief are constitutively defined by the norms which govern them, yet many pessimists are committed to the claim that there is some additional norm which governs aesthetic belief (a norm which, perhaps inter alia, renders aesthetic judgements formed on the basis of testimony illegitimate). I contend that the pessimist's position here is untenable. I will argue that we should reject the conjunction of these two claims. If aesthetic judgements are genuine beliefs, then they must, contra many pessimists, be governed by the same norms as other beliefs. Let's begin by focusing on a kind of pessimism (*BP*) which endorses both *AB* and *AN* and investigating how well this fits with different accounts of the nature of belief.

Accounts of the nature of belief typically explicate that nature—and differentiate beliefs from other psychological states—by appeal to constitutive norms, aims, or functions.[22] I will focus on norm-based accounts but have already argued elsewhere (Robson 2017) that these arguments easily generalize to other approaches. According to norm-based account of the nature of belief, one is permitted to believe that P iff the belief that P meets a particular standard.[23] The most prominent candidates for the relevant standard are that P is true and that the belief that P would qualify as knowledge.[24] In this section, I argue that neither norm is conducive to accepting *BP*. The proponent of *BP* can readily accept either standard as necessary for legitimate belief, but they must deny that a belief's meeting either the truth or knowledge standard is *sufficient* for its being licit.

The first case, where we take truth as the general norm for belief, is rather straightforward. Recall, that the pessimist is not a complete sceptic when it comes to aesthetic knowledge. They accept that there is some aesthetic knowledge and, a fortiori, some true aesthetic belief. Given this, it is a short step to the claim that some true aesthetic beliefs are formed on the basis of testimony. Consider a paradigm instances of an aesthetic truth; the claim that the ceiling of the Sistine Chapel is beautiful. I can conceive of no reason—other than the acceptance of a very strong version of descriptive pessimism (which I argued in §3.4 we should reject)—for resisting the claim that someone *could* form this belief on the basis of testimony. And, since the belief in question is clearly true, there is, therefore, no general barrier to someone who relies on aesthetic testimony meeting the truth norm. This would mean that the pessimist must either reject the truth norm for aesthetic judgements or else deny that aesthetic judgements are beliefs. Either way, assuming that we take the truth norm to hold for beliefs in general, they would be committed to rejecting *BP*.[25]

We might think, though, that appealing to a knowledge norm would serve the *BP*ist better here. It would seem a natural move for them to claim that the additional norm they postulate is an epistemic one and that it is *this* norm which

---

[22] For aim-based accounts see e.g. Steglich-Petersen (2006) and McHugh (2011). For function accounts see e.g. Millikan (1984) and Price (n.d.).

[23] I present the relevant norms here as permissive rather than injunctive since I take there to be some serious worries concerning injunctive norms, particularly injunctive truth norms, according to which we ought to believe P iff P meets the relevant standard (worries of this kind are presented by Bykvist and Hattiangadi 2007). I thank Ema Sullivan-Bissett for bringing this issue to my attention. Those not convinced by such worries should feel free to treat the relevant norms as injunctive if they prefer since this makes no substantive difference to my arguments in this chapter.

[24] Knowledge norms are defended by e.g. Bird (2007) and Williamson (2005). Truth norms by e.g. Shah and Velleman (2005) and Whiting (2013a, 2013b).

[25] An anonymous referee for the Press suggests that things can't be that simple since even advocates of truth norms would take there to be something problematic about e.g. true beliefs formed on the basis of asking a magic eight ball. This is a complex issue. The truth norm itself wouldn't render these beliefs problematic but (as discussed in e.g. Whiting 2013b: 129–30) advocates of the truth norm will often also embrace further derivative norms, norms designed to help guide our deliberations in arriving at true beliefs. It is not clear that such derivative norms will help the pessimist, though, since they often concern how an agent should go about forming their beliefs, rather than whether the beliefs themselves are licit. Regardless, appeal to these further norms won't help the truth norm theorist here (for reasons discussed below).

undermines the legitimacy of aesthetic beliefs formed on the basis of testimony. It is important to remember, though, that some of the most prominent recent defenders of pessimism would not be happy with a move of this kind. I have sometimes talked as if the debate between the optimist and the pessimist concerned whether aesthetic knowledge was available on the basis of testimony but, as I stressed in §1.7, this is intended merely as a convenience to ease exposition. The pessimist is not committed to there being any *epistemic* difficulty with reliance on aesthetic testimony. Indeed, the recent trend amongst pessimists has been to reject unavailability pessimism in favour of some version of unusability pessimism.[26] For the time being, then, I will restrict the focus of my argument to those *BP*ists who also claim that the additional norm on aesthetic belief is a non-epistemic one. That said, the sociological observation that unavailability forms of pessimism are currently somewhat out of vogue is hardly an argument against such views.[27] As such, I will turn later, in §3.7, to consider whether an appeal to knowledge norms can rescue the unavailability pessimist's position from the objection at hand (it can't).

Given the assumption that the extra norm which the pessimist appeals to is non-epistemic, it is easy to see the problem which those who defend *BP* encounter. They are, after all, committed to the claim that there are instances in which it would be illegitimate to form an aesthetic belief on the basis of testimony even when the belief in question would qualify as knowledge. So, once again, the pessimist must reject either *AB* or *AN*.

I have argued that—setting aside some possible caveats I will address in the next section—*BP* is incompatible with both truth and knowledge norms of belief. And, given that these are the two leading contenders for the correct belief norm, this is a significant cost to the kind of pessimism under discussion. The problems here go much deeper, though, since *BP* also comes into conflict with other putative norms of belief. It is a central tenant of *BP* that the (constitutive) norms operative with respect to aesthetic judgement differ substantially from those in place with respect to mundane judgements about, say, snips and snails and puppy dog tails. As such there is nothing—given the assumption that we ought to differentiate beliefs from other psychological states by appeal to the norms which govern them—to justify our classifying *both* kinds of judgements as beliefs. And, since everyone is happy to classify snip, snail, and puppy dog tail judgements as beliefs, we have excellent reason to reject *BP*.[28]

---

[26] There are, of course, exceptions such as Whiting (2015).
[27] Indeed, I will argue in Chapter 5 that there are good reasons for pessimists to prefer unavailability views.
[28] Well, everyone excluding those who hold certain extreme views—such as eliminative materialism—but advocates of these views will, of course, reject *BP* on independent grounds.

3.7. Objections and Replies

I have argued, then, that *BP* doesn't provide us with a tenable position concerning aesthetic judgement. Any state constituted by the kinds of norm which *BP* proposes would not be a genuine belief and so we must reject either *AB*, *AN*, or both. In this section, I will suggest some reasons for thinking that this conclusion is premature and argue that they are not persuasive.

One obvious objection to my position concerns my arguments with respect to the knowledge norm. I have noted that there has been a recent trend amongst pessimists to reject unavailability versions of their view, but don't my arguments here show that aspiring pessimists have reason to buck this trend? Perhaps, but a return to the unavailability view wouldn't do much to help the pessimist in this respect.

Consider first the unavailability pessimist who accepts *BP*. A pessimist of this kind will be committed to justifying their pessimism by appeal to some additional epistemic *norm* governing aesthetic belief. This view may seem attractive since it allows the pessimist to retain *AN* while also endorsing the influential knowledge norm of belief. Their position is, however, rather less promising than it may initially appear. A pessimist of this kind may respect the letter of the knowledge norm, but their view is not in keeping with its spirit. Knowledge norms, as with norms of belief more generally, are intended to set '*the* standard of appropriateness for belief' (Williamson 2000: 47, emphasis mine)—a standard which is taken to be entirely topic neutral. Given this, any epistemic norm which we propose as a *constitutive* norm of aesthetic judgement must be taken (by those who accept *AB*) to be part of *the* standard of appropriateness for aesthetic belief. Once this standard is established, though, we are faced with a close variant of the kind of dilemma we encountered repeatedly in the previous section. If the same standards of appropriateness apply to mundane beliefs, then the pessimist is not really proposing an *additional* norm. If, on the other hand, the standard they are suggesting is one which applies to aesthetic judgements alone then it is, again, difficult to see why we should count these as genuine beliefs since they are not evaluated by the same constitutive standards as belief.

Of course, the unavailability pessimist is likely to respond by insisting that both kinds of judgement are still governed by the same standard, the standard of *knowledge*, but this is unconvincing. Consider a pessimist who maintains that the standard for knowledge of mundane matters is that a true belief possesses some feature *F*—such as being sensitive, being safe, or being formed by a reliable process—and that in the aesthetic case the standard is that a true belief possesses *F and* that it is formed in accordance with *AP*. It seems evident that we really have two distinct constitutive standards here; one for aesthetic judgements and one for mundane judgements. The pessimist cannot render these into a single standard simply by insisting that we class both of them as standards for knowledge. Indeed, I can think of no reason why we should take the proposed standard for aesthetic belief to be an epistemic one at all (given how different it is from the standard for knowledge in non-aesthetic matters).[29]

A second potential response begins with the observation that, in presenting my arguments against *BP*, I have assumed that we should treat the norm constitutively governing belief as both necessary and sufficient for a belief's being licit. It might be suggested, though, that those who accept *BP* would be better placed rejecting this claim in favour of the view that the relevant norm provides a necessary but not sufficient condition for the beliefs in question being legitimate. This would allow the pessimist to maintain that, while there is (and could be) only one *constitutive* norm of belief, there are multiple non-constitutive norms which sometimes render beliefs illegitimate even when they satisfy the constitutive norm.

Why would someone be inclined to accept a view of this kind? The most likely motivation comes from drawing an analogy with debates concerning norms of assertion.[30] As I will discuss further in §6.2, merely allowing that some activity or state is governed by a single constitutive norm does not entail that there are never any other relevant norms in place. Proponents of a knowledge norm of assertion, for example, may claim that, in some sense, S may properly assert P iff S knows P but this doesn't prevent them from accepting that there is also something problematic about certain assertions which meet this standard (that they are impolite or violate Gricean maxims or...). One way of accounting for this apparent conflict is for those involved in such debates to claim that a particular standard isn't sufficient for an assertion to be legitimate tout court but merely for it to be *epistemically* sufficient.[31] More needs to be said, of course, to explain the exact nature and significance of this distinction, but I won't attempt to fill in the blanks here. What matters isn't precisely how such a division should be formulated, but whether the *BP*ist could plausibly say something in this spirit with respect to their norms of belief. There are two compelling reasons to think that they could not.[32]

First, as Daniel Whiting points out, a key difference between assertion and belief is that the former, but not the latter, is a social act. Whiting (2013a: 187) argues that supplementary norms of assertion concerning Gricean maxims etc. exist

---

[29] Similar difficulties arise for Hopkins's (2000) claim that there are different epistemic norms for testimony in mundane and aesthetic cases.
[30] Analogies of this kind are already commonplace (see e.g. Williamson 2000: 255–6).
[31] For discussion see e.g. Lackey (2011). The terminology here isn't ideal since it seems to presuppose that the relevant constitutive standard is an epistemic one.
[32] This is not to deny that there can be multiple extrinsic 'reasons for believing' in the sense of Adler and Hicks (2013: 141–2).

[p]recisely because asserting is 'external', rather than 'internal', it is, if not necessarily a social act, then necessarily a potentially social act. As a result, in evaluating an assertion, one might have to take into account the effect it might have on others, the expectations and needs of one's interlocutors, the part that speech act might play in the unfolding conversation, and so on. Evidently, all these considerations are foreign to the assessment of belief.

The thought here is roughly that additional norms on assertion are generated by the social role which our assertions play (in e.g. accurately communicating information in a relatively concise fashion) but that mere believing typically plays no such social role.

Second, the norms which pessimists propose are—unlike Gricean maxims, rules of etiquette, and so forth—typically taken to be, in some sense, constitutive. To be an aesthetic judgement, the pessimist claims, is to be governed by (or at least tend to be governed by) the further norms they propose. Thus, while Gricean norms of assertion can comfortably coexist with a constitutive knowledge norm of assertion, the *BP*ist's own constitutive norms of belief will necessarily clash with any other proposed constitutive norm.

3.8. Beyond BP

Given the failure of these objections, we are left with my earlier claim that *BP* is untenable. My arguments thus far have, however, been entirely dependent on two key assumptions, assumptions which some pessimists may wish to reject: first, that the pessimist construes aesthetic judgements as being beliefs (in a straightforward cognitivist sense); second, that the pessimist takes aesthetic judgements to be governed by some additional norm. That is, I have been targeting a particular form of pessimism (*BP*) rather than pessimism itself. This is certainly correct but, in this section, I will demonstrate that the reach of these arguments is surprisingly broad.

Let's begin by considering the claim that it's possible to adopt a plausible pessimist position while completely rejecting *AN*; that is, that we can account for the failings of aesthetic testimony by appealing to the same standards which govern testimony in mundane cases. It might be objected that any such position would merely count as a rather pessimistic kind of optimism rather than a genuine form of pessimism. Recall, for example, Hopkins's (2011: 139–42) claim that the difference between pessimism and optimism is that the former, but not the latter, proposes some additional norm of belief concerning aesthetic judgement.[33] As

---

[33] See also Hopkins (2006) and Gorodeisky (2010: 53).

I made clear in §1.6, though, I am not convinced by this line of thought and am willing to accept that someone may be a genuine pessimist while rejecting *AN*. Further, while I concede that such pessimists would be immune to the letter of the constitutive arguments I have offered, I do not find this concession to be particularly worrying for two reasons. First, the vast majority of pessimists *do* endorse some version of *AN*. Second, it is difficult to see how any of the candidates for the correct norm of belief in standard cases could bar us from routinely acquiring legitimate aesthetic beliefs on the basis of testimony. I have already indicated that we can clearly (assuming that there are aesthetic beliefs at all) arrive at true aesthetic beliefs via testimony and that it is difficult to see how someone could apply a standard knowledge norm—with no additional normative requirements for aesthetic knowledge via testimony—that prevented such beliefs often counting as knowledge (without also committing us to some general scepticism regarding aesthetic judgements or judgements formed on the basis of testimony).

Next, let's consider whether the pessimist is really committed to *BP*. I mentioned in §1.3 that, for the sake of convenience, I would generally talk as if aesthetic judgements were straightforwardly beliefs but that I would highlight key instances where this assumption had a significant impact on my arguments. Doesn't the current discussion provide us with just such an instance, though, since the cogency of its central argument is entirely dependent on this assumption? With respect to the letter of the argument, framed as it is in terms of belief, this is undoubtedly true. When it comes to the overall spirit of the argument, though, things are rather more complicated.

Certainly, I do not mean to suggest that arguments of the kind I have offered are relevant to every possible understanding of 'aesthetic judgement'. It is clear, for example, that some of the views discussed in the previous chapter—such as those which construe aesthetic judgement as a particular kind of appreciation—would be immune to the arguments I have offered. I have already argued, though, that such accounts provide little prospect for a version of pessimism which is both plausible and non-trivial. I will focus, then, on pessimists who thinks of aesthetic judgements in the way I have suggested that they should—that is, roughly, as the mental correlates of aesthetic assertions—but who still deny that such judgements are beliefs.

Even here, it seems that there are still easy options for the pessimist looking to avoid the worries I have raised in this chapter. Consider, for example, the novel kind of cognitive state, 'uliefs', which Alison Hills (2015) has appealed to in the moral testimony debate: states which stand to understanding as beliefs stands to knowledge. Hills is led to postulate such states by considerations that run somewhat parallel to those presented in this chapter. Recall that Hills's view is that the constitutive norm of moral judgement is understanding rather than knowledge, a view which, when combined with the acceptance of a knowledge norm of belief, quickly leads to the view that moral judgements can't be beliefs. Still, Hills thinks (for reasons I won't explore here) that we should nonetheless regard moral judgements as cognitive states, and so postulates uliefs as a new kind of belief-like, but understanding-normed, state.[34] Someone inclined towards the view that uliefs play this role with respect to moral judgement may well be tempted (see Hills 2017, 2022) to extend this claim to the aesthetic case as well. If, however, a pessimist takes aesthetic judgements to be uliefs, then my arguments in this chapter would pose no threat to them. They could merely claim that aesthetic judgements are of different kind to mundane judgements and, as such, it would be unsurprising (indeed required) that they are subject to a different constitutive norm.

While all this is true, there are also some compelling reasons to be suspicious of the appeal to uliefs. Postulating an entirely new kind of mental state is—as Currie and Ichino (2012) argue in a related context—certainly not something we should do lightly. Doing so would require an expansion in the number of distinct mental states in our ontologies, and it would also entail considerable revisions to our best theories of the mind (both within philosophy and in other disciplines). Further, this reluctance should be particularly pronounced in the present case since this new mental state isn't postulated on the basis of any empirical observations but purely to shore up a controversial philosophical thesis. Still, this doesn't show that such a radically revisionary move isn't *sometimes* required. Had it transpired that pessimism really was as firmly established as some have thought—and as Hills (2010) takes the parallel position in the moral case to be—then this may motivate giving serious consideration to an appeal to aesthetic uliefs (or some similarly radical proposal). One key lesson of this work, though, is that pessimism has nothing like this kind of standing. Further, even those who disagree with my general stance with regards to the plausibility of pessimism should still regard the pessimist's needing to postulate an entirely new kind of mental state as a significant cost.

What it seems the pessimist needs, then, is an already widely accepted species of mental state which is distinct from belief, but which also presents us with a plausible candidate for identification with the mental correlates of aesthetic assertion. Some pessimists will likely claim that there is a readymade solution here, the mental states postulated by various expressivist theories in meta-aesthetics. The expressivist will typically appeal to conative states which are already accepted as (virtually) uncontroversial elements of our mental makeup and there is already an expansive literature defending the plausibility of such states as the mental correlates of some assertions. We have already seen in §2.4 that some pessimists, such as Scruton (1976) and Todd (2004), have maintained that all pessimists should be expressivists. I argued that this claim isn't supported by the kinds of

---

[34] Hills's view is rather more nuanced than I have presented it as being. For a full explication and defence of it see Hills (2009, 2015).

constitutive considerations which Scruton and Todd advance, but I now appear to have reached the same conclusion by a different route—a conclusion which I am in fact happy to accept. I don't think that you should be a pessimist but, if you are going to be one, then expressivist-pessimism is likely your best bet. Does this mean that expressivist-pessimists have licence to completely disregard the worries I have raised in this chapter? Not quite.

In order to assess the extent to which the expressivist-pessimist is able to sidestep my arguments in this chapter, it is important to recall the distinction between different senses of 'belief' touched on in §2.4. Let's begin with Sinclair's (2006: 249) 'minimal beliefs'. In essence, all that is required for a mental state to qualify as a belief in the minimal sense is that it can serve as the mental correlate of a sincere assertion: that is, that it is a judgement in my sense. The expressivist-pessimist will not want to reject the claim that aesthetic judgements, in my sense, are beliefs in this sense (since this is a mere truism). This doesn't make them vulnerable to my arguments in this chapter, though, since there is no reason to hold that all states which qualify as beliefs in this minimal sense share a common constitutive norm.[35] But, of course, the expressivist cannot rest content with the claim that aesthetic judgements are minimal beliefs. If they want their position to present us with a genuine alternative to cognitivism then they need to spell out what claim it is that the cognitivist is making, and they're denying, with respect to such judgements. One way of doing so is to distinguish some further sense of 'belief' which Sinclair (2006: 249) terms 'robust belief', a sense in which the cognitivist will claim that aesthetic judgements are beliefs but in which the expressivist will deny this. Whether my arguments pose any threat to the expressivist will hang on how this further sense of 'belief' is explicated.

One suggestion is that robust beliefs are differentiated from the kind of judgement which the expressivist appeals to in that the former, but not the latter, are subject to a particular constitutive norm (such as a norm of truth or knowledge). If this were what distinguishes the two, then my arguments would, of course, be irrelevant to the expressivist. There is, however, good reason for the expressivist to be concerned about drawing the distinction in this manner. Consider truth norms first. Most expressivists are going to allow that the judgements they appeal to can be true in a deflationary sense (according to which e.g. '*Guernica* is harrowing' is true iff *Guernica* is harrowing). Indeed, some expressivists—including Blackburn (1988)—seem inclined to think that this deflationary account is the only legitimate understanding of the truth predicate. Similarly, sophisticated expressivists frequently offer us accounts of how the judgements they focus on can count as knowledge. They maintain, for example, that 'the primary function of talking of "knowledge" is to indicate that a judgment is beyond revision'

---

[35] Indeed, Hills's uliefs, which she explicitly assigns a different constitutive norm, would still qualify as beliefs in this sense.

(Blackburn 1998: 318) or that calling a judgement 'knowledge' is to indicate that it should be relied on in some particular sense (Gibbard 2003: 227).[36] Further, once we accept these claims, it seems extremely likely that the judgements in question might standardly be subject to some kind of censure for failing to meet these standards. At this point, though, we seem to have come very close to granting that the kind of judgement which expressivists postulate is constitutively governed by something like a truth or knowledge norm. If this is the case, then it would seem that—contrary to what has been suggested—the expressivist really would take aesthetic judgements to be beliefs (not just in a minimal sense but in the 'robust' sense of being governed by the same constitutive norm). An expressivist-pessimist of this kind would, therefore, have to give some further account of what separates their view from that of their cognitivist opponent. And, more relevantly for my purposes, they would find themselves faced with the very same arguments that I have already offered against cognitivist versions of pessimism.

All this shows, though, is that we can construct a position which is consistent with many of the claims made by sophisticated defenders of expressivism and which falls victim to my arguments in these last few sections. Are there any concerns for the expressivist pessimist's general position? It seems to me that there are competing considerations here. On the one hand, the expressivist needs to differentiate the kinds of judgement they are postulating from the states which their cognitivist opponent identifies with aesthetic judgements, and an appeal to different constitutive norms would be one, though not the only, means for doing so.[37] On the other hand, the more fundamental they take the difference between their judgements and the kind of judgement the cognitivist proposes to be, the harder it becomes for the sophisticated expressivist to overcome persistent challenges to their view. For example, the less like robust beliefs the expressivist's judgements are, the harder it is for them to overcome (aesthetic analogues of) the Frege-Geach problem, and more generally, to explain the various belief-like features which they are prone to ascribe to aesthetic judgements. I will not, however, attempt to settle this issue here since reaching any remotely satisfactory resolution would require developing and defending a fully blown version of aesthetic expressivism.[38] Instead, I will simply note that it is by no means obvious that the aesthetic expressivist really is immune to the arguments I have offered.

Let's assume, though, that there are plausible versions of aesthetic expressivism which can successfully sidestep my earlier argument. This may well show that pessimists should be expressivists, but it doesn't show that expressivists

---

[36] For some worries concerning these accounts of knowledge see Chrisman (2010).
[37] Other methods would be to appeal to the typical role which the corresponding assertions play or, as Sinclair (2006) does, to differences in non-constitutive function between the two kinds of state.
[38] For one attempt at such an account see Sinclair and Robson (forthcoming).

(or anyone else) should be pessimists. I argued in §2.4 that there is no reason to think that optimism is *ruled out* by expressivism, and my arguments in subsequent chapters are intended to show that there are compelling reasons for everyone, expressivists included, to prefer optimism to pessimism. Again, therefore, I intend—terminological convenience aside—to remain neutral in what follows between cognitivism and various expressivist views.

3.9. Constitutive Optimism?

In this chapter I have not only argued that there is a presumption in favour of optimism but presented a constitutive argument for optimism—an argument which, I claim, rules out many of the most prominent pessimist views. Yet, I have also noted that I will be going on in subsequent chapters to offer a sustained argument for my preferred version of optimism. Some might question, though, why I have any need to do so. If I am confident of my constitutive argument in the last few sections, what need is there to offer any further argument for optimism?

A partial response can be offered by noting that, as discussed in the previous section, I don't take the arguments I have offered to show that *all* extant forms of pessimism are ruled out by considerations relating to the nature of belief. In particular, I have left open the possibility that some expressivist forms of pessimism may be able to escape this challenge. Further, while I have suggested there are significant costs to doing so, there is nothing *in principle* to prevent someone from proposing a new form of pessimism based on a novel kind of mental state (indeed, my discussion of the ulief case indicates that this approach isn't merely hypothetical). Noting the availability of such positions highlights the importance of my arguments in subsequent chapters in helping to rule out *all* forms of pessimism as plausible positions.[39] Further, I am familiar enough with my discipline to expect that, when it comes to the remaining versions of pessimism, my arguments in this chapter will prove controversial. Give this, it will be useful to offer further considerations in favour of optimism as well as highlighting the particular ways in which I believe that key pessimist arguments go wrong. Of course, if what I've said so far has already left you thoroughly convinced of optimism, so much the better for me. Others, please read on.

---

[39] And, of course, I will also be aiming to show that we should prefer my own version of optimism over other (typically more moderate) versions which also aren't ruled out by the arguments I've offered thus far.

4
Pessimism and the Appeal to Cases

4.1. Pessimism and Cases

Why is it that so many aestheticians have found pessimism to be such an attractive view? As with any philosophical position, there are doubtless many different motivations which could be offered (we have already encountered some of these and will explore others at length in later chapters). It is, however, common practice amongst pessimists to anchor their defences of pessimism on our intuitions regarding various hypothetical cases. In what follows, I will refer to the kind of intuition which the pessimist seeks to elicit in such cases as 'pessimistic intuitions'.[1]

In §4.2, I present some standard examples of the cases which pessimists are wont to adduce and survey some empirical evidence which suggests that pessimistic intuitions concerning such cases are indeed widespread. I then go on to consider two lines of argument against using such intuitions to motivate pessimism. First, in §4.3, I note that there are reasons—even bracketing general concerns regarding the epistemic standing of intuitions—to view our intuitive judgements in such cases with suspicion. Second, I argue that the optimist can actually offer convincing accounts which allow them to endorse many of these pessimistic intuitions. In §4.4 I consider some extant optimistic attempts to accommodate such intuitions and argue that they are unsuccessful. I then go on, in §4.5–§4.7 to flesh out my own contextualist optimist account, arguing that it can successfully incorporate many pessimistic intuitions. Finally, in §4.8, I briefly consider how the optimist might respond to some additional sources of pessimistic intuitions.

4.2. Pessimistic Intuitions

To begin to appreciate the kinds of cases I have in mind consider the following illustrative examples:

> As I leave work, I meet someone entering the building.... She tells me that Hockney's recent portraits are lifeless. In response, I form the belief that

---

[1] It is important to note that this terminology should not be taken as a concession that the intuitions in question really do favour pessimism. Indeed, I will be arguing that they do not.

Hockney's recent portraits are lifeless. In this way, on the basis of testimony, might I come to know that the portraits are lifeless? (Whiting 2015: 91)

If you tell me that some film you have seen is excellent, it is far from clear that I can legitimately adopt your view. Your testimony might motivate me to watch the film, but it does not give me the right to the belief that the film is excellent. I will not have that right until I have seen the film myself. (Hopkins 2011: 138)

Your friend knows a lot about art. You want to know whether the Rothko Chapel is a masterpiece. So you ask her, and she tells you that the Rothko Chapel is a masterpiece, and you believe on that basis that it is. (Hazlett 2017: 49)

Suppose the editor of *Sight and Sound* gives Evelyn a piece of "pure" aesthetic testimony, e.g. that *Citizen Kane* is a great film—one of the greatest films of all time. It would be odd for her simply to take his word, to form a confident opinion that it is excellent. (Hills 2022: 22)

There are, of course, various important differences between these cases. In some we are explicitly told what belief we do (or should) form, in others we are not. Some concern aesthetic judgements in Sibley's sense, whereas others are focused on aesthetic verdicts, and so forth. However, the crucial commonality is that we are clearly intended to judge that it would be illegitimate to form a testimonial belief in each case.

What should we say concerning such cases? One might expect that, qua optimist, I would maintain that the individuals in these examples really can come to legitimately believe the truth of the relevant aesthetic claims. Given the rather minimal descriptions involved, though, such a claim would be premature. Most obviously, it is not even stipulated in these examples whether the claims in question are, as a matter of fact, true. As such, the optimist should not conclude that the relevant individuals *do* possess knowledge, but only that they *may* do so if certain further conditions are met. For many optimists, myself included, the relevant conditions will just be the standard conditions for testimonial knowledge concerning mundane matters. This is perfectly compatible with maintaining that, in many cases, including certain precisifications of the cases just outlined, these conditions are not met.

That said, I suspect that even such qualifiedly optimistic intuitions will be relatively rare. By far the more likely intuition—and the one which the authors above clearly intended to elicit—is that, irrespective of the precise details of the cases outlined, the individuals in these cases do not attain knowledge on the basis of testimony. (If my suspicion here is mistaken, though, and the reader feels no such pull, then so much the better for my overall argument.) For the remainder of this chapter, therefore, I will assume that my readers share the intuition that there is some important disanalogy between the cases described above and apparently equivalent non-aesthetic/non-testimonial cases, one which rebounds to the deficit of aesthetic testimony, and ask what we should make of this.

It is also important to note that the pessimist's case need not merely rely on an appeal to the intuitions of individual readers. One of the clearest lessons from recent work within 'experimental philosophy' is that the intuitions of professional philosophers—who, I will assume, comprise the majority of my readership—often differ markedly from those of the folk (see e.g. Tobia et al. 2013 and Weinberg et al. 2010). Of course, there is (to say the least) no consensus when it comes to such divergences as to whether, and to what extent, we should favour the intuitions of philosophers or of the folk. I take no side on these issues here. What is important to note, though, is that we don't have to speculate about what the folk think on this particular issue since empirical data are available.

The data in question primarily come from a series of experiments by Meskin, Liao, and Andow (n.d.) which asked participants to answer various questions relating to cases of both aesthetic and mundane testimony. They were, for example, asked how confident they were, based on assertions presented as part of a film review, that the film in question possessed various aesthetic properties (such as being beautiful) and various mundane properties (such as being set in Taiwan). The results showed a clear difference when it came to the confidence subjects placed in the two kinds of testimony. A difference which, unsurprisingly, favoured mundane testimony over aesthetic testimony.[2] Their work also showed a clear devaluing of aesthetic testimony—compared to both mundane testimony and first-hand aesthetic judgement—as a source of *knowledge*. For example, they found that participants were (i) significantly more likely to judge that an individual presented in a vignette could know that a sculpture was beautiful on the basis of first-hand experience than on the basis of testimony and (ii) significantly more likely to think that they could know that a sculpture was large on the basis of testimony than that they could know that it was beautiful.[3]

It is, however, important not to overstate the asymmetries which these results highlight. While participants certainly took there to be something problematic about aesthetic testimony (compared to both mundane testimony and first-hand aesthetic judgement), their responses hardly indicated a straightforward acceptance of pessimism. Participants were generally willing to assign *some* epistemic value to aesthetic testimony, and the majority of them stopped short of endorsing the thought that testimony is straightforwardly incapable of providing us with

---

[2] Participants were asked to rate how confident they were in various claims about a film on a 100-point scale ranging from 'not at all' to 'completely' confident. The average level of confidence in a statement based on aesthetic testimony was 71.21 whereas it was 90.48 for a statement based on mundane testimony.

[3] On a seven-point scale (from 'strongly disagree' that the subject knows to 'strongly agree' that they do), the average rating was 5.9 for first-hand aesthetic judgement, 4.2 for non-aesthetic testimony, and 3.41 for aesthetic testimony.

aesthetic knowledge.[4] For example, while answers to the knowledge question in the aesthetic testimony case were—in contrast to non-aesthetic testimony and first-person aesthetic cases—below the mid-point of the scale (3.41 on a seven-point scale) they were still far closer to the mid-point than the bottom end of the scale.[5] On the face of things, then, it seems that these results support a somewhat moderate position in the aesthetic testimony debate. What is less clear, though, is whether this position is closer to the kind of moderate pessimism defended by, for example, Andow (2014) and Hazlett (2017) or to the kind of moderate optimism defended by Meskin (2006). I will not, however, attempt to settle this issue here since the relevant point for my purposes is that the position in question will clearly be considerably more pessimistic than the kind of extreme optimism I am defending.

We have seen, then, that folk intuitions and, I will continue to assume, the intuitions of most philosophically trained readers concerning various cases are at least somewhat pessimistic. Given this, there is no need for me to enter into the question of whether the intuitions we are tracking here are intended to be those of the former or the latter (I suspect that different pessimists will have distinct targets). What does need addressing, though, is how the optimist should account for them. There are, broadly speaking, three possible responses which the optimist could offer. First, we could simply accept that these intuitions *do* provide a powerful motivation for accepting pessimism. While this concession would certainly provide something of a blow to the optimist, it is by no means clear that it would be a fatal one. Indeed, in the next chapter I will argue that even the optimist who makes this concession can still maintain that the overall balance of intuitions, regarding a more complete range of cases within aesthetics, clearly favours optimism. Second, we could argue that, while intuitions regarding such cases do favour pessimism, the support which this offers the pessimist is minimal at best. Finally, we could concede that we should adopt the verdicts which our pessimistic opponents offer in these cases but argue that these can be incorporated within an optimistic framework. In the next section I will briefly consider arguments in favour of the second response before turning, in the remainder of the chapter, to put forward a specific version of the third response.

4.3. Rejecting Pessimistic Intuitions

How might one go about rejecting the evidential value of pessimistic intuitions? I will avoid considering the 'nuclear option' of denying that intuitions have any

---

[4] Nor is this merely a worry for the unavailability pessimist. Andow (2018: 43–4) found similar results when it came to the issue of whether someone could properly judge something to be the case on the basis of (aesthetic) testimony.

[5] Again, Andow (2018: 43–4) found similar results when it came to proper judgement.

(significant) evidential value within philosophy, since most of the rest of this work will, in one way or another, be taken up with discussing competing intuitions.[6] Those who are radically sceptical of appeals to intuition should, given that they won't be susceptible to any of the standard motivations for pessimism I will discuss, have sufficient reason to accept optimism based on the theoretical considerations adduced in the previous chapter.[7] I will focus instead on the question of whether there are specific reasons to be sceptical of the evidential value of the particular intuitions we are discussing.

A useful place to begin here is with a return to the various arguments, discussed in §2.3, for being suspicious of appeals to folk belief in the debate concerning aesthetic testimony. These reasons seem, mutatis mutandis, to be relevant when considering pessimistic intuitions. First, there is the standard difficulty of ensuring that our intuitions really do concern judgements (in our sense) rather than appreciation, assertion, or so forth. Second, we need to ensure that people's intuitions concern the beliefs which they *should* form rather than those which they *would* form. We have, after all, already seen in the previous chapter that people are often disposed to underestimate the extent to which they do, as a matter of fact, rely on (aesthetic) testimony. Third, there is the difficulty that these intuitions may be rooted in the (tacit) acceptance of some philosophical thesis—such as folk relativism or crude emotivism—which we have clear independent reason to reject.[8]

Finally, there is the worry that the tendency to devalue aesthetic testimony in the relevant cases may be (in part or in whole) the result of a general undervaluing of testimony. I will focus on this last concern in a little more detail since it is—with respect to folk intuitions at least—not merely speculative. Returning to the empirical work just discussed, Meskin, Liao, and Andow (n.d.) found that their participants were far less willing to attribute knowledge of non-aesthetic matters on the basis of testimony than on the basis of first-hand experience (4.02 compared to 6.2 on a seven-point scale). Indeed, the gap between first-hand and second-hand cases in non-aesthetic matters was far larger than that between aesthetic and non-aesthetic testimony (3.41 compared to 4.02). It seems, then, that

---

[6] Though see e.g. Weinberg (2007), Cappelen (2012), and Deutsch (2015).
[7] With the exception of those intuition sceptics, such as Cappelen (2012: 1), who also deny that genuine appeals to intuition are widespread in philosophy. Such sceptics might well regard the kinds of argument I will go on to discuss as perfectly legitimate, but merely deny that they genuinely concern intuitions. For those in this group, I invite you to paraphrase appeals to 'intuition' into your own preferred lexicon.
[8] This final response would likely be most useful in explaining away the intuitions of the folk rather than of philosophers (who would explicitly reject such theories). However, even philosophers may sometimes find themselves tacitly endorsing a theory which they explicitly reject (by way of comparison, consider how often experts in statistics can lapse into tacitly adopting forms of statistical reasoning which they know to be fallacious). The other responses I'm considering appear to me to be applicable to both kinds of intuition.

folk pessimistic intuitions are at least partially explained by a general distrust of testimony.[9]

Given this, it should be clear that a case can be made for the unreliability of pessimistic intuitions. Even if these worries ultimately prove to be misguided, though, this wouldn't show that our pessimistic intuitions provide unambiguous support for pessimism itself. On the contrary, I will argue in the remainder of this chapter that at least one optimistic approach (my own, naturally) is able to accommodate the truth of many of these intuitions.

4.4. Accommodating Pessimistic Intuitions

It may initially seem rather strange to claim that the optimist can accommodate (some of) these pessimistic intuitions. On reflection, though, it should be clear that optimism as such is perfectly compatible with accepting many pessimistic intuitions. Consider, for example, Meskin's (2004, 2006) unreliability optimism. On Meskin's view it is, ceteris paribus, harder to get testimonial knowledge in aesthetic cases than in mundane cases. However, the extra difficulties with the former can be explained purely in terms of the *kinds* of factor which sometimes prevent us from achieving testimonial knowledge even in mundane cases. In particular, Meskin (2006: 120–4) claims that the key difference is the relative paucity of qualified aesthetic judges. While many (though by no means all) of us are qualified to comment on many (though by no means all) mundane matters, few of us come close to meeting the criteria, set out by, for example, Hume (1757/1875), for being a true judge concerning aesthetic matters. An optimist who accepted this account would, therefore, have no difficulty accommodating various pessimistic intuitions.

Still, I am not convinced by this account and, importantly, by Meskin's defence of the second asymmetry thesis. Meskin (2006: 123) defends this asymmetry by claiming that an individual is 'much more likely to know the extent to which he or she meets the requirements for being a true judge than the extent to which another person meets those requirements'. Given this, combined with the epistemic importance Meskin places on identifying appropriate Humean judge, we are far more likely to arrive at aesthetic knowledge via first-hand experience than via testimony. However, the evidence suggests that, contrary to Meskin's contention, we are actually remarkably unreliable when it comes to assessing our own abilities.[10] In particular, we consistently overestimate our abilities in various areas (with the majority of people famously taking themselves to be better than average

---

[9] Though I will argue in §5.8 that the experimental work in question doesn't support the claim that this is the whole story.

[10] I discuss this phenomenon, and its implications for aesthetic epistemology, at length in Robson 2014b.

students, friends, drivers, romantic partners, and much more besides).[11] Further, this general pattern extends to include our assessment of our abilities in areas at least analogous to aesthetic judgement (Kruger and Dunning 1999).

Meskin attempts to strengthen his case here by appeal to another key source of testimonial failure in mundane cases: dishonesty. He suggests (2006: 123) that the important role our perceived abilities as aesthetic judges play in determining our social status gives us strong motivation towards insincerity with respect to signalling our own abilities as aesthetic judges. Further, while insincerity of this kind is a paradigmatic defeater for testimonial warrant, it provides no reason to doubt an individual's first-hand aesthetic judgements. To support this insincerity explanation, Meskin (n.d.) quotes Kieran (2010: 255)'s claim that many people are, at least to some degree, snobs about the aesthetic, 'driven to deceive others or...prone to self-deception because what matters to them most is appearing to be the 'right' sort of person'. I agree with Kieran here, as I will discuss further in Chapter 6, but not with Meskin's interpretation. Rather, of the two inclinations Kieran identifies, I hold that the tendency to self-deception is liable to be far more prevalent. It would, I suggest, be very rare to find a snob who is consciously lying about their aesthetic preferences to others while being entirely (or at least reasonably) self-aware concerning their true preferences.[12] This is not, of course, to suggest that conscious deception doesn't occur in the aesthetic realm (it certainly does) nor even to suggest that people aren't somewhat more inclined to lie about aesthetic matters than about, say, the colours of medium-sized objects in their immediate vicinity. The thought is merely that the kind of widespread long-term deception Kieran and Meskin are pointing to here would almost invariably be accompanied by some degree of self-deception. If this is the case, then the phenomena Meskin points to would serve as a defeater for first-hand aesthetic beliefs as well as those formed on the basis of testimony.

A further worry is that the unreliability account doesn't seem able to capture the full range of pessimistic intuitions. Consider the following case:

APPRECIATOR: I am someone for whom art appreciation is very important. On the basis of the testimony of many reliable critics, I form the belief that the painting in the next room is hauntingly beautiful. I could easily investigate the matter for myself (by walking a few feet and looking at the painting) but I choose not to do so.

---

[11] For overviews of relevant evidence see e.g. Dunning et al. 2004.
[12] Technically someone who is a straightforward self-conscious deceiver wouldn't even count as a snob on Kieran's account since 'aesthetically irrelevant social features' do not 'play a causal role in [their] appreciative activity in coming to judge the value of *x qua* aesthetic object' (2010: 244). Instead, such factors merely play this role in their reporting of their (putative) judgements to others. However, the relevant concern here is about the prevalence of such individuals rather than how best to label them.

86 AESTHETIC TESTIMONY

I take it that many of those who encounter APPRECIATOR will feel the pull of the pessimistic intuition that my belief in this case is problematic. Yet, this case—along with others discussed by e.g. Hazlett 2017: 49—provides us with explicit assurances as to the reliability of the testifiers. Given this, the unreliability optimist appears bereft of any means by which to explain such intuitions. Is there an optimistic account which can do better, and accommodate our pessimistic intuitions concerning a wider range of cases? In the next three sections I will suggest that there is. My explanation of this view will, however, proceed via a rather indirect route. The route begins with a return to the debate between unavailability and unusability pessimists.

4.5. Unusability Pessimism and Non-Epistemic Norms

Recall that unusability pessimists allow that the epistemic standing of beliefs formed on the basis of aesthetic testimony is often precisely as the optimist takes it to be. They will typically allow, then, that if we *were* to form the relevant aesthetic belief in APPRECIATOR (and parallel cases) then this would—assuming the belief in question is true and that various Gettier-style worries don't arise—qualify as knowledge.[13] However, they then go on to claim that the beliefs in question are still illegitimate since they violate some non-epistemic norm of belief formation, that is, some norm which would not determine 'whether the belief the recipient is offered would count as knowledge' (Hopkins 2011: 147).

One obvious response is to insist that there aren't, and indeed couldn't be, any non-epistemic norms of belief formation. As Hopkins himself phrases the worry, 'Belief aims at truth, and aspires to the status of knowledge. Epistemic norms determine whether it hits this target. How can belief be governed by non-epistemic norms, norms that govern something other than whether it counts as knowledge?' (Hopkins 2011: 145). I am inclined to believe that Hopkins's imagined opponent has things right here but, for the purposes of my argument in this chapter, such an uncompromisingly position is not required. For the time being, then, I will not be arguing that non-epistemic belief norms are incoherent, nor even that there are no such norms.[14] Rather, my aim will merely be to demonstrate that there is no reason to posit non-epistemic norms of the kind the unusability pessimism proposes (and I will raise some objections to doing so in the

---

[13] For simplicity's sake I will assume in what follows that the unusability pessimist agrees with the (extreme) optimist regarding the epistemology of all of the relevant cases. There is, however, nothing to prevent someone from claiming that aesthetic knowledge is unavailable in some of these cases and merely unusable in others.

[14] The most plausible candidate is pragmatic justification norms such as those discussed, but ultimately rejected, in Feldman and Conee (1985: 22–3). Unusability norms, however, are clearly not intended to be pragmatic ones, so even if we already accept such norms then Hopkins would still be asking us to introduce a novel norm type and my argument would remain essentially unchanged.

next chapter). Doing so will, I believe, highlight a promising strategy for the optimist looking to accommodate pessimistic intuitions.

In responding to this objection, Hopkins (2011: 146) presents what he takes to be a relatively uncontroversial example of a non-epistemic norm of belief formation: a norm which is analogous to those he advocates in the aesthetic case, and which is violated in scenarios such as EXPERT.

> EXPERT: I am an expert in a particular field, but I form many important beliefs in this area solely through accepting the testimony of other experts who I (correctly) take to be my epistemic superiors. I have the ability to easily investigate these issues for myself but refrain from doing so.

What has gone wrong in EXPERT? According to Hopkins, we typically judge that an expert is, in some sense, a person who 'ought to settle for herself questions in her domain of expertise' (2011: 146). If I am an expert in philosophy then, even if all the other experts (including many I rightly judge to be my epistemic superiors) unanimously tell me that some philosophical proposition P is true, I cannot legitimately believe that P without investigating the matter for myself.[15] Yet, Hopkins claims, there need not be any *epistemic* fault here. If these other experts genuinely know that P then—absent defeaters—their unanimous testimony is surely enough to make knowledge that P available to me and to allow a non-expert to legitimately believe that P (i.e. to believe P without violating any norm, epistemic or otherwise). Hopkins hopes that we will take two lessons from this case. First, that there are some cases where non-epistemic usability norms govern the formation of belief. Second, that we are already accustomed to applying norms of this kind. I will argue that Hopkins fails to establish either part of this claim.

One objection Hopkins considers to his interpretation of cases like EXPERT is that the relevant phenomena could just as easily be handled by appealing to an epistemic, but contextually sensitive, norm of belief. To this end, Hopkins considers, and rejects, two possible contextualist positions. The first holds that something about cases like EXPERT raises the standard for knowledge to the extent that mere testimony cannot reach it. However, as Hopkins (2011: 148) points out, if the problem is purely a quantitative lack of sufficient warrant for knowledge, then it is not clear why I should think that investigating the issue for myself would do more to close this gap than acquiring further testimony from my epistemic superiors. A second contextualist strategy maintains that something about the context in EXPERT 'dictates directly what methods of belief formation are

---

[15] It is, of course, a challenge to think of any substantive philosophical claim which does enjoy this level of agreement. I will, however, ignore this complication so as to present Hopkins's position as strongly as possible.

appropriate' (ibid.) and, in particular, dictates that those beliefs can't be formed on the basis of testimony alone. In response, Hopkins argues that this is merely a terminological variant of the unusability position rather than a genuine alternative to it. This response strikes me as rather too quick. If the imagined contextualist means by 'appropriate' something like 'required for a belief to count as knowledge', then their position would be an epistemic one and thus manifestly distinct from the unusability account. However, while such a position would present a genuine alternative, it would also, absent independent motivation, be a worryingly ad hoc. Rather than pursuing such a position here, then, I will turn in the next section to propose a different contextualist epistemic norm which is violated in EXPERT.[16]

4.6. Contextualism and Expertise

Before presenting my account, though, it is important to briefly outline some key general features of epistemic contextualism. To get a sense of these, let's start with a famous pair of cases from DeRose (1992: 913).

> *Bank Case A.* My wife and I are driving home on a Friday afternoon. We plan to stop at the bank on the way home to deposit our paychecks. But as we drive past the bank, we notice that the lines inside are very long, as they often are on Friday afternoons. Although we generally like to deposit our paychecks as soon as possible, it is not especially important in this case that they be deposited right away, so I suggest that we drive straight home and deposit our paychecks on Saturday morning. My wife says, "Maybe the bank won't be open tomorrow. Lots of banks are closed on Saturdays." I reply, "No, I know it'll be open. I was just there two weeks ago on Saturday. It's open until noon."

> *Bank Case B.* My wife and I drive past the bank on a Friday afternoon, as in Case A, and notice the long lines. I again suggest that we deposit our paychecks on Saturday morning, explaining that I was at the bank on Saturday morning only two weeks ago and discovered that it was open until noon. But in this case, we have just written a very large and very important check. If our paychecks are not deposited into our checking account before Monday morning, the important check we wrote will bounce, leaving us in a very bad situation. And, of course, the bank is not open on Sunday. My wife reminds me of these facts. She then says, "Banks do change their hours. Do you know the bank will be open tomorrow?" Remaining as confident as I was before that the bank will be open then, still, I reply, "Well, no. I'd better go in and make sure."

---

[16] Those not interested in the details of this account can skip to §4.8. I provide a brief summary of key aspects of my view in §5.8 before going on to evaluate it in contrast to opposing positions.

DeRose aims, in discussing these cases, to accommodate three apparently conflicting intuitions; that what he says in *Bank Case A* is true, that what he says in *Bank Case B* is also true, and that if he knows in *Bank Case A* that the bank will be open then he also knows this in *Bank Case B* (1992: 914).

The ingenious solution which contextualists offer here is to propose that the meaning of 'know' shifts between the two cases.[17] The thought here is not that 'knows' is straightforwardly equivocal like 'bank' or 'duck', nor even that it used analogically as when we describe both a person and certain kinds of food as 'healthy'. Rather, the claim is that 'knows' behaves, in some important respects, like certain standard context-sensitive words such as 'tall' or 'near'.[18] So, the contextualist proposes, just as the same person can truly be described as 'tall' by one individual (perhaps discussing their career as a jockey) and as 'not tall' by another (perhaps discussing their hobby as a basketball player), they can truly be described by one attributor as 'knowing that P' and another as 'not knowing that P'. This is because these two attributors may well be in relevantly different contexts, contexts which pick out different standards for 'knows'. The reason, then, why both of DeRose's assertions are true is that they are made in distinct contexts which differ in relevant respects. Yet, whatever context we are in it will always be true that 'If DeRose knows in *Bank Case A* then he knows in *Bank Case B*' since this attribution will be judged according to a single standard for knowledge (whichever standard applies in the particular attributor's context) which DeRose either meets in both cases or fails to meet in either.

What factors cause the attributor's context to shift in relevant respects? Contextualists offer a range of different answers at this point but DeRose himself (1992: 914–15) suggests two factors which he takes to be relevant. First, the importance of being right has shifted greatly between the two contexts, thus making the standard for true knowledge attributions significantly higher. Second, a new potentially knowledge-undermining possibility—the bank having changed its hours such that it is no longer open on Saturdays—has become conversationally salient in *Bank Case B*. This possibility will, DeRose (1992) suggests, need to be ruled out if the individual in such a context is going to meet the relevant standard for knowledge.

Key to the contextualist's story here is that there are two importantly different kinds of factor which are—to use DeRose's (2009: 188) terminology—required for a particular true belief to 'count as knowledge';[19] that is, for an assertion that 'S knows that p' to be true in a particular conversational context. The first of these, subject factors, concerns the subject of a particular knowledge attribution and the second, attributor factors, concerns the individual who is making the relevant

---

[17] What I offer here is merely a rough guide to the relevant contextualist position. For a much more complete exposition of the view see DeRose (2009: 3–44).
[18] This isn't to say that 'knows' is precisely parallel to 'is tall' (see DeRose 2009: 169 for discussion).
[19] I thank Tom Crawley for reminding me of this useful terminological move.

attribution (of course, in some cases a single individual is both subject and attributor). DeRose (1992: 921–2) explains the difference as follows.

> Attributor factors set a certain standard the putative subject of knowledge must live up to in order to make the knowledge attribution true: They affect *how good an epistemic position the putative knower must be in to count as knowing*. They thereby affect the truth conditions and the content or meaning of the attribution. Subject factors, on the other hand, determine whether or not the putative subject lives up to the standards that have been set, and thereby can affect the truth value of the attribution *without* affecting its content: They affect *how good an epistemic position the putative knower actually is in*.

In DeRose's view, then, the subject's epistemic position does not change one iota when the stakes change or when new possibilities become salient in the attributor's conversational context, even though these changes can affect whether the subject counts as knowing. What has shifted isn't the subject's epistemic standing but, rather, the standard for knowledge which is being contextually determined within the attributor's conversational context (and, therefore, the standard which that subject needs to meet to count as knowing in that context).

This point is very important for several reasons. Not least of these is that it allows the contextualist to avoid the counterintuitive conclusion that we can improve our epistemic position with respect to some matter by coming to regarding the topic of our investigation as less important. As contextualists such as DeRose (2009: 188) are always keen to stress, the 'contextualist does not hold that whether a subject knows or not can depend on non-truth-relevant factors' such as the perceived importance of the matter at hand. An investigator may, through caring less, go from a position where they cannot truly assert of themselves 'I know that P' to one in which they can (and therefore come to 'count as knowing') but this is only because the meaning of 'know' has shifted between the two contexts of attribution. They no more gain knowledge through caring less than they would gain height by standing next to shorter people.

So, how can this general view be applied in the case of EXPERT? It is a common feature of a number of prominent epistemic theories, in particular contextualist ones, that for someone to count as knowing P they have to rule out all *relevant* alternatives to P. Crucially, though, all relevant alternatives here don't typically include all alternatives simpliciter.[20] In *Bank Case B*, for example, DeRose would have to rule out the possibility that the bank has recently changed

---

[20] I say 'typically' since contextualists will often allow that there are certain, highly sceptical, contexts where someone *would* have to rule out all alternatives to P to count as knowing P (see Cohen 1988: 94–7).

its hours—since his wife's raising this possibility, perhaps in combination with the raised stakes, makes it relevant—but not the possibility that the bank itself is merely an illusion generated by a Cartesian demon. Importantly, though, the class of relevant alternatives can often include possibilities which are very unlikely and, crucially, ones which are no more likely (and, indeed, sometimes significantly less likely) than some non-relevant alternatives.

To illustrate this, consider a contextualist interpretation of Dretske's famous (1970) zebra example (one which Dretske himself would not accept).[21] According to this interpretation, certain aspects of a context—most obviously appropriate conversational moves—can make it the case that, in order to count as knowing that some animals are zebras, I must rule out the possibility that the animals are cleverly disguised mules. Yet, merely demonstrating that they are not disguised mules provides little in the way of warrant for my belief that they are zebras since there are dozens of equally probable alternatives (that they are disguised ponies, etc.) which I have not ruled out.[22] For some contextually determined reason, though, I do not have to rule these other alternatives out in order to count as knowing that the animals are zebras.[23] Something similar is, I claim, occurring in EXPERT.

Hopkins argues that in cases where enough of an expert's epistemic superiors claim that P, she should believe that she has 'as great a warrant or justification for the belief testified to as she can reasonably hope to attain by working things out for herself' (2011: 148). Given this, there would be no *epistemic* reason for her to carry out her own investigations before believing P. Now, if all that mattered for the contextualist was the overall level of warrant for a belief then I concede that Hopkins would be largely in the right here. It is, perhaps, something of an exaggeration to claim that investigating these issues for herself would do *nothing* to boost the expert's overall epistemic standing but—given the right degree of testimonial support—it does seem that any extra epistemic boost which first-hand investigation might provide would be close to negligible. However, on the view I am proposing—as with most extant versions of contextualism—the quality of the subject's overall epistemic state isn't the only relevant factor. In particular, as we have seen, it is sometimes required that, in order to count as knowing, a subject must be able to rule out a very specific alternative. As a consequence of this, it

---

[21] Dretske (1970) takes this case to provide a counterexample to epistemic closure since he believes that we can know that an animal is a zebra without knowing that it isn't a cleverly disguised mule.

[22] It may well be that, in a world where nefarious zookeepers have, unbeknownst to the general public, labelled a great many disguised mules (but not ponies, etc.) as 'zebras', this alternative would be made relevant owing to its likelihood of being true (rather than on the basis of the factors I suggest). However, the relation of such 'subject factors' to relevant alternatives isn't relevant to the kind of contextualist position I am discussing (see DeRose 1992: 918–23).

[23] The contextualist can also allow that 'what counts as "ruling out" an alternative can vary with context' (DeRose 2009: 31). I will not, however, consider this complication here.

may even turn out that someone in a lower overall epistemic position counts as knowing, while someone in a superior overall epistemic position does not, because only the former is able to rule out this particular alternative.

Let's consider how this applies to EXPERT. It is neither impossible nor even unheard of for an individual who investigates some issue for themselves to overturn an established belief that has been enthusiastically endorsed by many giants in their field. Gettier was a relatively unknown academic with no prior publications when—if we accept the standard history of twentieth-century epistemology—he refuted a view of knowledge endorsed by a raft of philosophical heavyweights dating back to Plato.[24] One alternative to the truth of each piece of testimony I receive in EXPERT will be that, if I were to investigate the issues for myself, I would discover that some alternative view is, in fact, correct. And, in contexts where this alternative becomes relevant, I would have to rule it out in order to count as knowing that the claim in question is true. The only sure-fire way of doing this, though, is to actually carry out my own investigations.[25] Of course, as Hopkins (2011) points out, it would—given sufficient numbers of experts holding the conflicting view and sufficient epistemic superiority on their part—be a serious breach of intellectual humility to think that this alternative is particularly likely to be realized. However, according to the contextualist story I am proposing, it is not required that we think an alternative particularly probable in order for it to become relevant (think again of the likelihood that the alleged zebras really are disguised mules).

What makes this alternative a *relevant* alternative though? I propose that the following key features of EXPERT are important here. (i) That the result of the investigation is seen as important by the one attributing knowledge. (ii) That ruling out such alternatives demands no spectacular effort on the part of the would-be knower (as would be required if they had to e.g. develop expertise in an area with which they were previously unfamiliar). (iii) That some feature(s) of the way in which the case is presented tends to make the alternative in question conversationally salient (in this case, the explicit mention that I refrain from carrying out my own investigation when I could easily do so).

If the story I have outlined above is plausible, then it undermines Hopkins's appeal to EXPERT to provide an independently acceptable example of non-epistemic norms of belief formation. The question, therefore, becomes whether it *is* plausible. One strategy for rejecting my story would be to offer various

---

[24] There are—as discussed at length in Le Morvan (2017)—reasons to be sceptical of this standard story. However, the point for my purposes is that such a phenomenon is possible, not that any particular reputed instance of it is actual.

[25] Well, this isn't quite right. It may well be that enough (and good enough) testimony would make the chances of this alternative being realized sufficiently remote that it no longer counts as relevant. I will discuss a case of this kind in §5.8.

objections to the epistemic contextualism on which it is based. I will not, however, attempt to respond to these worries here for two reasons.

First, my own view is that the most prominent objections to contextualism have already been addressed successfully elsewhere, and I have nothing new to contribute to these extant defences.[26] This judgement is, of course, controversial but it must at least be conceded that contextualism is far from lacking in support and is, at the very least, a 'live option' within epistemology.[27] Second, contextualism's leading rivals each offer their own accounts of, for example, bank cases which could easily be adapted to apply to EXPERT (and APPRECIATOR). An account very closely paralleling the one I have could easily be offered by contextualism's leading rival in epistemology, interest relevant invariantism (as defended by e.g. Stanley 2005 and Hawthorne 2004). According to the interest relevant invariantist, there is, contra the contextualist, a single standard for knowledge but some of the factors the contextualist highlights (most prominently the importance of the issue at hand) play a part in determining whether this standard is met.[28] More traditional invariantists will deny that such factors are relevant to whether someone counts as knowing, but will tend to offer other explanations of the peculiarities of the contextualist's cases. Perhaps the most influential response of this kind is offering so-called 'warranted assertibility manoeuvres', according to which our intuitions about a difference between the bank cases reflects a difference in what can be legitimately asserted rather than a difference in what is known (see e.g. Brown 2006). And, again, accounts of this kind could easily be adapted to the cases under discussion here.[29]

Of course, even bracketing general concerns over contextualism, we are not yet in a position to judge that my account of EXPERT is more (or even equally) plausible than the one Hopkins offers. There are, however, compelling reasons to accept something like my epistemic contextualist account. Most obviously, it allows us to maintain the claim that belief is exclusively governed by epistemic norms (the importance of which should be clear from the previous chapter). I will not attempt to defend my account of this particular case in detail though.[30] My primary concern in this chapter isn't with explaining EXPERT itself but with showing how the lessons we learn from it can be applied to the debate between the optimist and the pessimist. It is to that task that I now turn.

---

[26] By e.g. Cohen (2001), Lewis (1996), and De Rose (1992, 2009, 2018).
[27] For evidence of its prominence see <https://philpapers.org/surveys/results.pl>.
[28] Though, on their view, it is the importance to the subject (rather than the attributor) which is key here.
[29] I won't attempt to provide detailed versions of such accounts here, though, since I believe that the contextualist position enjoys a number of advantages over its rivals (as we will see in §5.8).
[30] Though some of the arguments I offer against unusability pessimism in the next chapter will also apply, mutatis mutandis, to Hopkins's interpretation of EXPERT.

4.7. Contextualist Optimism

A very similar contextualist explanation can also be provided for (many of) the pessimistic intuitions we are considering in this chapter. When someone tells me that the painting in the next room, or the film showing at the local cinema, possesses some aesthetic property and I merely acquiesce to their view, without investigating the matter for myself, there is a widespread intuition that I am violating some norm of belief formation. As with EXPERT, though, I suggest that the norm violated is a purely epistemic one. This may initially seem a strange claim to make. As an optimist, and an extreme optimist at that, shouldn't I deny that any norm at all is violated here? Not quite. To reiterate a point I made in §4.2, it is not required that the optimist (even the extreme optimist) allows that we count as knowing in every cases which the pessimist adduces. Rather, all that the extreme optimist requires is that the account they give of such cases is compatible with the denial of the two asymmetry theses regarding aesthetic testimony. I will argue that a certain kind of contextualist position meets this standard.

To see how this can be done, let's start from the case which I labelled APPRECIATOR. My suggestion here is that my discovering, upon investigating the matter for myself, that the work is not, contrary to the reports I have received, hauntingly beautiful is a relevant alternative in this case. Meaning that, on my proposed view, it is an alternative which I need to rule out in order to count as knowing that the painting is hauntingly beautiful. Yet, as was the case with EXPERT, this is not simply a question of my overall epistemic position and so I cannot come to count as knowing merely by receiving additional testimony.[31] What makes this alternative relevant here though? Again, there are different accounts which could be given but I'll focus on the three factors I have suggested as important in EXPERT. First, aesthetic matters are of great importance to the attributor since I am the attributor in this case and I have stipulated that I care very much about aesthetic matters.[32] Second, I have stressed how very easy it would be for me to rule out this alternative by merely walking to the next room. Finally, my description of the case makes my sceptical alternative conversationally salient by suggesting the possibility of my going to check the painting for myself.

It might be objected that my description of the case never explicitly mentioned any suitable alternative (such as my discovering upon investigating the matter for myself that the work is not hauntingly beautiful) and so it isn't clear why we should take any such alternative to be relevant. This omission is, however, a deliberate one intended to illustrate the important general point that explicit statements of alternatives are comparatively rare even in paradigm contextualist cases.

---

[31] Again, this isn't quite right and I will discuss some exceptions in §5.8.
[32] I even wrote a book about them.

Consider, for example, that DeRose's wife doesn't explicitly highlight an alternative but merely points out that 'Banks do change their hours'. Yet, this fact—and indeed this particular bank's changing its hours—is compatible with the bank's still being open tomorrow. The sceptical alternative is clearly that the bank has changed its hours such that it no longer opens on Saturdays, but this is never explicitly mentioned.[33]

Given this, we are able to give a contextualist (and purely epistemic) explanation for the problematic nature of the belief in APPRECIATOR. It might be objected, though, that the fittingness of this explanation is merely an artefact of the way I chose to set up APPRECIATOR and that it is much less clear that an explanation of this kind can be applied—and still less that it *should* be applied—to the pessimistic intuitions which I presented in §4.2. More generally, it will not have escaped notice that (for the most part) I have merely presented my contextualist optimist position rather than arguing for it. This is no accident, and a full defence of my position would require a rather broader view, one which takes into consideration not only the standard cases which have been the focus of this chapter but a range of other cases which are often overlooked in these debates. I will present these cases in the next chapter and argue that—in combination with some of the considerations already raised above—they provide a powerful argument in favour of my contextualist optimist view.

There is, however, still one question that remains to be addressed in this chapter; why do I think that this view counts as an optimistic one? After all, I have accepted that, when it comes to cases such as APPRECIATOR, the subject does not count as knowing. Isn't this precisely the verdict which the (unavailability) pessimist would propose? It is, but the crucial difference lies in the kind of story I have offered to account for this result. One important difference is that the reasons I have offered for accepting this verdict are not specific to the domain of the aesthetic. Rather (as my discussion of EXPERT and other non-aesthetic cases illustrate) the very same factors which shift the epistemic context in APPRECIATOR also do so in mundane cases.[34]

A truly pessimistic explanation would require an acceptance of the two asymmetry theses, and the explanation I have offered appeals to neither. Recall that the contextualist factors I am highlighting here don't make the slightest difference to how good a subject's epistemic position *is* but merely to how good their epistemic position needs to be (in order for a particular attributor to judge that they count

---

[33] Similarly, in Cohen's famous (1999: 59) airport case, the worries raised about whether the passenger counts as knowing when the plane will leave, based on their itinerary, are that it 'could contain a misprint' and that the airport 'could have changed the schedule at the last minute'. Both of which are compatible with the plane's still leaving at the time reported on the original itinerary.

[34] EXPERT itself may not concern mundane matters since there are general worries about expert testimony in areas like philosophy (see Ranalli 2020) but other cases, such as DeRose's bank cases, clearly do.

as knowing) in a particular context. Given this, there is no reason for the contextualist-optimist to posit any epistemic difference between the subjects in the pessimist's core cases and those in parallel cases of mundane testimony (or of first-hand aesthetic judgement). The only remaining question is how a contextualist-optimist can explain why it seems so much easier to make certain sceptical alternatives conversationally salient in cases of aesthetic testimony (an issue which I will address in §5.8). For now, though, I will leave such considerations aside in order to briefly survey some further cases which may initially be taken to favour pessimism.

4.8. Some Further Cases

I have focused in this chapter on arguing that the optimist is able to accommodate our pessimistic intuitions regarding a common class of cases. It is, however, important to note that these are not the only appeals to pessimistic intuitions in the literature. In particular, it is sometimes proposed that there are case where some agent's behaviour on the basis of aesthetic testimony is intuitively problematic—in a way which parallel behaviour in a non-aesthetic case would not be—and that pessimism provides the only (or at least the best) explanation for this. In this section I want to briefly highlight two arguments of this kind.[35]

One prominent class of cases concerns the apparently problematic nature of certain aesthetic assertions, assertions such as 'J. M. Coetzee's *Slow Man* is a great novel, but I never read it' (Gorodeisky 2010: 53) and 'the film is absolutely superb, although I have never seen it' (Andow 2014: 211). These assertions seem problematic but, the pessimist argues, their problematic nature would be inexplicable given the truth of optimism. If we are able to know that a film we haven't seen is superb on the basis of testimony then why can't we assert this? Cases of this kind are found throughout discussions of aesthetic testimony and, I believe, provide the most powerful motivation in favour of accepting some form of pessimism. Given the importance of this argument, though (and the difficulty of responding to it), I will defer full consideration of it until Chapters 6 and 7.

---

[35] Cases of this kind would be easy to generate if we accepted a principle such as Always Fully Possess (according to which 'if you possess p as a reason, then you possess p as a reason to react in all the ways that p recommends': Lord 2016: 7). Whiting (2015) offers an argument—from the inability to rationally appreciate an object on the basis of aesthetic testimony to a lack of knowledge in such cases—based on something like this principle. I believe, however, that there is good reason (as Lord 2016 demonstrates) to reject this principle, along with the particular argument Whiting offers, but this doesn't show that all arguments of this general kind fail. If Lord is right, as I believe he is, then it isn't always the case that someone who possesses a reason, P, where P is a reason to φ, possesses P *as a* reason to φ. However, it is clear that they sometimes do. My belief that pizza is delicious gives me a (pro tanto) reason to acquire pizza and my beliefs about Harriet Tubman's life give me reason to admire her. Merely rejecting Always Fully Possess does not, therefore, give us a blanket reason to reject all arguments of this kind.

A different kind of argument is presented by Thi Nguyen, based on a case he calls 'Private Display'.

> I am fabulously wealthy. I wish to hang a picture in my bedroom, so that I may be surrounded by beautiful things. I have an opportunity to purchase a Turner painting for a relatively good price. I am assured by artists and art historians that I trust that the painting is of the utmost beauty and sensitivity, a real landmark. I study it for a long time and fail to register its beauty in any way. But still, I trust my artist friends, the art historians, and especially the fact of their consensus, and hang the painting in my bedroom for the rest of my life, not because I'm hoping to see the beauty for myself—I have given up on that—but because I am confident that it is in fact beautiful, and that it therefore does make my bedroom more beautiful, even though I cannot see it for myself.   (2017: 25)

Although Nguyen himself is far from being a straightforward pessimist (2017: 36), this case could easily be put into service by a pessimist who maintains that it is their view which best enables us to explain what is problematic about the behaviour of this hypothetical version of Nguyen (Wealthy-Nguyen).[36]

A pessimist friendly explanation would, I assume, proceed in something like the following manner. In (virtually) any mundane case where I am looking to settle the truth of some important issue it would be problematically presumptuous for me—as a mere neophyte in the relevant domain—to place my own judgement ahead of that reached by a consensus of experts. In this case, by contrast, it seems that it is deferring to the relevant experts, and thus hanging the painting which they assure me is oh so beautiful, which is problematic. In order to explain what is problematic here, then, we need to appeal to some pessimistic norm which requires that my beliefs, and corresponding actions, concerning a painting's beauty cannot be based on testimony (expert or otherwise). If beliefs formed in this manner were unproblematic, then Wealthy-Nguyen's actions would be similarly unproblematic. However, since there is clearly an issue with Wealthy-Nguyen's actions, there must also be something wrong with the beliefs themselves.

What should we make of this account? It is certainly clear that Wealthy-Nguyen has acted in a bizarre fashion. What is less clear, though, is that the strangeness of Wealthy-Nguyen's behaviour is best explained by appeal to pessimism. After all, the account which the pessimist offers here is not the only explanation available. Consider, for example, the following story which the optimist might offer. Wealthy-Nguyen's behaviour is strange not because it is based on a problematic belief but, rather, because it either fails to achieve the end he desires or else is based on an exceedingly anomalous desire.

---

[36] Nguyen himself suggests (2017: 36) that the positions which I and my fellow optimists put forward are unable to account for this.

When we are told that Wealthy-Nguyen desires to be 'surrounded by beautiful things' we might naturally interpret this as shorthand for some quotidian desire, such as the desire to enjoy the pleasure of being surrounded by beautiful things or the desire to appreciate the beauty of these objects. If this were the case, though then it would be clear why his behaviour is so bizarre. He has shelled out large quantities of money in order to achieve a result (satisfying these desires) which he knows he will not achieve. Let's assume, then, that Wealthy-Nguyen really does have the straightforward desire to be surrounded by beautiful things. Here we can simply note that such a desire is eccentric to say the least.[37] Consider for a moment the psychology of someone who desires (for its own sake) to fill their bedroom with beautiful objects, even though they know they will never appreciate these. Such a person strikes me as no less aberrant that someone who desired to fill the basement of his local Denny's or the Mariana Trench with beautiful objects. I am not suggesting that it is impossible for someone to have any of these desires but merely that someone who possesses them—at least to the degree that they would be willing to spend large sums of money to satisfy them—would be highly psychologically abnormal. The presence of such a curious desire can, therefore, be used to explain why we find Wealthy-Nguyen's behaviour so bizarre without the need to impugn any of his beliefs as illegitimate.

As with the other cases discussed, though, merely placing another explanation on the table doesn't show that we should accept this explanation over the one which the pessimist proffers.[38] In the next chapter, I will undertake the task of weighing up these competing explanations and arguing that the optimist (and especially the contextualist optimist) has the advantage.

---

[37] Provided, that is, that we cannot view this as merely an instrumental desire. Someone who desires the presence of beautiful things in the service of some other aesthetic goal—e.g. that of learning to appreciate and enjoy them over time—or of some non-aesthetic end—such as impressing potential romantic partners with their good taste—would not strike me as remotely abnormal. However, it would also seem unproblematic (epistemically speaking) for such an individual (provided they don't, as Wealthy-Nguyen does in the first respect at least, already know that these further ends won't be achieved) to take the further step of buying and displaying the painting.

[38] Indeed, things are even less straightforward here since, as I will discuss in the next chapter, Nguyen presents this case as part of a pair with a second case which he takes to elicit rather different intuitions.

5
Optimism and the Appeal to Cases

5.1. Pessimistic Intuitions and Optimistic Intuitions

In the previous chapter I sketched an optimistic account which, I argued, can accommodate many pessimistic intuitions. In this chapter, I aim to show that an account of the kind should be preferred to any account which the pessimist can offer. I will do so by appealing to intuitions concerning a wider range of cases in aesthetics and arguing that, overall, my contextualist optimist account provides the best explanation for these. In §5.2 I briefly outline a range of, often unduly neglected, cases in which our intuitions tell powerfully in favour of optimism. In §§5.3 and 5.4 I consider, and reject, some attempts by pessimists to either explain away or accommodate these intuitions. I then move on, in §5.5, to investigate some other aspects of our aesthetic practice which appear to favour optimism. §5.6 offers an assessment of the unusability pessimist's ability to respond our optimistic intuitions (and of their position more generally). In §§5.7–5.8 I tackle the question of which view of the epistemology of aesthetic testimony is best able to account for our intuitions regarding the full range of cases surveyed in these last two chapters. In doing so, I argue for two main conclusions. First, that standard optimistic accounts of these intuitions are to be preferred to pessimistic ones. Second, that the contextualist optimist account I outlined in the previous chapter is even better placed than extant forms of optimism.

5.2. Optimism and the Variety of Aesthetic Judgements

Many discussions of the value of aesthetic testimony—including my own discussion in the previous chapter—centre around 'toy cases' such as APPRECIATOR. In considering such cases, we are typically asked whether you can come to know, on the basis of testimony alone, that some unfamiliar presently existing artwork possesses a particular aesthetic property. It is for this reason that I dedicated so much space in the previous chapter to considering case of this kind—cases where pessimism concerning aesthetic testimony is typically regarded as the intuitive view—and arguing that my contextualist optimist view can accommodate these pessimistic intuitions. In this section, I will approach matters from the other direction, considering what we might regard as some of the optimist's core

Aesthetic Testimony: An Optimistic Approach. Jon Robson, Oxford University Press. © Jon Robson 2022.
DOI: 10.1093/oso/9780192862952.003.0006

cases—cases, that is, where optimistic intuitions appear commonplace.[1] I will focus primarily on three representative examples: judgements concerning lost artworks, judgements of natural beauty, and judgements of what I term 'aesthetic common knowledge'.

Let's begin by considering testimony concerning lost works.[2] This testimony we receive with respect to particular works which are, for various reasons, no longer extant and which we are unable to assess vicariously by means of some surrogate such as a photograph or reproduction. A particularly compelling example of this kind is presented by Brian Laetz (2008: 355).

> Like many interested in the history of ballet, I have read various things about the life and career of Vaslav Nijinsky. And I happen to accept much of what I have read. Among other things, I believe that he was born in Ukraine, had an affair with Sergei Diaghilev, starred in *Petrushka*, choreographed *The Afternoon of a Faun*, suffered from mental illness, and died in 1950. 1 accept all of this, and much else, solely on the basis of testimony,...But I believe other things about him as well, among them, that he was a brilliant performer—graceful, dynamic— one of the greatest danseurs of Russian ballet. This too, I accept on nothing more than the word of others. And, again, it is clear that I could have no other basis for doing so.

The intuition that aesthetic beliefs of this kind are legitimate is widespread and—as we will see in §5.6—is even endorsed by some prominent pessimists.

Next, let's consider cases involving making assertions regarding natural beauty. Again, our doing so on the basis of testimony is often regarded as intuitively unproblematic. For example, Friend (2008: 159) asks us to consider the following quote from the novel *Thunderball*: 'New Providence, the island containing Nassau, the capital of the Bahamas, is a drab sandy slab of land fringed with some of the most beautiful beaches in the world.' Friend then goes on to claim that a reader who is properly informed about the style of Fleming's writing would, and should, believe the content of this quote. Crucially, though, she does not present this claim in relation to the debate over aesthetic testimony. Rather, the point she is making concerns the general issue of learning from fiction and could easily have been illustrated using a mundane example. This seems to indicate that Friend— and, anecdotally, various others who I have heard discuss the paper in question— didn't regard the added aesthetic element as generating any additional difficulties. Again, I think that this is an intuition which will be widely shared. Similarly, I do

---

[1] Paralleling my usage of 'pessimistic intuitions' in the previous chapter, my use of this phrase is intended to leave it open whether the intuitions in question can be accommodated within a pessimistic framework.

[2] I use the phrase 'lost works' but it is important to note that some of the examples discussed involve particular performances, rather than work itself, no longer being extant.

not think that there is anything intuitively problematic with my believing (as I in fact do) on the basis of testimony that the Grand Canyon and the Aurora Borealis are far more breathtakingly beautiful than photographs and other surrogates can convey.

A third kind of case which elicits optimistic intuitions involves judgements of what I will call 'aesthetic common knowledge'.[3] There are certain aesthetic claims—concerning, for example, the beauty of Shakespeare's sonnets, the excellence of Caravaggio's paintings, and the relative superiority of Mozart's music to Salieri's—which are generally known amongst certain segments of our society. Typically these are claims which are taken to, in some sense, have passed the 'test of time'. In some cases, this knowledge will arise (at least in part) from relevant first-hand experience of the objects in question but it is highly counterintuitive to claim that it must *always* do so. Consider the case of someone who has never encountered—either directly or via surrogates—Shakespeare's plays or Beethoven's music for themselves. Would it really be plausible to suppose that such an individual doesn't know anything about the aesthetic qualities of these works? Clearly there will be a widespread intuition that—presuming they are aware of the enduring reputation of these works—it would not. Indeed, Jerrold Levinson (2005: 213) goes so far as to classify the judgement that 'the Adagio of Beethoven's Third Symphony' possesses certain aesthetic properties 'on the basis of centuries of testimony' as a paradigmatic example of a legitimate second-hand judgement.[4]

5.3. Rejecting Optimistic Intuitions

I have claimed, then, that there are various cases which tend to garner optimistic intuitions. The obvious question to ask here—paralleling the question I raised concerning the optimist and pessimistic intuitions in §4.3—is how the pessimist should respond to these. Again, two broad kinds of response are available. First, pessimists could opt for a hard-nosed approach and argue that the intuitive judgements about such cases are simply mistaken. Second, they could propose that these optimistic intuitions can be accounted for within a pessimistic framework. In this section, I will consider each of these strategies in turn.

It is clear—especially in light of my arguments for a presumption of optimism in Chapter 3—that the pessimist looking to reject these intuitions owes us some explanation for their doing so, but providing such an explanation is no easy matter. In particular, it is worth noting that some of the justifications I considered for

---

[3] I discuss these cases at length in Robson (2019).
[4] Complications arise here since the particular property that Levinson appeals to (sadness) is not, in contrast to most of those discussed in the literature, a straightforwardly evaluative one. However, Levinson's arguments are clearly intended also to apply with respect to judgements concerning evaluative aesthetic properties.

rejecting pessimistic intuitions in the previous chapter simply cannot be adapted to undermine optimistic intuitions. In some cases, the reasons for this are obvious. We cannot appeal to a general scepticism about testimony to explain the intuitive acceptability of testimony in particular cases and if we were really making judgements about appreciation, rather than belief, then this would only stand to make our optimistic intuitions in such cases even more mysterious (given the trivial unavailability of appreciation via testimony which I discussed in §2.6). Some other explanations may initially appear more promising but even these don't survive close scrutiny.

Consider first the claim that people are judging what they would believe in such cases rather than what they *should* believe. While it is certainly *possible* that this is happening, it doesn't seem particularly plausible since, as I have already discussed in §2.6, there is compelling empirical reason to believe that people tend to underestimate their reliance on testimony (aesthetic and otherwise). Something similar applies with respect to the claim that these optimistic intuitions only arise because we are in the grip of some mistaken theory. There are, as we have seen in §3.2, some important pieces of aesthetic 'folk theory' which would, if true, tell strongly in favour of pessimism. By contrast, I cannot think of any view of this kind which might be appealed to in order to explain away optimistic intuitions.

There are, however, other options which remain open to the pessimist. One tactic would be to deny that some (or all) of the judgements I have discussed are genuinely aesthetic. In my view, the most promising response along these lines draws inspiration from Jane Fairfax in the following dialogue from *Emma*.

> "Oh! those dear little children. Jane, do you know I always fancy Mr. Dixon like Mr. John Knightley. I mean in person—tall, and with that sort of look—and not very talkative."
> "Quite wrong, my dear aunt; there is no likeness at all."
> "Very odd! but one never does form a just idea of anybody beforehand. One takes up a notion, and runs away with it. Mr. Dixon, you say, is not, strictly speaking, handsome?"
> "Handsome! Oh! no—far from it—certainly plain. I told you he was plain."
> "My dear, you said that Miss Campbell would not allow him to be plain, and that you yourself—"
> "Oh! as for me, my judgment is worth nothing. Where I have a regard, I always think a person well-looking. But I gave what I believed the general opinion, when I called him plain."[5]

---

[5] The Jane Fairfax case is discussed in detail in Blackburn (1998: 60).

We see in this dialogue that Jane has so little confidence in her own aesthetic judgement—at least as it pertains to the appearances of various gentlemen—that she refrains from reporting her own views in favour of presenting the 'general opinion'.[6] And, the pessimist might suggest, something very similar is happening in the cases I have discussed. That is, that our intuitions here don't concern the claim that some object possesses a particular aesthetic property but, rather, the claim that this object is generally viewed as possessing it. There are, however, several reasons to be suspicious of this kind of 'self-effacing' account (I will focus on how this strategy would proceed in the lost works case, but the worries here apply, mutatis mutandis, to other cases).

A first obvious concern is that this self-effacing account would commit us to the view that claims about lost works mean something very different in our mouths than they did in the mouths of contemporary critics. The optimist, by contrast, has no need to appeal to any such widespread, and previously unremarked upon, ambiguity. Yet, these additional complications are the least of the pessimist's worries here. Consider, for example, the following exchange.

A: Nijinsky's dances were graceful.
B: No. That's what most people thought but they were actually mistaken.

This seems like a paradigm case of aesthetic disagreement, but the pessimist would be forced to deny that there is any genuine disagreement here. If A is really only claiming that Nijinsky's dances were generally regarded as being graceful, then this is already something which B explicitly endorses (and parallel difficulties arise for other candidate self-effacing paraphrases).[7]

Given these difficulties, I return to my earlier claim that the pessimist has no good explanation to offer to accompany their rejection of optimistic intuitions. The pessimist may, however, simply take this as providing added impetus to search for a workable version of the second kind of response; a response which aims to accommodate these intuitions within a broadly pessimistic framework.

5.4. Accommodating Optimistic Intuitions

What are the prospects for this kind of pessimistic response? It is clear that an extreme pessimist, who maintains that we are *never* able to legitimately form aesthetic judgements on the basis of testimony, will be unable to accommodate any

---

[6] Or at least she intends to do so. I don't mean to commit myself to the claim that her intentions here *are* sufficient to successfully alter the meaning of her assertions.
[7] I'm assuming here that we don't take B's response to be similarly self-effacing since interpreting it this way would implausibly render their—entirely unremarkable—assertion self-contradictory.

of these intuitions. However, the prospects for a more moderate pessimist initially seem more promising. Indeed, we have already seen (in §1.4) that it is commonplace for pessimists to allow that there are exceptions to their general prohibition on forming aesthetic judgements on the basis of testimony. Still, there are difficulties here in justifying these putative exceptions in a manner which is neither arbitrary nor ad hoc. What is it, for example, about claims concerning past artworks which permits these, but not those concerning their presently extant equivalents, to be formed on the basis of testimony? This is a task which becomes even more difficult when we consider the heterogeneity of the optimistic cases I have outlined. (I will argue in §5.6 that the unusability pessimist's attempts to accommodate optimistic intuitions is, at best, a mixed bag. For now, though, I'll focus on the unavailability view.)

One proposal is that aesthetic testimony is, for whatever reason, peculiarly epistemically weak, to the extent that it is rarely able to provide us with warrant sufficient for knowledge, but not so weak that it is *never* capable of doing so. It seems plausible, for example, that our testimonial warrant for various claims concerning the excellence of Mozart's music is—given the centuries-long critical consensus on this matter—strong enough to compensate for whatever epistemic deficiencies aesthetic testimony is burdened with. However, accounting for the other examples I've discussed (along with the optimistic practices I will discuss in the next section) is rather more of a challenge. It seems, for example, that we should expect that our epistemic position regarding lost works will, all else being equal, be significantly worse than that with respect to many extant works we've never seen. We will typically have access to far fewer sources of direct testimony regarding lost works (especially long-lost works) and will often lack the ability to cross-examine these testifiers and their epistemic credentials.

In addition to these particular worries about which optimistic intuitions it can accommodate, there is also the concern that this proposal itself is radically underspecified (indeed, it is little more than a restatement of the unavailability pessimist's view). The unavailability pessimist still owes us some explanation for the peculiar weakness of aesthetic testimony; perhaps aesthetic matters are just really difficult, or perhaps widespread dishonesty or disagreement within aesthetics makes it very difficult to come by aesthetic knowledge on the basis of testimony. The difficulty here, though, is in putting forward a version of these answers which is able to respect both of our asymmetry theses. As mentioned in Chapter 1, cases of mundane testimony vary in a range of epistemically relevant respects, including how much disagreement and deception there is regarding a particular topic. Given this, we would need some reason to think not only that it is harder to arrive at knowledge that *Paddington 2* is a wonderful movie on the basis of testimony than it is to acquire knowledge of the current time on this basis, but that it is also more difficult to arrive at knowledge of the former than of mundane matters more generally.[8] Similarly, the reason offered would have to be one which doesn't also entail scepticism about first-hand aesthetic judgement. I have already argued (in §4.4) that appeals to widespread aesthetic deception don't do the job here (given the frequency with which these are accompanied by self-deception) and appeals to disagreement seem similarly problematic. If these dissenting voices are enough to undermine my dependence on your judgement that the work is beautiful, then why aren't they also enough to undermine my reliance on my own judgement?

5.5. Optimistic Practices

As well as accounting for our intuitions in these cases, optimism also seems better placed than pessimism to account for various aspects of our aesthetic practice. The standard example here (described in e.g. Gorodeisky 2010: 60 and Hopkins 2011: 153) concerns someone choosing to engage with an unknown artwork on the basis of a friend's assurance that the work is excellent. However, such 'friendly recommendations' aren't the only kind of testimony which frequently influences people's actions. Many of us allow ourselves to be guided in our viewing choices by reviews from professional critics as well as the aggregated review scores found on websites such as Metacritic and Rotten Tomatoes.[9]

It might seem obvious that the optimist has a clear advantage in explaining such behaviour. If, on the basis of relevant testimony, I can *know* that the work in question is indeed excellent then this would explain why my action of engaging with it, rather than some less well-received alternative, is rational. If, on the other hand, I cannot know this, then it might be suggested that my behaviour is irrational at best and inexplicable at worst. As things stand, though, this is rather too quick. After all, it is not as if the pessimist must regard the testimony which such recommendations provide as entirely without merit. They may, for example, claim that it leads to a reasonable suspicion that the work is excellent and that such a suspicion, given the absence of any contrary indications, may well be enough to make it rational to choose to engage with that work.

---

[8] This point highlights a limitation of some recent empirical work on aesthetic testimony—by e.g. Andow (2018) and Meskin et al. (n.d.)—which tends to focus on a contrast between aesthetic testimony and a very limited range of mundane judgements (often ones which seem especially amenable to testimonial knowledge).

[9] The force of some of these cases is weakened by the fact that I am restricting my discussion to the instance of pure testimony. For example, it may be that the role of the critic is, as Carroll (2009: 8) claims, providing 'evaluation grounded in reasons', and that we can gain knowledge not by accepting the critic's testimony but by considering the reasons they provide. However, there is clearly a widespread practice of acting merely on the basis of, say, a high Rotten Tomatoes score.

106 AESTHETIC TESTIMONY

This line seems plausible in many cases—watching a certain film at your local multiplex, purchasing a particular novel at a second-hand bookshop and so forth—where the costs involved are rather minimal. However, as Keren Gorodeisky (2010: 60) reminds us, we

> might spend a lot of money on getting tickets to a concert, on the basis of the testimony of [a] musically informed and trustworthy friend, according to whom the concert is superb. And if we are deep lovers of art, we might also make flight reservations and go all the way to Berlin in order to see Alfred Menzel's paintings, about whose greatness we read in a book by the art historian Michael Fried. Would it be reasonable to make such efforts if what the testimony here gave us were mere... suspicion?

Yet, the pessimist—or, rather, the unavailability pessimist since Gorodeisky presents this argument as part of her defence of unusability pessimism—might object that the contrast between knowledge and mere suspicion is a false dichotomy.[10] There is a variety of epistemic positions between suspicion and full-blown knowledge, some of which may legitimize our going to considerable lengths to view the work in question. The unavailability pessimist might allow that these recommendations can provide us with a significant degree of warrant for the belief that the work is excellent, or that they allow us to *know* that it is probably excellent, or... The worry, though, is whether they are really able to concede that it is commonplace for recommendation to enable us to move this far towards knowledge without being able to take us all the way. After all, if a single recommendation can provide us with a significant degree of warrant then (as Hopkins 2011: 141 argues) it is difficult to see why enough recommendations of the right kind aren't able to provide us with knowledge.

It seems, then, that the unavailability pessimist is committed to denying that recommendations can provide us with much in the way of warrant for our aesthetic judgements. Given this, they also appear committed to regarding our ordinary practice of acting on these recommendations—at least in cases where doing so is somewhat costly to us—as deeply suspect. This conclusion would force them to be revisionary with regards to our ordinary practice in a way which the optimist—and, if Gorodeisky and Hopkins are to be believed, the unusability pessimist—is not.[11]

Despite the prominence they have been given, our responses to recommendations aren't the only aspect of our aesthetic practice which appears to favour the

---

[10] Even more so given that the original quotation describes the suspicion in question as 'unjustified' (Gorodeisky 2010: 60).

[11] I will argue in the next section that the unusability pessimist's response to such cases is also unconvincing.

optimist. Laetz (2008: 361–2) points to our tendency to enlist the testimony of others in reaching a judgement concerning a piece about which our own initial feelings are ambivalent. And Nguyen (2017: 22–5) highlights the various roles which testimony plays within aesthetic education (in, for example, helping us to determine which art forms it is worth investing our limited time and energy in familiarizing ourselves with). Further, an even wider range of practices can be identified once we turn our attention towards less quotidian contexts. Neilson (n.d.) considers at length the ways in which aesthetic testimony may legitimately be relied upon as part of legal proceedings.[12] Similarly, Nguyen (2017: 26) presents the following 'Public Display' case.

> I run a small local museum and I am offered a chance to obtain a... painting for a very good price. I am assured by [those] that I trust that the painting is of the utmost beauty and sensitivity, a real landmark. I study it for a long time and fail to register in any way its beauty. But still, I trust [the testimony I have received] and hang the painting in my museum, not because I am hoping to see the beauty for myself—I have given up on that—but because I am confident that it is in fact beautiful and that it does in fact contribute to the aesthetic value of the art contained in my museum, even though I cannot see it for myself.[13]

As stated, I don't think that pessimists of any stripe need find this case particularly threatening since it may be that our curator isn't especially motivated by aesthetic concerns but merely wants to buy a work which is generally well regarded (and so likely to attract more visitors). Let's assume, though, that (as Nguyen 2017 goes on to suggest) they are concerned with acquiring works which are 'aesthetically valuable, or important, or worthwhile'. Even with this further assumption in place, the curator's actions still seem permissible, and this does begin to generate a puzzle for the pessimist.[14] Indeed, saying that expert testimony is permissible in this case strikes me as something of an understatement. Rather, I think it would be *illegitimate* for the curator in Public Display to reject expert testimony in these matters and to rely entirely on their own judgement.

Again, I do not mean to suggest that this list is exhaustive. On the contrary, I believe that there are many other aspects of our aesthetic practice which the optimist could appeal to. However, these examples present us with a good representative sample, and the pessimist might reasonably hope that a successful explanation

---

[12] Something which, as I will discuss further in §6.7, famously occurred in the trial following Penguin Books' publication of *Lady Chatterley's Lover* where the testimony of a slew of literary critics was called upon to help determine whether the work possessed sufficient literary merit to escape a charge of obscenity.
[13] I have altered Nguyen's example a little since it originally featured a case of aesthetic common knowledge (concerning the value of Turner's paintings) and I wanted to remove this further complication.
[14] Nguyen (2017: 26) contrasts this case with the private display case discussed in §4.8.

of these practices can be applied (mutatis mutandis) to whatever other examples the optimist might adduce. The question, then, is whether such an explanation can be provided. In the next section I will consider at length what an unusability pessimist might say in response to these practices as well as to the optimistic intuitions discussed in §5.2.

5.6. The Unusability Account

The unusability pessimist often maintains that their view can succeed where unavailability pessimism fails, but in this section I will argue that the appeal of the unusability view has been significantly overstated (since Hopkins (2006, 2011, n.d.) has presented by far the most developed version of the unusability position, I will focus primarily on his defence of the view).

Key to Hopkins's attempt to accommodate optimistic intuitions is his claim that, while the non-epistemic pessimistic norms he proposes are themselves exceptionless, these norms lapse under certain conditions (2011: 153).[15] According to Hopkins (2011: 153–4), the effect of the non-epistemic norm he proposes 'is to require one either to think aesthetic matters through for oneself (at the least, to experience for oneself the object in question), or to remain agnostic'. However, he suggests that it just isn't feasible (given our practical aims) to suspend judgement concerning the merits of the various films which we are deciding between. And, since we clearly cannot employ our own judgement prior to making this choice, we are not able to abide by either of the unusability pessimist's disjuncts. However, since we cannot abide by the unusability norm in this particular case, then—given the plausible principle that ought implies can—we are no longer obligated to follow this norm and can, therefore, legitimately form a belief regarding the film's merits purely on the basis of testimony. This permission is, however, only temporary. Once we have seen the film for ourselves the recommendations we have received 'should count for nothing in [our] assessment of it' (2011: 154).

Hopkins's account of this particular case is certainly ingenious, but it also raises some immediate concerns. In particular, the application of the 'ought implies can' principle here is rather suspect. Typically, this principle is taken to concern cases where we are literally unable to comply with a putative norm, not merely those where doing so would conflict with some relevant practical aim of ours. It would not do, for example, to claim that the norm against lying lapses merely because

---

[15] He primarily focuses (2011: 153) on the example of someone choosing to view a particular film on the basis of a friendly recommendation but it is clear that he intends the lessons here to apply rather more broadly.

we happen to have a practical interest in deceiving others.[16] Still, I don't think that the case against Hopkins is decisive here. He may, for example, argue that this modified version of ought implies can doesn't apply to every norm whatsoever but merely to norms of a certain kind (indeed, I take this to be what he *is* suggesting in Hopkins (n.d.)). Regardless, though, my primary concern won't be to consider how plausible the 'norm lapse' account is in this particular case but, rather, to ask whether it can be put to work in accommodating other optimistic intuitions and practices.

It's clear that there are going to be some limits to applicability of such an account (I cannot, for example, think of any remotely plausible means of extending it to cover judgements of natural beauty) but there are other cases where the norm lapse explanation has some prima facie plausibility. Hopkins himself suggests (2011: 154) that his account might be expanded to explain our optimistic intuitions concerning 'works now lost'. He doesn't expand on this remark, but I take it that he intends something like the following. In the pessimist's core cases, we always have the option of disregarding any testimony we are offered in favour of investigating the work for ourselves (indeed, it is often presented as a trivial matter for us to do so). In lost work cases, by contrast, things are different. We are unable to form any judgement concerning these works by conducting our own investigation and so cannot be under any obligation to do so.

Yet, this line of reasoning only seems persuasive if we accept that we *must* form some judgement concerning a lost work rather than, as the other disjunct of Hopkins's norms dictates, remaining agnostic. It is unclear, though, why we should take this to be the case. Hopkins's explanation for the impermissibility of agnosticism in the recommendation case is based on the link between belief and action. If I'm aiming to watch a good but unfamiliar film this evening (rather than a poor or mediocre one) then forming, and acting upon, a belief based on suitable testimony seems to be my only reliable method for achieving this goal.[17] By contrast, our assessment of lost works won't typically link up with action in this way. We are, for obvious reasons, not faced with the choice of which lost works to interact with or to display in galleries and, more generally, our judgements concerning these works will standardly be of a purely theoretical kind. Of course, we could always claim that the relevant aim is 'acquiring true beliefs concerning these works' but it is clear that the unusability pessimist doesn't want their norm to lapse whenever this aim would be better served by disregarding it.

Can this kind of story do a better job when it comes to explaining some of our other optimistic practices, such as the actions of the curator looking to fill their

---

[16] It may well lapse in cases where the practical consequences are bad enough—consider the famous 'axe murderer' objection to Kantian ethics—but that hardly applies here. And even in such cases, it's not clear that the norm really lapses (rather than, say, being overridden).

[17] Of course, this oversimplifies things somewhat by excluding other methods of belief formation (such as induction). However, any such method would also violate the wider norms Hopkins proposes.

gallery with beautiful works? I don't believe that it can. Consider the curator in Nguyen's 'Public Display' case. They certainly have the *option* of relying on their own aesthetic judgement, so it is not clear why the norm in question would lapse. Of course, taking this option would involve acting on a mistaken judgement but, again, a norm which lapsed whenever this was the case would begin to look rather toothless.[18]

Finally, let's consider the case of aesthetic common knowledge. Hopkins (n.d.) suggests that there will be some cases in which the weight of testimonial evidence becomes overwhelming and that, in such instances, we may be psychologically unable to refrain from forming the relevant aesthetic belief (and so unable to abide by either disjunct of his proposed norm). Further, it seems plausible that someone's being faced with the kind of centuries-long critical consensus concerning a work we find in common knowledge cases would often prove overwhelming in this way. Indeed, I agree with Hopkins that the position of someone who acknowledges that the evidence—whether testimonial or otherwise—in favour of an aesthetic judgment is overwhelming but still refuses to form that judgement seems very difficult to maintain (both rationally and psychologically). However, while this account does provide the unusability pessimist with some success in accounting for cases of aesthetic common knowledge, it also helps to highlight a deeper worry for their position.

We have seen that position of the person facing overwhelming testimonial evidence but refusing belief is, to say the least, a precarious one. I would suggest, though, that they are not alone here. It is, recall, a commitment of the unusability pessimist's view that there can be cases where I have sufficient warrant for some belief on the basis of testimony but where I'm still not permitted to form the belief in question. Again, though, such a position seems deeply precarious from both a rational and a psychological point of view. There is clearly (as discussed in e.g. Adler 2003, Chignell 2010, and Horowitz 2014 a very close link between taking myself to have sufficient warrant for a belief and actually forming that belief. The exact nature of this connection is a controversial matter, and one which I won't attempt to adjudicate here, but the underlying thought is that there would be something anomalous about an individual who took themselves to have sufficient warrant for the belief that *P* but who still refused to believe that *P* (indeed, some take this position to be straightforwardly incoherent). It seems, then, that there is clear motivation for Hopkins to apply his norm lapse account to any case where someone takes themselves to be in the position to know some aesthetic truth on the basis of testimony. Given this, though, the unusability view becomes a

---

[18] It might be objected that making the wrong choice would frustrate the curator's practical aims, such as attracting visitors to their museum, in a significant way. However, our focus here is only on the curator's attempts to acquire works of art qua aesthetic objects rather than on any other aims they may have in acquiring such works.

somewhat self-effacing one. The norms of belief they propose only hold in those cases where we are not fully attending to then.

This self-effacing character isn't merely an unattractive feature of the unusability pessimist's view but it also undermines their ability to account for our pessimistic intuitions. Imagine that we were to supplement the cases from the previous chapter with the assurance that the individuals involved patiently took stock of their epistemic standing regarding the aesthetic judgements in question. Doing so would not, I take it, make our intuitions about these cases any less pessimistic. Yet, it seems that if—contra the unavailability pessimist and my own contextualist optimism—they were in a strong enough epistemic position to count as knowing in these then this, combined with their clear assessment of their own epistemic state, would virtually (perhaps actually) compel them to form the relevant judgement. Given this, it seems that the unusability pessimist must allow that their norms lapse and, therefore, that there is nothing illegitimate about forming these judgements.

To sum up, I have argued that the unusability pessimist is able to accommodate some (though by no means all) of the optimistic intuitions which stymie their fellow pessimist but that this advantage comes at a significant cost. This is in addition to the costs which (as we saw in §4.5) the unusability view encounters in postulating an entirely new species of non-epistemic belief norm. All of which is to say that we should be strongly disinclined to accept their view if there is any plausible alternative on the table. Is there?

5.7. Weighing Things up

In these last two chapters I have surveyed a wide variety of intuitions concerning different cases of reliance on aesthetic testimony as well as discussing some ways in which both optimists and pessimists might seek to respond to these. We now need to ask which theory of the epistemology of aesthetic testimony is best able to deal with the totality of these intuitions. In this section I will argue that standard versions of optimism fair better than either unusability or unavailability pessimism. In the next section, I argue that my own contextualist optimist view performs best of all.

I have already highlighted that an extreme unavailability pessimist will meet very little success in accommodating the optimistic intuitions and practices we have considered thus far, but other unavailability pessimists seem in a more promising position. I argued in §5.3 that a less extreme unavailability view—according to which it is possible but typically prohibitively difficult to arrive at aesthetic knowledge via testimony—can accommodate cases of aesthetic common knowledge, and a view of this kind may also vindicate the practice of acting on certain widespread recommendations (consider, for example, a film with an exceptionally high score on both Metacritic and Rotten Tomatoes). It's much harder to see, though, how such a view would be able to explain other intuitions (such as those concerning lost works) and practices (such as out willingness to act on a lone friendly recommendation).

Yet, we shouldn't get too carried away in vilifying unavailability views. Indeed, I think that—the waning popularity of such views amongst pessimists notwithstanding—they should be preferred to unusability views for two main reasons. First, they avoid any complications concerning the existence and nature of any new non-epistemic norms of aesthetic judgement. Second, they are able, as I suggested in the previous section the unusability view may not be, to straightforwardly accommodate the pessimistic intuitions discussed in the previous chapter. So, there is good reason to prefer the unavailability view to the unusability view, but how does it compare to (standard versions of) optimism?

One obvious advantage of optimistic views is that they are, unsurprisingly, able to deal very well with the optimistic intuitions and practices which I have discussed. Consider, for example, a very simple (invariantist) version of optimism which denies both asymmetry theses. Such a view would have no difficulty allowing that we can legitimately arrive at judgements concerning natural beauty, lost works, and the like on the basis of testimony. Similarly, there will be nothing puzzling about practices such as following friendly recommendations. On the flipside, there is the equally predictable concern that they will struggle to accommodate the pessimistic intuitions from the previous chapter. We might think, though, that (as with the unavailability pessimist) their position could be strengthened by making it less extreme. A moderate optimist could simply maintain that there are some additional difficulties in acquiring legitimate aesthetic belief on the basis of testimony which aren't overcome in the pessimist's core cases. I don't think such a move would ultimately be worth it, though, since any benefit would be offset by no longer leaving it as a 'sure thing' that these more pessimistic forms of optimism can accommodate the optimist's own core cases.

It may seem, then, that we are left with a rather predictable standoff. The optimist does a better job of accounting for our optimistic intuitions, while their pessimistic opponent is better placed to accommodate pessimistic intuitions. Of course, if there really is a dead heat here, then that would be perfectly in line with my overall conclusion, since I argued in Chapter 3 that our default position in the absence of any compelling reason to endorse pessimism, should be optimism. However, any suggestion of a standoff here is premature.

First, as I argued in §4.3, the optimist who rejects pessimistic intuitions has a range of prima facie plausible justifications for doing so. By contrast, I argued in §5.3 that the pessimist will have a difficult time explaining away any optimistic intuitions which they wish to reject. Given this, the optimist's failure to accommodate pessimistic intuitions is far less damaging than the pessimist's inability to accommodate optimistic intuitions. Second, the range of intuitions which the pessimist flouts is considerably broader. We have seen that the pessimist's core cases tend to be rather narrowly constrained to those concerning presently extant, but non-canonical, artworks. By contrast, the optimist's core cases include examples as diverse as aesthetic common knowledge regarding canonical works, judgements of natural beauty, and judgements concerning past works. Further, we have already seen that there is a range of optimistic practices which the pessimist has difficulty accommodating. By contrast, it is difficult to think of any significant aesthetic practice which even prima facie favours the pessimist.[19]

I have argued, then, that standard invariantist versions of optimism do a better job than various pessimist accounts when it comes to the overall range of intuitions. Yet, it is still true that standard versions of optimism accrue something of an intuitive cost in, for example, having to reject the kinds of intuition which the pessimist's core cases tend to elicit. Further, these are costs which I argued, in the previous chapter, are not shared by my contextualist optimist view. In the next section, I go on to argue that this kind of contextualist optimism provides the best overall explanation for our full range of intuitions concerning testimony in aesthetics.

5.8. Defending my Account

In §4.7 I outlined my contextualist optimist account of various intuitions concerning the pessimist's core cases. This account appealed to three key features of these cases which, I suggested, tended to raise the contextually salient standard for knowledge in these cases by raising some relevant alternatives which couldn't (standardly) be ruled out on the basis of testimony. These features are (i) that the result of the investigation is seen as important by the one attributing knowledge; (ii) that ruling out such alternatives demands no spectacular effort on the part of the would-be knower (as would be required if they had to e.g. develop expertise in an area with which they were previously unfamiliar); (iii) that some feature(s) of the way in which the case is presented tends to make the alternative in question conversationally salient. In the previous chapter, I showed how each of these applied in my own sample case, APPRECIATOR, but it is more of a challenge to demonstrate that any of these apply in the kinds of cases which actual pessimists present (see §4.2).

---

[19] Well, that's not quite true. There are two putative practices which might appear to fit the bill here (i) our practice of refraining from forming aesthetic judgements on the basis of testimony and (ii) our practice of refraining from making various aesthetic assertions (such as 'the painting is beautiful') on the basis of testimony. However, I have already argued in Chapter 3 that (i) fails to identify a genuine aesthetic practice and I will go on to argue in the next two chapters that (ii) ultimately fails to motivate pessimism.

In order to respond to this challenge, let's return to one of our representative examples.[20] 'Your friend knows a lot about art. You want to know whether the Rothko Chapel is a masterpiece. So you ask her, and she tells you that the Rothko Chapel is a masterpiece, and you believe on that basis that it is.' (Hazlett 2017: 49). It's easy to see how (ii) is met in this case. While visiting the Rothko Chapel itself would likely require a considerable journey for most readers, a plethora of surrogates (including a range of detailed photographs and a video tour) can be accessed online in seconds. (i) is, admittedly, rather less clear. We are explicitly told that you have an interest in knowing about the masterpiece status of the chapel—so we know you don't regard the issue as entirely lacking in import—but it's not clear just how much this issue is intended to matter to you. One thing that is worth mentioning in this context, though, is that discussions of aesthetic testimony typically take place amongst philosophers of art, a group who (I assume) tend to have a greater than average concern for matters of artistic value.[21] Why think (iii) is met here, though, since there isn't even a hint in Hazlett's presentation of the possibility of investigating the issue for yourself? There are two things to say in response. First, it's important to stress that I didn't mean to suggest that each of the trio of features I suggested needed to be present in a case for the kind of explanation I am proposing to be applied. APPRECIATIOR is deliberately intended to highlight a case where all three features are clearly present—just as DeRose's bank cases are designed to highlight each of the key features he highlights as relevant for the contextualist—but each of the features can also be contextually relevant in isolation. Second, and less concessively, I think there is good reason to hold that (iii) can actually be applied in this case.

In order to see why I take this alternative to be psychologically salient in such cases, it will be useful to consider a contrast with the optimist's core cases. At first glance, it may seem that my contextualist optimist is at a disadvantage, compared to an extreme but invariant optimist, in terms of accommodating optimistic intuitions.[22] The latter can, after all, straightforwardly allow that we *do* count as knowing in these cases (just as, they will claim, counterintuitive as this may be, that we count as knowing in the various pessimistic core cases). The former, by

---

[20] The lessons I adduce here should be easily applicable to other pessimistic core cases.
[21] Anecdotal evidence suggests that philosophers of art tend to be rather more inclined towards pessimism than philosophers in other subdisciplines, but I'm not aware of any empirical work on this question.
[22] I won't consider optimistic practices in this section since, so far as I can see, the contextualist-optimist can just give the same account as any other (reasonably extreme) optimist of these—that is, that these practices are entirely reasonable given the epistemic benefits which testimony affords. Remember that the contextualist optimist doesn't claim that any of the attributor factors they point to actually reduce our epistemic standing but merely that they influence whether it is appropriate to say of someone in that epistemic position that they count as knowing (this may, however, provide us with a reason to favour the contextualist version of optimism I have outlined over an interest relevant invariantist alternative).

contrast, needs to explain why we count as knowing in these optimist-friendly cases but not in those outlined in the previous chapter.

Some optimistic intuitions are relatively easy to account for. In lost work cases, for example, it will be very rare that either (i) or (ii) applies. These cases typically aren't ones where our judgements carry any practical import and they are not, for obvious reasons, ones in which we are able to investigate the matter for ourselves (easily or otherwise).

Cases of aesthetic common knowledge are rather more complicated. It is certainly possible for me to examine these works for myself, and someone could easily raise the standard sceptical alternative concerning these works (that if I were to investigate them for myself, then I would discover that they don't actually possess the aesthetic properties they are reputed to have). There is, however, reason to doubt the effectiveness of such a move. I suggested in the previous chapter that the only method for ruling out such an alternative would be to actually investigate matters for myself, but also noted that this was something of an oversimplification. While, on most contextualist views, it is certainly *possible* to generate contexts in which we would have to rule out, so to speak, every world in which I discover that the consensus was false upon investigating these matters personally, this isn't standardly required whenever this alternative becomes salient. Consider, for example, that 'every world' here would include those very distant worlds where it turns out that this apparent consensus is based on a centuries-long conspiracy designed to deceive early twenty-first-century aestheticians. This is something which, I take it, no one would want to maintain that I typically need to rule out to count as knowing. Rather, most contexts in which an alternative is raised are ones in which I would only have to rule out certain possible worlds in which that alternative is true. In *Bank Case B*, for example, DeRose could rule out the sceptical alternative in question by calling the bank to confirm their opening hours even though this doesn't rule out a world in which the bank has changed its hours (such that it is no longer open on Saturdays) but wishes for some Machiavellian reason to mislead him concerning this. Returning to the aesthetic case, it seems likely that the scale and duration of the consensus regarding certain works will—while not ruling out *all* possibilities in which this alternative is true—be enough to rule any version of this sceptical alternative which would typically be relevant. Consider, for example, Hume's (1757/1875: 255) worry that widespread contemporary testimony in praise of some present artist is often the result of the propensity of '[a]uthority or prejudice' to give 'a temporary vogue to a bad' artist.[23] Concerns of this kind seem relevant when it comes to testimony surrounding many contemporary works, but they clearly don't apply when it

---

[23] It is worth noting that while the factors which Hume and Sibley highlight generate sceptical worries for many instances of aesthetic testimony, I see no reason to think that the factors which they mention wouldn't be at least as problematic for parallel cases of first-hand judgement.

comes to the long-lasting consensus regarding canonical works. And something similar applies to many other sceptical scenarios. As Sibley (1968: 50–1) puts the point,

> possibility of error with a case that has elicited long-lasting convergence decreases as possible explanations of error become more obviously absurd; e.g. we could not sensibly reject a centuries-spanning consensus about *Oedipus* as being the result of personal bias, enthusiasm for a novel style, or passing fashions or fads. I do not mean that, in *other* cases, there is always some reason for doubt; only that the long-attested cases may virtually exclude the *theoretical sceptic's* doubt as absurd.[24,25]

A similar explanation can also be offered when it comes to many of our judgements concerning the aesthetic value of nature since, once again, it would be hard to appeal to the kinds of sceptical consideration which Hume (and others) adduce as explanations for the general consensus concerning the beauty of sunsets.

We have seen, then, that there are important differences between the optimist's core cases and the core cases of their pessimistic opponents. In addition to this, I will now argue that there is a further relevant distinction when it comes to (iii), such that it is typically much easier to make the kinds of sceptical alternative I am considering conversationally salient in the pessimist's core cases that in the optimist's core cases or, for that matter, in most cases of mundane testimony.

So, what can make an alternative conversationally salient? One common suggestion involves what Lewis (1996: 559) terms the 'rule of attention' according to which any alternative which is so much as mentioned in the attributor's conversational context becomes *eo ipso* salient (and so must be ruled out to count as knowing).[26] Yet, even if accepted, this controversial rule it wouldn't be relevant here since I have been focusing on cases where the sceptical alternative in question is never explicitly mentioned. Further, a rule of this kind would clearly be of no help to the optimist since it is entirely neutral in terms of the domain under discussion (and so would apply just as much in mundane cases as aesthetic ones). What we need to consider, then, is what besides explicitly mentioning it might make a sceptical alternative relevant to the attributor. An obvious response here would be that a sceptical alternative becomes more salient if it is one which is more likely to occur to attributors who are discussing the matter or, at least, when

---

[24] Importantly the claim being made here only concerns the value of works included within the canon and says nothing about those which are excluded from it. It is undoubtedly the case that (as discussed in e.g. Eaton 2008: 878–9) many works have been excluded from the canon in large part due to aesthetically irrelevant factors such as the gender, race, or class of the artist.

[25] In this respect, then, the aesthetic case differs from the philosophical one. Philosophical consensus, when it does occur, tends not to be especially stable across different times and cultures.

[26] Lewis's own discussion (1996: 559) focuses on the conditions under which an alternative can't be 'properly ignored' rather than those under which it is relevant.

it is one which is likely to occur to them *and* which they inclined to regard as sufficiently likely to be of concern given other aspects of the conversational context (something that would, for example, virtually never be the case when it comes to the possibility of a centuries-long aesthetic conspiracy).

Now, why might we think that my sceptical alternative—that if I investigate the matter for myself, then I will discover that the testimony I have received is mistaken—is more likely to meet this standard in the pessimist's core cases than in cases of mundane testimony (and, indeed, of first-hand aesthetic judgement). It is here that many of the pessimist's own ideas become surprisingly helpful to my account. I have suggested in §3.2 that there are various reasons why many individuals may, as a matter of psychological fact, tend to be suspicious of appeals to aesthetic testimony. Not only do they underestimate the epistemic credentials of testimony in general, but they are also inclined to note factors such as the widespread disagreement that arises over aesthetic matters or the tendency towards snobbish deception in aesthetics, as well as to endorse views such as crude relativism about the aesthetic. I have, of course, argued that these points are of no help to the pessimist since they either are almost certainly mistaken (as is the case with crude relativism) or else fail to highlight a genuine epistemic difference between testimony and first-hand aesthetic judgement (as is the case with worries about various kinds of bias and prejudice). However, what matters here isn't whether these factors really generate significant support for pessimism (they don't) but whether they have a tendency to make it easier for certain kinds of sceptical alternative to become salient in cases of aesthetic testimony. I will argue that they do.

To see why, I'll focus on the case of aesthetic disagreement but much of what I say can be applied mutatis mutandis to many of the other factors mentioned.[27] The pessimist's core cases often concern works about which there is, or is at least likely to be, widespread disagreement. Further, it seems clear that disagreement of this kind is frequently apt to generate sceptical worries concerning the epistemic status of testimony. Given this, the mere mention of reliance on aesthetic testimony in these cases will likely cause various sceptical alternatives to occur, and to be regarded as reasonably plausible, by many of those considering them (even more so if we include the slightest hint at the possibility of investigating these issues for oneself instead). This kind of widespread disagreement is, by contrast, absent in most mundane domains. Further, while I have argued that disagreement of this kind *should* be equally threatening to first-hand aesthetic judgement, we have seen that (for whatever reason) this threat just doesn't tend to be regarded as salient in the same way. The pessimist's core cases here also contrast with cases concerning nature and aesthetic common knowledge where disagreement is, and is known to be, much less endemic. As such, it will plausibly be far more difficult

---

[27] I focus on disagreement since there is empirical evidence (Andow 2018) to suggest that concerns about widespread disagreement in aesthetics correlate with a tendency towards pessimistic intuitions.

to render these sceptical alternatives conversationally relevant (just as it would be with respect to the sceptical alternative in DeRose's cases in a world where banks are known to be extremely cross-temporally consistent in their opening hours).[28,29]

I have now presented you with some further details of my contextualist optimist account and the story it offers to account for both our pessimistic and our optimistic intuitions. Why should we accept a story of this kind though? The answer is remarkably simple. The contextualist optimist is able to accommodate a broader range of intuitions than both the pessimist and the more traditional optimists, and we can do so solely by appealing to some common aspects of a view, epistemic contextualism, which is already widely accepted for independent reasons. Given this, I regard it as providing by far the best explanation of our full range of intuitions concerning aesthetic testimony.

To finish this chapter, though, I should reiterate that my primary aim in this work is to convince you of the truth of optimism in general rather than of my own preferred contextualist optimistic view. And those who are unconvinced by my arguments in this last section—or who are already committed to rejecting contextualism on independent grounds—should remind themselves of my conclusion from the previous section that standard versions of optimism should still be preferred to any version of pessimism. Preferred, that is, in terms of their ability to accommodate the intuitions I have been discussing in these last two chapters. In the next chapter, I turn to some further considerations which are often taken to favour pessimism.

---

[28] Unless, of course, we can do so by merely mentioning them. I will not, however, pursue this possibility for the reasons already given.
[29] It is not clear that this kind of story will apply in lost works cases, but I have already highlighted some other important disanalogies between these and the pessimist's core cases.

6
Pessimism, Assertion, and Signalling

6.1. Aesthetics and Assertion

One of the strongest arguments in support of pessimism relates to a puzzling feature of our aesthetic discourse. Certain kinds of assertion, unproblematic in mundane domains, are typically ruled as impermissible when it comes to aesthetic matters. I can legitimately assert that postboxes in Australia are red, that Justin Bieber's sophomore album lasts a little over thirty-eight minutes, and that arsenic is extremely poisonous, despite the fact that I have never seen, heard, or imbibed the relevant items. By contrast, utterances such as '*The Diving Bell and the Butterfly* is an extremely moving film' (Lackey 2011: 257), and 'It's such a wonderful novel; insightful and moving, with the most beautiful and bewitching language' (Robson 2012: 4), appear extremely problematic in the mouth of someone who has not experienced the works in question for themselves.[1] Examples such as these are typically taken to license the general claim that it is illegitimate to make assertions concerning the aesthetic properties of an object in the absence of first-hand experience of the object itself. Thus, Mary Mothersill (1994: 160) claims that 'the judgment of taste (speech act) presupposes, through the avowal that it implicates, first-person knowledge of the object judged' and Simon Blackburn (1998: 110) states that if 'I have no experience of *X*, I cannot without misrepresentation answer the question 'Is *X* beautiful/boring/fascinating...?'[2]

This claim regarding aesthetic assertion has been drafted into the service of arguments for a surprisingly broad range of views. Blackburn (1998), for example, employs it as part of an argument for quasi-realism concerning normative judgements and Lackey (2011: 157–8) to argue against the claim that assertion is constitutively governed by a knowledge norm.[3] Most commonly, though, this claim is discussed as part of an argument for pessimism.[4]

---

[1] I will qualify this claim in some significant respects later.
[2] Lackey (2011: 157–8), Gorodeisky (2010: 53), Franzén (2018: 669), and Hills (2022: 22) make comments in a similar vein.
[3] While I will not focus on such claims in this chapter it is important to note that, if the arguments I offer here are cogent, then they will also undermine the arguments which Blackburn and Lackey offer. The account of the phenomenon I will offer is, contra Blackburn, compatible with aesthetic judgements being straightforwardly cognitive and, contra Lackey (2011: 265), does not explain the relevant impropriety in terms of the 'asserter's epistemic relation to that which she asserted'.
[4] See e.g. Blackburn (1998: 110–12), Gorodeisky (2010: 53), and Ninan (2014).

Such 'arguments from assertion' proceed roughly as follows. It is perfectly acceptable to assert most propositions on the basis of testimony, but it is impermissible to do so with respect to aesthetic claims, and the only (or at least best) way to adequately explain this is to endorse pessimism. Stated in such schematic terms, arguments from assertion doubtless look rather hasty but I will suggest in this chapter that—once properly formulated—they provide one of the most formidable challenges to optimism. In §6.2 I briefly survey some issues relating to norms of assertion in aesthetics (and elsewhere). In §6.3 I outline in detail what I take to be the strongest instance of an argument from assertion. I then demonstrate that this argument presents a powerful challenge to the optimist's view which, if left unanswered, would significantly undermine the plausibility of optimism. In subsequent sections I argue that the optimist is able to provide a plausible, and non-ad hoc, explanation for the infelicity of the relevant assertions. §6.4 proposes an optimistic response to arguments from assertion in the form of a rival explanation which draws analogies with some influential work concerning the role of signalling in aesthetic creation. In §§6.5 and 6.6 I further clarify this account by responding to some potential objections. §6.7 argues that there are independent grounds for accepting the signalling account I propose, as well as considering applications for this account in areas beyond the immediate debate concerning aesthetic testimony.

6.2. Norms of Assertion

There is an ongoing philosophical debate as to what constitutes, in some fundamental sense, a legitimate assertion. These debates are concerned with the truth of claims such as; 'to be an assertion is to be improper if the speaker does not know what is asserted' (Weiner 2007: 187), 'someone who knowingly asserts a falsehood has thereby broken a rule of assertion, much as if he had broken a rule of a game; he has cheated' (Williamson 1996: 489) and 'assertion is that speech act that (normatively) requires knowledge of its content' (Hindriks 2007: 393). I will refer to such fundamental norms as 'constitutive norms of assertion'. For the purposes of this work, I will make no claims concerning the correct constitutive norm of assertion (in aesthetics or elsewhere). In what follows, I will mostly talk as if some kind of knowledge norm is the correct constitutive norm in all cases but the explanation I will offer is neutral between the knowledge norm and its leading rivals.[5]

In addition to such constitutive norms of assertion, though, there are other rules governing what it is—in some sense—appropriate to assert at various points

---

[5] I will also assume, for ease of exposition only, that belief and assertion are both constitutively governed by norms rather than having, say, constitutive aims or functions.

in a conversation. These additional rules include various Gricean conversational (and conventional) maxims as well as social rules concerning 'tact, prudence, and concern for the feelings of others' (Hopkins 2011: 145). I will denote the totality of rules governing what it is appropriate to assert, incorporating both the correct constitutive norm of assertion and these supplementary rules, as simply 'norms of assertion'.[6]

So, what norm—or norms—explain the impermissibility of the aesthetic assertions discussed so far? An obvious explanation seems to be available to the pessimist at this point. There are two norms active in the relevant cases. First, the constitutive knowledge norm of assertion (playing its typical topic-neutral role) and second some norm of aesthetic belief which prevents the corresponding beliefs from qualifying as knowledge in certain circumstances. What are these circumstances though?

The examples I have surveyed thus far—along with much of the discussion in the literature on aesthetic belief—suggests that the requisite additional condition is that we have first-hand experience of the object in question.[7] So, perhaps, the norm that the pessimist requires is something like *AP*. I say 'something like' because, even setting aside such controversial issues as the epistemic standing of aesthetic testimony, there are clear counterexamples to the unqualified claim that aesthetic belief is illegitimate in the absence of first-hand experience: counterexamples involving, for example, exact reproductions or photographs of the object, perceptual imagination, and so forth.[8] Of course, one might attempt to revise the experience condition for aesthetic knowledge in such a way as to accommodate these proposed counterexamples but there are, as I have argued at length elsewhere (Robson 2013), compelling reasons—independent of debates concerning aesthetic testimony—to be sceptical of the success of any such project. That said, I am well aware that my position here is by no means uncontroversial and that *AP* remains widely popular (in spirit if not in letter). As such, I will leave to the pessimist the project of specifying the precise nature of the broader norm(s), if any, which they take to govern aesthetic belief. Instead, I will tentatively propose what I hope will be a relatively non-controversial—though consequently somewhat underspecified—norm of aesthetic assertion, which, I will suggest, can be explain by appeal to various different pessimistic norms.

AF: In order to properly assert an aesthetic proposition (P) an agent must possess sufficient warrant for legitimately believing P on the basis of the operation of their own aesthetic faculties.

---

[6] Of course, many of these rules, such as Grice's maxims, govern not only assertion but communication more broadly.
[7] See e.g. Todd (2004), Hopkins (2006a), and Goldman (2006).
[8] For detailed discussions of some of these cases see Hopkins (2006a: 93) and Livingston (2003: 262).

Both sides of the aesthetic testimony debate should, I maintain, accept that *AF*—or some norm very like it—is operative with respect to aesthetic assertion (or rather, for reasons I will outline in §6.5, that it is operative by default).[9] The price of maintaining this level of neutrality is that *AF* is deliberately underspecified in some key respects. I have, for example, made no comment as to how aesthetic beliefs acquire warrant, nor explained precisely what it takes for an individual's warrant to be based on the operation of their own aesthetic faculties. Further, I have not indicated whether *AF* will be satisfied in various problem cases concerning inferences, less than perfect duplicates, and the like.

AF should appeal to the pessimist since it captures much of what motivates principles such as *AP*.[10] Those who have discussed *AP* (and other related principles) in a favourable light tend to highlight problems—concerning the absence of principles of taste and so forth—for our employing our own aesthetic faculties, or at least employing them to much effect, in the absence of first-hand experience. On the other hand, the most uncontroversial counterexamples to the letter of *AP* focus on cases where our own aesthetic capacities can be usefully employed even in the absence of such experience.[11] And, of course, the pessimist will typically think that these restrictions on aesthetic belief carry over to aesthetic assertion. Given this, it seems likely that any suitably refined pessimistic principle regarding assertion will include—perhaps among other restrictions—some norm broadly in the spirit of *AF*. Indeed, as I discuss further in §7.1, for many pessimists *AF* will be something of a freebie as it is simply entailed by a combination of their existing norms of aesthetic belief alongside a constitutive, and topic-neutral, norm of assertion.

One might legitimately wonder, though, why an optimist should accept anything even broadly in the vicinity of *AF*. Shouldn't we, rather, be inclined to claim that there are no additional norms on aesthetic assertion and, a fortiori, no norm of the kind I have suggested? After all, if there are no such norms then the optimist will have no case to answer with respect to arguments from assertion. If it is not impermissible to assert that '*The Diving Bell and the Butterfly* is an extremely moving film' on the basis of testimony, then it is not an advantage for pessimists (quite the reverse in fact) that their account of aesthetic belief—combined with independently plausible constitutive norms of assertion—predicts this impermissibility. In my view, though, the optimist should be extremely reluctant to adopt this line since the assertions in question really *do* seem problematic. The view that such assertions are illegitimate isn't limited to pessimists but, rather, is widely

---

[9] For the sake of brevity, I will omit the 'or some norm very like it' qualification in what follows.
[10] And is even closer in spirit to the alternative pessimistic principle which Hopkins (2011: 149) advances, according to which 'having the right to an aesthetic belief requires one to grasp the aesthetic grounds for it'.
[11] Hopkins (2006a) provides a useful overview of such issues.

shared both by optimists (such as Robson 2012: 4, Meskin 2004: 76) and by those with no obvious axe to grind in such debates (Lackey 2011: 257, Ninan 2014). Of course, some optimists might ultimately resolve to reject appearances here but biting this bullet would be a significant cost and one which, I will argue, they are not compelled to accept. As to why the optimist should accept *AF* in particular, rather than some alternative further norm of aesthetic assertion, it is my hope that the account I will offer shortly (and defend in the next chapter) will provide a convincing response to that challenge.

The dialectic in the remainder of this work, then, will concern what broad kind of account provides the best explanation for *AF*. The standard pessimistic story and the optimist-friendly account I will be defending provide examples of two competing classes of explanation for the relevant data. The former tries to explain the infelicity in question by means of epistemic factors which relate to the nature of the aesthetic judgements themselves.[12] The latter, by contrast, will explain the infelicity by appeal to broadly pragmatic factors. According to such accounts the assertions in question aren't problematic because of the status (epistemic or otherwise) of the corresponding beliefs but, rather, because of what the assertions themselves implicate or presuppose. In what follows, I will refer to these two species of explanation as 'epistemic explanations' and 'pragmatic explanations', respectively. Most of the remainder of this chapter will be taken up with outlining and motivating my preferred pragmatic explanation. Chapter 7 will argue that we should prefer pragmatic explanations of this kind to epistemic explanations.

6.3. The Argument from Assertion

I am now in a position to present in detail what I take to be the strongest instance of an argument from assertion (which I will term simply 'the argument from assertion'). I have claimed that various aesthetic assertions are illegitimate when made in violation of *AF* and that the pessimist has a readily available explanation for this.[13] The explanation in question goes as follows. An agent who does not possess sufficient warrant for legitimately believing an aesthetic proposition on the basis of the operation of their own aesthetic faculties (because they, say, failed to abide by some properly formulated version of *AP*) will not possess sufficient warrant simpliciter. As such, the agent will not *know* the proposition in question,

---

[12] I frame the dialectic here in terms of epistemic norms of belief but an unusability pessimist could easily reframe much of what is said in terms of non-epistemic belief norms.

[13] To be rather more precise, such an explanation is available to the pessimist who endorses some more general norm of aesthetic belief which parallels the restrictions *AF* places on aesthetic assertions. I will, therefore, focus on pessimists of that kind in what follows. Pessimists who don't postulate such a general norm seem to encounter much the same difficulty as the optimist here.

meaning that, given a constitutive knowledge norm of assertion, they cannot properly assert it.[14]

Optimists, by contrast, encounter significant difficulty in explaining the impropriety of violating *AF*. We are committed to the claim that we regularly come to possess aesthetic knowledge via testimony and, as such, we cannot avail ourselves of the convenient appeal to a constitutive knowledge norm which the pessimist makes. This might not appear especially problematic since—as already discussed—we can clearly violate norms of assertion (in the wider sense) even when asserting that which we know. However, non-constitutive norms, at least of the kinds discussed earlier, also appear powerless to explain the relevant impropriety. In particular, the four categories of conversational maxim which Grice (1989: 26–9) identifies are manifestly incapable of accounting for the infelicity of the assertions in question. Indeed, bringing conversational considerations into play appears to make matters worse. Consider, for example, that certain qualified versions of the relevant assertions ('Phil says the melody was graceful', 'it must be very beautiful', 'apparently it was a good play', etc.) all appear perfectly permissible on the basis of appropriate testimony. If, however, I know the unqualified form of these propositions then asserting the qualified versions would violate Gricean maxims by deliberately making my contributions less informative—and in many cases less relevant—than they could otherwise have been. Similarly, I can see no general explanation available for the impropriety in considerations pertaining to 'tact, prudence and concern for the feelings of others' (Hopkins 2011:145).

We have seen, then, that the pessimist has a simple and readily available explanation for the impropriety of aesthetic assertions made in violation of *AF*. If, therefore, the optimist cannot provide such an explanation, this will constitute a powerful strike against their position. I will argue, however, that the antecedent of this conditional does not hold and that (appearances notwithstanding) the optimist can satisfactorily account for the impermissibility of the relevant assertions. The remainder of this chapter will be dedicated to presenting this explanation.

6.4. The Appreciative Signalling Account

The explanation I propose begins with the claim that one important function of aesthetic assertion—and *mutatis mutandis* aesthetic discourse more generally—is to signal that the individual making these assertions possesses certain valuable

---

[14] It is worth noting that this explanation is only superficially dependent on my earlier decision to assume a constitutive knowledge norm of assertion. Variants of this argument could easily be produced to accommodate many other proposed constitutive norms of assertion (concerning e.g. warranted belief or true warranted belief). There are exceptions here (most obviously constitutive truth norms of assertion) but I will assume, for the sake of charity, that the pessimist subscribes to a suitable norm.

attributes. To see how an account of this kind might be developed it will be useful to draw an analogy with the kind of story which Gregory Currie (2011), Stephen Davies (2010), Dennis Dutton (2009), Geoffrey Miller (2000), and others have told concerning the creation of objects of aesthetic appreciation. The bare bones of such stories proceed roughly as follows:[15]

> *Creative Signalling Account (CSA)*: The universal (or near universal) tendency among human cultures to produce objects of aesthetic appreciation is explained (at least in part) by the fact that in performing such activities individuals signal their possession of certain desirable attributes.

This basic CSA story can be fleshed out in various ways depending on how a particular theorist answers certain crucial questions. What exactly is being signalled (creativity, craftsmanship, protean intelligence)? What purpose does the signalling serve (mate selection, social advancement)? Is CSA meant to explain human artistic activity tout court or merely some particular aspect of it? It isn't necessary for present purposes to provide answers to any of these questions, but it will be useful to look in a little more detail at one influential CSA account in order to gain a better understanding of how such stories function.

According to this account, our practice of aesthetic creation originated as the result of the evolutionary process of sexual selection. While the production of artworks does not itself typically contribute anything to an individual's evolutionary fitness, producing artworks (or at least artworks of a certain kind and quality) enables them to reliably signal to potential mates that they possess other qualities which are fitness enhancing. These artworks are analogous to the peacock's tail, the stag's antlers, and the bowerbird's construction of intricate bowers, in that each of these signals to an individual's conspecifics that the individual in question possesses certain evolutionarily valuable qualities and is thus (ceteris paribus) an attractive mating prospect. As Geoffrey Miller (2000: 168) puts it, we 'find attractive those things that could have been produced only by people with attractive, high-fitness qualities such as health, energy, endurance, hand-eye coordination, fine motor control, intelligence, creativity, access to rare materials, the ability to learn difficult skills, and lots of free time'.[16]

While this account is useful for illustrating the kinds of claim which some proponents of CSA make, it is important to note that CSA itself does not commit one to any particular account (or, as some critics would have it, 'just-so story') either of how the relevant signalling system arose or of how it presently functions. In particular, it should be stressed that, while many advocates of CSA claim that the

---

[15] For a somewhat different kind of evolutionary account see Dissanayake (2001).
[16] Naturally this brief summary cannot do justice to the intricacies of such views. For an influential and accessible sustained defence of one view of this kind see Dutton (2009).

relevant creative activities originated as evolutionary adaptations, I don't take CSA itself to be committed to this claim for several reasons. First, as Davies (2010) argues, the claim that the relevant practices at present play a fitness indicating role is compatible with holding that these practices originally arose as a result of other factors (perhaps as spandrels or random non-adaptive mutations) and only later acquired their role as signals of fitness. Second, CSA as such is not committed to regarding the relevant signalling systems as fully (or even partially) explained by biological rather than, say, sociological factors.

CSA is a story about the production of artworks (and perhaps other objects of aesthetic appreciation) but producing artworks is neither the only aesthetic activity nor even the only one which requires the employment of the kind of desirable capacities signalled in CSA. On the contrary, much of our ordinary aesthetic engagement will also necessitate their deployment. To judge, via the application of one's own aesthetic faculties, that an object possesses certain aesthetic qualities—and even more so to understand why this is so—will often require a great deal of skill, and perhaps even creativity, on the part of the appreciator. This is especially true when the object in question is a complex artwork. To appreciate for oneself the value of works such as *Vertical Earth Kilometer*, *L.H.O.O.Q*, or *Boundary Functions* will require knowledge of the artistic traditions within which such creations arose along with some intricate imaginative engagement.[17] Nor is this phenomenon confined to works of conceptual art. Fully appreciating a great work of literature, for example, may require the ability to interpret various symbols, to follow complex plots, and to draw plausible psychological inference as to the motivations of the work's various characters.[18] Indeed, there is reason to think that a full appreciation of certain art forms requires one to have some familiarity with producing (and not merely appreciating) works of that kind.[19]

I propose, then, that one important reason why we engage in art appreciation, critical discourse, and related practices is to signal to our conspecifics that we possess various desirable skills and traits such as those enumerated earlier. According to this 'Appreciative Signalling Account' (ASA) by correctly identifying the intention behind a work of conceptual art, sifting the original from the merely novel, or identifying the underlying themes in a complex symbolist tome, we employ (albeit typically to a lesser degree) many of the same abilities which artists employ in their creative acts. These qualities, it has already been argued—in numerous variations of CSA—are judged to be valuable by our conspecifics.

Yet, reliance on such signalling becomes problematic when we consider our ability to appeal to aesthetic judgements formed on the basis of testimony.

---

[17] For descriptions and philosophical discussions of these works see Konigsberg (2012: 165), Shelley (2003: 364), and Lopes (2009: 26), respectively.
[18] See Currie (1998).   [19] See Montero (2006: 237).

Consider, for example, a situation where someone totally devoid of taste finds themselves with easy access to the views of a cooperative and well-informed critic. In such a case, they could use the critic's testimony to perfectly track the view of someone with excellent taste and then reliably transmit these views to others. To illustrate this point, consider the following case of Matthew Kieran's.[20] Kieran reports observing an individual standing at the bar after an operatic performance and listening intently to a fellow opera-goer as she describes in learned terms the ways in which the evening's performance instantiated, or failed to instantiate, various aesthetic properties. This individual then returned to his own table and repeated these profound pronouncements almost word for word. Kieran's verdict with respect to this case—one which strikes me, and many others, as eminently plausible—is that the opera-goer is acting improperly in making the assertions he does. The interesting task is to explain why this is so. We can, I think, safely stipulate that the opera-goer actually believes the claims he makes and that he meets those conditions which would normally (i.e. in non-aesthetic cases) suffice for testimonial knowledge. The pessimist will have their usual explanations for the impropriety; the opera-goer's beliefs are not formed in the right way and, as such, the corresponding assertions are improper.[21] According to ASA, by contrast, the opera-goer's violation of AF is problematic not because he doesn't know the propositions he asserts but rather because he is attempting to pass off this knowledge as the deliverances of his own aesthetic faculties and thus signalling that he possesses some desirable features which he actually lacks.[22] On this account the problem with his pronouncements is closely analogous to the worries which Dutton highlights with respect to artistic forgeries—they both 'misrepresent artistic performance' (1983: 186). Indeed, proponents of ASA may wish to classify the opera-goer's assertions as literally a kind of forgery; he misrepresents the results of a piece of aesthetic labour (a critical judgement) as his own when it is really the work of another.

Or so the story goes, and it is a story which—in my view—has a great deal of prima-facie plausibility. As presented, though, it doubtless strikes many as being extremely speculative. Before turning to motivate this account, though, it is worth pausing to consider three initial objections.

---

[20] Kieran has presented this case in a number of talks concerning the influence of snobbery on aesthetic judgement.
[21] I agree with Tormey (1973: 38), then, when he claims that such an individual is flying 'under false colors' and in danger of being 'caught out' (just not with his pessimistic explanation of this fact). It may be objected that, since he has first-hand experience of the work, he would not violate a principle in the spirit of AP. However, AP-style principles typically require not only that an individual in question undergoes the relevant experiences but that their judgements are *based* on such experiences.
[22] Of course, neither the pessimist, nor the optimist who embraces ASA, is committed to the claim that the feature they highlight is *all* that is wrong with the opera-goer's behaviour.

6.5. Some Initial Objections

A first worry is that it seems implausible to imagine that people generally go around intending to send signals of this kind (Kieran's opera-goer might be an exception here) or that they refrain from making certain assertions because of an awareness that doing so would violate *AF*. I agree that these claims would be implausible but, fortunately, ASA is not committed to making them. People's conformity to various linguistic rules almost always outstrips their understanding of such rules (think, for example, of Grice's maxims or the rules for ordering different adjectives) and this case is no exception. ASA offers an explanation for the existence of a particular linguistic practice but doesn't presuppose that any of those involved in it are aware of the practice itself and, still less, that they are consciously motivated to follow it.

The second worry is that ASA only succeeds if we take the opera-goer's asserting that, for example, '[t]here were serious balance problems, too, with some of the singers struggling to project over even this instrumentation, and the gravitational centre of ensembles was awkwardly skewed',[23] to suggest that he has arrived at this judgement by employing his own aesthetic faculties. Surely, though, this would only be the case if *AF*, or some similar norm, were already in place to ensure that such assertions could not properly be made on the basis of testimony. As such, we need some independent account of the origins of *AF* before we can appeal to the 'misrepresented artistic achievement' explanation. In order to respond to this worry, we need to look in depth at a third objection.

The objection in question proceeds as follows. It is standardly assumed that, in order for a signalling system to be reliable, signals must be prohibitively expensive to fake.[24] Yet, it does not seem that any such costs are present with respect to ASA, quite the reverse in fact. For a genuine expert to be in a position to signal their laudable skills as an aesthetic appreciator they will frequently be required to expend significant effort in familiarizing themselves with the nature and history of the works they are discussing (as well as the works themselves). By contrast, the faker needs only have access to a few impressive sounding pieces of testimony which they repeat more or less verbatim. Given this, we need some explanation as to how such a signalling system would ever achieve (or even approximate) reliability. Fortunately, such an explanation can be offered, and this explanation will also help us to appreciate how a norm such as *AF* may have arisen. Crucially for my defence of ASA, there is a sense in which misleading signalling has the potential to be very costly indeed. To see how, we'll need to examine another instance of misleading signalling: straightforward lying.

---

[23] Words which he could take from *Opera Review*'s review of *Don Giovanni: The Opera* <http://www.opera.co.uk/view-review.php?reviewID=112>.

[24] Though this assumption has been contested, see e.g. Smith (1994).

As with the example just discussed, lying initially seems to carry few costs and offer many benefits. Perhaps there is some additional cost to the liar in signalling what is not the case—their lie may require them to construct and sustain a plausible narrative which is typically not an easy task—assuming a reasonable level of skill on their part, though, such costs will likely pale in comparison to the manifold benefits that they could obtain from deceiving their conspecifics. Given this, it would seem that lying will typically be in an individual's best interests, which would create significant pressure towards making insincere assertions and (via a linguistic version of Gresham's law) a complete disvaluing of normal assertion. There are, however, mechanisms in place which prevent this outcome. Those who lie—or rather those who lie and are detected—are subject to all manner of sanctions. Individuals known to be dishonest may be ostracized by their group, be the subject of unflattering gossip, or even faced with legal penalties. More directly, the liar will lose the benefit of having their assertions regarded as plausible. Sanctions of this kind are widespread across time and culture; indeed, as Hauser (1992) discusses, they may not even be unique to our species.

A story parallel to that offered in the lying case can also be told concerning aesthetic assertions of the kind presented in Kieran's opera example. Were the opera-goer's tricks to be discovered by his fellows then he would doubtless be subject to all manner of censure and mockery. Sanctions of this kind can't be enforced, however, if we have no reliable way to distinguish between (i) statements of ordinary critical judgements based on evaluating the work through the operation of one's own aesthetic faculties, (ii) fraudulent imitations of such statements, and (iii) legitimate attempts to pass on aesthetic information acquired via testimony (distinctions which roughly mirror those between genuine artworks, forgeries, and legitimate reproductions).

We can now begin to see how a norm such as *AF* might have arisen in aesthetics (and so respond to our second objection as well). One simple and effective strategy for marking these distinctions would be to apply a norm of this kind to unqualified aesthetic assertion. This norm could then lead to something like the following taxonomy. When making unqualified aesthetic assertions, we signal that we have arrived at a critical judgement based on the application of our own aesthetic faculties. If we have done so then this signal is accurate, if not then it is misleading and—assuming we are not, as I have suggested in §3.3 we often are, mistaken concerning the source of our aesthetic judgements—qualifies as a fraudulent attempt to pass off the fruits of someone else's aesthetic labour as our own. What of someone who wants to legitimately transmit an aesthetic belief formed on the basis of testimony? How should they transmit their belief that an object has an aesthetic property without illegitimately signalling that this judgement is the output of their own aesthetic faculties? Simple, they qualify their assertion in some way—such as adding an 'everyone says that...' or 'it must be the case that...' rider—which makes it clear that the judgement is warranted but that this warrant was not acquired via the application of their own aesthetic faculties.[25]

This strikes me as a good strategy for differentiating the three relevant species of aesthetic assertion, but it is important to stress that is by no means the only one. There are many other possible conventions governing aesthetic assertion which could be—and, I will suggest, sometimes have been—successfully adopted to balance the relevant desiderata. The problem we are presented with is that of establishing and policing a reliable signalling system concerning our abilities as aesthetic appreciators while also maintaining a reasonably efficient system of communication. This is a problem which, I maintain, arises across all (or virtually all) human cultures but the strategy of addressing this problem by adopting a further norm on aesthetic assertion, such as *AF*, need enjoy no such ubiquity. To put it another way, the norms of assertion I am proposing here are not intended to be constitutive norms delineating what it is to be an aesthetic assertion. Individuals in a different culture, where some other convention is active, would still literally be making aesthetic assertions.[26]

An example of such a convention would be one in which speakers are always required, even in non-aesthetic cases, to give some indication as to the source of their beliefs but which also enables them to do so in ways which aren't overly cumbersome. One instance of this is already found in languages such as Wintu where flagging of the (putative) source of one's beliefs is automatically accomplished by grammatical means.[27] A study of how attitudes to aesthetic belief and assertion operate in societies where these languages are spoken would be extremely useful evidence in addressing the argument from assertion (as well as the optimist/pessimist debate more broadly). Sadly, though, such evidence is, to the best of my knowledge, not presently available and so I will focus on the conventions which, I maintain, are operative within my own linguistic community.

6.6. A Further Worry

With these claims in place my outline of ASA is almost complete, and I will turn in the next section to offer some reasons for regarding it as non-ad hoc and prima facie plausible. Before doing so, though, it is worth pausing to address one lingering worry. I have presented ASA as an explanation for a particular practice—our

---

[25] See Hills (2020: 2). Of course, not all qualified instances of aesthetic assertion will carry the relevant locutionary force. If I say 'according to that well-known liar Fred the painting is beautiful' then I am clearly not signalling any agreement with Fred's claim. Exactly what force particular riders carry will be a complex matter influenced by both context and convention.

[26] I should also make clear, in response to a concern raised by Morgan (2017), that I take aesthetic assertion itself to be the same kind of speech act as assertions concerning mundane matters (differing, at a fundamental level, only in terms of its subject matter).

[27] For details see Schlichter (1986).

convention of not making aesthetic assertions in violation of *AF*—and the corresponding norm. 'Explanation' is, however, a notoriously promiscuous label and some might worry that my argument rests on an equivocation. ASA may offer an explanation for this practice in the sense of providing a causal explanation of how it arose but, my opponent maintains, as a merely causal account it will not—indeed *could* not—explain the practice in the sense of providing any normative justification for it. As such, it cannot furnish us with an answer to the normative question of why it is impermissible to make assertions in violation of *AF*.[28]

The first aspect of this charge is a perfectly legitimate one. ASA is, first and foremost, an etiological account; it explains our unwillingness to make assertions in violation of *AF* by offering a causal account of how such a convention might have arisen.[29] Further, it is also true that, in themselves, such accounts carry no normative force. There would, as I have already discussed, be nothing wrong with a society (actual or counterfactual) rejecting *AF* in favour of some alternative norm which met the relevant communicative desiderata. Nor would there be anything wrong—in any deep or fundamental sense—with a society which adopted no such norm. Rather, the disadvantages of refraining from doing so are purely pragmatic. Yet, isn't my aim in this chapter to explain the illegitimacy—rather than merely the inconvenience—of making aesthetic assertions in violation of *AF*? It is, and I will argue that it is a mistake to think that, just because my explanation is at its heart a causal one, it cannot contribute to explaining the impermissibility of assertions made in violation of *AF*.

So, where does the normativity enter into my account? Very late in the process, it turns out. If the explanation I have offered is correct, then it is easy to see how the convention of not making aesthetic assertions in violation of *AF* arose. Given that we have accepted the convention, though, it is also easy to make the further step to acceptance of a corresponding norm. Recall that, given the existence of the relevant convention, assertions made in violation of *AF* have a very real potential to serve as misleading signals. The relevant assertions (those made in violation of *AF*) are problematic, then, for the remarkably prosaic reason that—given the conventions presently operative in our society—they are liable to mislead our interlocutors in a variety of ways. Given this, there is no mystery as to why there is presently a norm against making such assertions. If, however, we were to abandon our current convention of not making aesthetic assertions in violation of *AF* then such assertions would no longer have the same potential to mislead and there would, therefore, no longer be any norm rendering them impermissible.

---

[28] I thank two anonymous referees of Robson (2015b) for pushing me to address this kind of worry.
[29] Strictly speaking my account, as with CSA, is compatible with the claim that the practice itself initially arose for some other reason(s) but now functions to prevent the kind of misleading signalling I discuss. I will, however, ignore this complication in what follows.

132   AESTHETIC TESTIMONY

This attempt to link the existence of a convention so closely to the existence of a corresponding norm may initially appear suspect but this phenomenon is relatively commonplace. Consider the presently existing conventions according to which people standardly sign their names only to those artworks which they themselves have created and avoid signing the names of others to their own works. Such conventions clearly have pragmatic advantages (most obviously in policing against forgeries). Further, given the existence of such conventions, it would (ceteris paribus) be problematically misleading for me to sign my name to your work or your name to my own. These conventions are, however, fragile and contingent things. Other conventions could easily have existed in their place, ones which allow someone to sign the name of an admired artist as a homage, or a master to sign their name as a seal of approval on their pupil's work. Indeed, as Lenain (2012: 67, 214–5) discusses, alternative conventions such as these *have* frequently been operative in other times and cultures. Further, it would be presumptuous (and straightforwardly mistaken) to criticize those in societies which follow these alternative conventions for violating any norm. As with the case of ASA, the norm only comes into force once a convention exists which would make these actions misleading.

6.7. Analogues to the Aesthetic Signalling Account

Having outlined ASA and responded to some initial concerns, the obvious question becomes whether there is any reason to believe that ASA is actually true. I believe that there is. In the next chapter I will argue at length that ASA does a much better job than rival pessimist accounts of *AF*. For now, though, I will focus on demonstrating that ASA isn't merely an ad hoc explanation for the relevant phenomenon but, rather, that there are independent grounds for accepting an account of this kind.

So, why think that my explanation for the existence of *AF* meets even this standard? First, while the kind of picture I am proposing is more prominent in aesthetic matters, it is not entirely unique to them. Assertions of other kinds can, given the right circumstances, serve similar signalling purposes. And, in such circumstances, it is not unusual to see norms at least somewhat parallel to *AF* being applied. Let's look at a concrete example. I suspect that we've all experienced conversations reminiscent of the following:

A: He said I was 'dyspeptic', what does that mean?
B: It means you are irritable or prone to indigestion.
A: You just looked that up!

A's final comment is intended as a form of criticism and (given appropriate circumstances) may well be a legitimate one. What is the charge though? Certainly not that B illegitimately acquired their belief about the meaning of the word 'dyspeptic' through testimony; without our accepting testimony on such matters, it is difficult to see how we could ever develop as competent language users. Yet it seems natural to judge that B is open to criticism here—provided that they retrieved the information in a surreptitious manner—why so? Again, a signalling explanation can be given. An ability to define a word which your co-conversationalists cannot is indicative of a larger than average vocabulary and a large vocabulary is an impressively accurate indicator of above average intelligence (among other desirable qualities).[30] The mere ability to use a dictionary, by contrast, is not indicative of anything of the kind.

Once we start thinking about such cases, further examples are not difficult to find.[31] Imagine an individual who skims through travel guides learning three obscure facts about every European country which they then trot out at dinner parties. Although they know the facts in question—and are not making any false claim concerning their overall level of geographical knowledge—there still seems to be some element of fakery here. This is because it is clear that their assertions will be taken as an indicator of an impressive repository of geographical insights. As such, they would typically be under some obligation not to assert these facts unless they were able to take appropriate steps to ensure that such misleading signals were not sent (by, for example, explicitly drawing attention to their limited repertoire of geographical titbits). So, again, it looks as if we spontaneously apply a norm somewhat analogous to *AF* here.

It could be objected, though, that these cases hurt rather than help the overall account I have offered. I have argued that, given the right context, utterances in other domains can serve signalling roles similar to those standardly played by aesthetic discourse. Yet, these areas are not standardly governed by any norm analogous to *AF* (in most instances it is perfectly legitimate to make assertions concerning the meanings or words or European geography on the basis of testimony). How can I explain this without undermining the account I have offered? The explanation lies, I maintain, in considering the functions which different kinds of discourse *typically* play. In most areas one of the primary reasons (often *the* primary reason) that we make assertions is to convey information to others. By contrast, the mere accumulation of aesthetic information is rarely of paramount importance in aesthetic discourse. In adopting an *AF*-style norm of assertion we are able to better maintain and police a policy against certain misleading signals but at the cost of some significant loss in our ability to convey information efficiently. Whether the gain outweighs the loss will vary from case to case, but I tentatively suggest that, while it will do so frequently in aesthetics, this will occur

---

[30] See Smith et al. (2005).
[31] E.g. many of the problematic assertions discussed in Lackey (2011) strike me as being of this kind and, as such, I believe that they fail to support Lackey's arguments against a constitutive knowledge norm of assertion.

much more rarely in most other areas of discourse. A good strategy, then, would be to have a norm such as *AF* operate by default with respect to aesthetic assertion (where signalling of the relevant kind typically plays a more central role than the transmission of information) but for parallel norms in other areas (where the reverse is the case) to be inactive by default.

All of this depends, though, on my earlier claim that the mere transmission of aesthetic information is rarely of paramount importance, a claim which may strike some as rather implausible. Aren't there large sections of the art world concerned with transmitting just such information? Most obviously, one might maintain that art critics are often primarily concerned with transmitting information about the aesthetic value of the artworks they discuss. This worry is, however, misplaced and the position put forward by the hypothetical objector importantly misrepresents the role of the critic. Even leaving aside controversial claims concerning signalling in aesthetic discourse, critics typically do much more than merely conveying information concerning the aesthetic properties of the artworks under review. They also seek—alongside a range of non-evaluative projects such as describing the work and its historical context—to provide us with reasons in favour of their evaluations and to assist us 'in discovering the value to be had from the works under review' (Carroll 2009: 14). Indeed. as Hopkins (2006b: 137) highlights, recent debates over the primary role of critical discourse have typically been between those who hold that it is a form of argument on the one hand and those who claim it is an aid to perception on the other. The claim that such discourse is primarily a vehicle for the transmission of aesthetic information barely gets a look in.

Still, I am sure that many readers will remain unconvinced by this appallingly brief argument. Fortunately, though, a more complete defence is not needed for my purposes. Recall that my aim is not to convince you that ASA is true but merely that it provides a plausible alternative to the pessimist's explanation of the impermissibility of assertions made in violation of *AF*. And since the pessimist qua pessimist is committed to the claim that we cannot transmit aesthetic knowledge via testimony they must also accept—assuming they do not wish to be unduly revisionary with respect to our current aesthetic practice—that the primary purpose of critical discourse is not the mere transmission of aesthetic information. If you are convinced that this claim misrepresents the role of the critic (or of others within the art world) then this will give you reason to be suspicious of ASA but it will also, and to an even greater extent, be a reason to be suspicious of the pessimist's rival explanation.

From now on, then, I will take it as common ground in this debate that the mere transmission of aesthetic information is rarely of paramount importance in aesthetic discourse.[32] To reiterate, though, I am only claiming that this is the

---

[32] There is also, as discussed in §1.7, good reason to believe that it is of little importance to many of our other aesthetic practices as well.

default position. I do not deny that there can be circumstances where the mere transmission of aesthetic information is of central importance, nor that there are non-aesthetic cases where the transmission of information is of little or no import. Indeed, I believe that a careful consideration of such non-standard cases actually helps to support ASA.

We have already seen that there are non-aesthetic cases where a norm somewhat similar to *AF* can arise and those who accept my account can easily see why this is so. To return to an earlier example, it is easy to think of certain dinner parties (particularly those held in nineteenth-century novels) as competitive displays where diners only broach a subject to demonstrate their superior insight into a topic or their sharper wit in discussing it. In these contexts, passing on or acquiring knowledge about a particular subject is unlikely to be regarded as a particularly important consideration in comparison to, say, social or romantic advancement. Given this, it is easy to imagine that norms of assertion similar to *AF* will be in play, and this appears to be exactly the kind of convention which we *do* find developing on such occasions.[33]

Next, let's consider a non-standard aesthetic case. In §6.2 I suggested that it should be uncontroversial that aesthetic assertions are governed by *AF* but also noted that this was something of an oversimplification. Put more precisely, my view is that *AF* is active *by default*. It is possible (indeed actual) for there to be contexts in which aesthetic assertions aren't governed by *AF*. Consider, for example, an interesting class of cases originally highlighted by C. A. J. Coady (1992: 292) and explored in much greater depth by Jenn Neilson (n.d.). Some statutes which allow a work of art to be censored on the basis of obscenity also allow a defence based on the claim that the work in question possesses significant aesthetic or artistic merit. This defence was famously, and successfully, deployed in the obscenity trial following Penguin books' 1960 publication of an unexpurgated edition of *Lady Chatterley's Lover*. In such cases, the primary concern of the trier of fact is (or should be) to determine the truth of the matter with respect to the value of the work. Given this, there would be nothing untoward in their making substantive comments with regards to the work's merit which aren't based on employing their own critical faculties.[34] On the contrary, it would be problematic if they *were* to pronounce their verdict entirely on the basis of their own firsthand reading of the work rather than relying (as happened to a significant extent in the *Lady Chatterley* case) on testimony from suitably chosen experts. Here, again, we have a non-standard context where the standard norms aren't in play

---

[33] I do not mean to suggest that the norms in question will be strictly parallel and there is, doubtless, much to be learned in exploring some disanalogies between different cases. I will not, however, pursue this project here.

[34] The jury in the *Chatterley* case were asked to read the novel but they weren't required to base their verdict on their own reading. Indeed, as we'll see in the next chapter, the conduct of the trial made it clear that they weren't expected to do so.

and, again, proponents of ASA can offer a straightforward explanation for why this is so.

Hopefully the examples I have adduced lend some credence to the thought that there is an important connection between *AF* and the presence of potentially misleading signals. Given this, along with my responses to objections in earlier sections, I hope to have discharged my duty of showing that ASA provides the optimist with a prima facie plausible, and non-ad hoc, explanation for *AF*. Having done so, I turn in the next chapter to consider how well this explanation stacks up against those offered by the pessimist.

7
The Debate Concerning Assertion

7.1. The State of the Dialectic

I have argued in the previous chapter that the argument from assertion provides a powerful challenge to optimism. The pessimist has an easy-to-hand explanation for a plausible norm of aesthetic assertion, *AF*, according to which properly asserting an aesthetic proposition (P) requires an agent to possess sufficient warrant for legitimately believing P on the basis of the operation of their own aesthetic faculties. The optimist, by contrast, appears to have none. Thankfully, though, I have also shown that the optimist is able to offer a prima facie plausible and non-ad hoc response to this argument. In doing so, I offered my own preferred account, the Appreciative Signalling Account (ASA). In order to come to any final conclusion concerning the argument from assertion, though, we will need to consider how well this explanation stacks up against the explanation which the pessimist offers.

An initial worry is that the pessimist's explanation ought to be preferred since it avoids reliance on any complex and controversial story to account for *AF*. On the pessimist's account, *AF* is merely a straightforward consequence of a topic neutral constitutive knowledge norm of assertion. As such, the pessimist might maintain, their view has the advantage since they can eschew additional commitments altogether. This claim would, however, importantly misrepresent the state of the dialectic. The pessimist maintains—as part of their explanation for *AF*—that we cannot achieve aesthetic knowledge on the basis of testimony and this claim is supported by appeal to further norms which *are* specific to the aesthetic realm.[1] As such, both parties in the debate are committed to postulating domain-specific norms in aesthetics and owe us some explanation for their existence. The question, then, becomes which account is overall most plausible. The issue of the general plausibility (or otherwise) of the pessimist's proposed norms of belief is, of course, one which I have addressed at length in earlier chapters. In the present chapter, therefore, I will be focusing exclusively on the specific issue of which side offers the best explanation of which aesthetic assertions are problematic

---

[1] A pessimist might object that their position is compatible with their not postulating any additional norms of belief. There are, however, two things to say in response here. First, very few contemporary pessimists actually endorse an account of this kind. Second, I cannot see any plausible way for a pessimist who holds this moderate view to account for the general claim that we cannot know the truth of assertions made in violation of *AF*.

(and why). My conclusion will, unsurprisingly be, that the optimist has the advantage here.

In §7.2 I outline the debate between two general kinds of explanation for the infelicity of the aesthetic assertions in question—epistemic and pragmatic explanations—and present the biggest challenge to my own preferred (pragmatic) explanation. §7.3 begins my defence of ASA by considering a range of cases (both aesthetic and non-aesthetic) where our intuitive reactions seem more easily explained by ASA than by the kind of epistemic explanation which the pessimist proposes. §7.4 focuses in depth on one non-aesthetic domain where a norm very much like *AF* seems to be in place: assertions concerning gustatory taste. I argue that the features of this case are best explained by a norm paralleling ASA and that this provides further motivation for accepting the proposed norm in the aesthetic case. §7.5 summarizes the state of the debate between ASA and its pessimist rival. §7.6 introduces, and rejects, a further rival to my account. §7.7 offers some concluding remarks.

Before I begin my defence of ASA, though, it's worth reiterating that my primary aim is to convince you of the superiority of a broadly optimistic explanation rather than of any particular optimistic account. Some of my discussion will depend on the specific details of ASA but much of it will be compatible with a range of other optimistic accounts (provided that they belong to the same general species of explanation as ASA).

7.2. Epistemic Explanations and Pragmatic Explanations

As I already mentioned in §6.2, ASA and the standard pessimistic story provide examples of two competing classes of explanation for the relevant data. One of these (epistemic accounts) tries to explain the infelicity in question by means of epistemic factors which relate to the nature of the aesthetic judgements themselves. The other (pragmatic accounts), by contrast, explains the infelicity by appeal to broadly pragmatic factors.[2] According to such pragmatic accounts, the assertions in question aren't problematic because of the status (epistemic or otherwise) of the corresponding beliefs but, rather, because of what the assertions themselves implicate or presuppose. Most of the remainder of this chapter will be focused on arguing that pragmatic explanations (and ASA in particular) are to be preferred to epistemic explanations.

To begin, consider a species of argument presented by Dilip Ninan (2014) and Franzén (2018) which provides the most pressing objection to pragmatic accounts. According to such arguments, we should reject the pragmatic interpretation of

---

[2] It is worth noting that pragmatic 'Warranted Assertability Manoeuvres' of this kind are commonplace elsewhere (see e.g. Brown 2006).

norms such as *AF* since there is no way for an explanation based on extant pragmatic features of language—such as implicature and presupposition—to account for the behaviour of such norms.[3]

Consider first conversational implicatures. As Franzén (2018: 3) notes, '[c]ancellability is generally taken to be a defining feature of conversational implicature'. It would standardly be problematic for someone who knows that Jack went up the hill to assert 'either Jack or Jill went up the hill', since this would violate the Gricean maxim of quantity, but there would be nothing infelicitous (rather than merely infuriating) for them to assert 'either Jack or Jill went up the hill, and I know which one'. By contrast, the oddness of asserting 'the painting is beautiful' in the absence of first-hand experience is in no way mitigated by asserting instead 'the painting is beautiful, but I've never seen it'. Indeed, we have seen that assertions of this kind are often used to motivate the argument from assertion itself.

What about conventional implicature? It is often taken to be a feature of such implicatures that they don't merely apply with respect to simple sentences of the relevant kind but that they 'project out' to cover various more complex sentences which use these simpler sentences as parts. Again, though, this doesn't appear to apply in the case at hand. To understand the contrast here, let's look at some concrete examples. The assertion 'he is poor but honest' conventionally implicates something like the claim that poor people tend to be dishonest. Further, as, for example, Christopher Potts (2005: 38) has pointed out, this implicature will carry over to cases involving qualifiers ('he is probably poor but honest'), embedding ('if he's poor but honest we'll still employ him'), and interrogatives ('is it true that he's poor but honest?'). By contrast, assertions such as 'it is probably beautiful' and 'if it's beautiful we should buy it' would be perfectly licit in circumstances where the straightforward assertion that 'it is beautiful' would violate *AF*.

So, what should the proponent of pragmatic accounts say to defend our appeal to some form of implicature (or related pragmatic phenomenon)?[4] It seems clear that critics of pragmatic explanations are correct when they claim that the problematic nature of the relevant assertions cannot be explained by appeal to the standard behaviour of either conversational or conventional implicatures.[5] Given this, advocates of pragmatic explanations have two options. First, they could claim that *AF* is explained by appeal to some standard form of implicature operating in a non-standard manner. Second, they could maintain that it is explained by

---

[3] Both Ninan and Franzén focus on an assertoric version of *AP* which they term 'the acquaintance phenomenon', rather than on *AF* itself. I have, however, adapted their arguments to more directly target *AF*.

[4] I will largely ignore the parenthetical complication in what follows and talk in terms of different kinds of implicature. It is important to note, though, that ASA (and pragmatic explanations more generally) are not committed to the relevant pragmatic feature being a form of implicature.

[5] As Ninan (2014: 299) and Franzén (2018) point out, similar worries arise for attempts to explain *AF* by means of some kind of presupposition.

a novel kind of implicature which has hitherto been neglected in both philosophy and linguistics.

With regards to the first option, it is important to note that there have already been numerous proposed counterexamples to the claim that implicatures always operate in the standard ways outlined earlier. Consider, for example, the following case from Weiner (2006: 128) concerning conversational implicature.

> Alice and Sarah are in a crowded train; Alice...is sprawled across two seats, and Sarah is standing. Sarah says to Alice, 'I'm curious as to whether it would be physically possible for you to make room for someone else to sit down.' The implicature is that Alice should make room. It is extraordinarily unlikely that Sarah really is curious about whether Alice is physically capable of moving, since it is mutually obvious that she is capable.... Suppose now that Sarah adds, 'Not that you should make room; I'm just curious.' This has the form of an explicit cancellation of the implicature. Nevertheless, the implicature is not cancelled.

Examples of this kind are, however, controversial (see e.g. Blome-Tillmann 2008) and I don't mean to commit myself to the claim that they present us with genuine counterexamples to the claim that cancellability is a constitutive feature of conversational implicature (though I am somewhat inclined to believe that they do). Rather, I merely intend to highlight that the constitutive cancellability claim is a controversial thesis about the nature of conversation implicatures rather than a universally accepted platitude.

What about the second line of response which aims to defend ASA by appealing to some previously untheorized species of implicature? Doubtless, appealing to an entirely new kind of implicature to defend pragmatic accounts will strike many as an implausibly ad hoc move but, again, I think it is important that we don't overstate the case here. Making a move of this kind would certainly be a significant cost to ASA but this cost may well be one which is worth paying. First, this move need not be an ad hoc one, fitted only to respond to the particular kinds of implicature I have argued *AF* generates. I have already suggested in §6.7, and will argue at length later in this chapter, that there are various non-aesthetic assertions which appear (given the right circumstances) to exhibit similar behaviour. Second, I hope to convince you that there are compelling reasons to judge that *AF* is best explained by the kinds of pragmatic factor which ASA appeals to. If this is right, and if we cannot account for *AF* by means of any extant form of implicature, then this would provide a strong motivation for postulating implicatures of a novel kind.

To summarize, both of the options available to proponents of pragmatic options such as ASA come with costs which, while not insignificant, are by no means fatal. In the remainder of this chapter, I will be arguing that the advantages of pragmatic explanations (and of ASA in particular) are significant enough to make such costs worth paying. I will not, however, take any stance as to which of the two options we should endorse.

7.3. A Wider Range of Cases

As with the kinds of intuitions discussed in Chapters 4 and 5, a great deal of the apparent plausibility which the pessimist's explanation of *AF* enjoys arises from focusing on a narrow range of cases. In this section, I highlight a range of cases which cause difficulties for the pessimist's approach—difficulties that, I will argue, ASA does not encounter.

One area where the optimist has the advantage over their opponents is in accounting for the non-standard cases I considered when motivating ASA in the previous chapter. That is, aesthetic cases where *AF* does not seem to be active as well as non-aesthetic cases where a norm paralleling *AF* looks to be in operation. I have already looked at one example of the former—concerning legal cases (such as the *Lady Chatterley* trial)—in §6.7.[6] This is, however, far from being the only example worth considering.

Another telling example concerns assertions regarding past artworks and past performances. Consider, again, Laetz's (2008: 355) assertion that 'Vaslav Nijinsky "was a brilliant performer—graceful, dynamic—one of the greatest danseurs of Russian ballet"'. If the standard norm of aesthetic assertion, *AF*, were active in such cases then assertions of this kind would clearly be problematic. Yet, most of us to do not take this to be the case. Moreover, given the truth of ASA, it is easy to see why *AF* would not be operative in these cases.[7] Flagging such assertions with relevant qualifiers to avoid sending misleading signals would be redundant since it will be clear to everyone in the conversation—provided they are suitably informed in the relevant historical respects—that the speaker does not know these things on the basis of applying their own aesthetic faculties. Asserting these claims would, therefore, no longer act as a potentially misleading signal.[8]

---

[6] A related case ('The Mapplethorpe obscenity trial') is discussed in Freeland (2003: 11).

[7] It might be objected that my discussion of past works provides the optimist with something of an embarrassment of riches here. After all, haven't I already proposed an optimist-friendly explanation of such cases in §5.8. This worry is, however, misplaced. There are two facts to be explained here: (i) the apparent permissibility of beliefs concerning past cases and (ii) the apparent permissibility of assertions regarding such cases. My earlier arguments concerned the former; my arguments here concern the latter.

[8] Again, there are non-aesthetic parallels here. Consider that a number of the problematic assertions which Lackey (2011) highlights would be perfectly legitimate in cases where it was common knowledge that the assertions could not possibly have been based on the speaker's own determinations.

A parallel discussion concerns what we might loosely call 'future work' claims (that is, future tensed claims about works which the speaker themselves is yet to engage with). It seems, for example, to be perfectly acceptable for someone to claim that a film which they haven't yet seen *will* be excellent on the basis of appropriate testimony to that effect. And, again, a proponent of ASA can explain this by the fact that such assertions typically lack any potential to misleadingly signal that the speaker has formed an aesthetic judgement in accordance with *AF*.[9]

What is the pessimist to make of these cases? We already saw in §5.4 that some pessimists make exceptions to their standard norms of aesthetic belief—and so, by extension, to their norms of assertion—when it comes to past works. Given this, some pessimists might be tempted to suggest that the additional cases I have been discussing merely highlight further exceptions. This response would, however, be unconvincing. I have already argued that the pessimist is unable to provide a convincing justification for making an exception for past works, and the other cases under consideration appear no less problematic. There is no reason to expect that knowledge of what *will be* beautiful will come any easier than knowledge of what *is* beautiful. And, given the stakes involved, the legal cases discussed should, if anything, be more epistemically demanding than many of the pessimist's core cases. This is not, however, to suggest that the pessimist has no options available to them.

One possibility would be to appeal to an assertoric version of the kind of self-effacing paraphrase discussed in §5.3. According to this proposal, these assertions aren't really about which aesthetic properties an object has but, rather, about which aesthetic properties they are taken by some relevant group—a group which does not include the speaker themselves—to possess. And there are certainly cases where this suggestion appears plausible. Consider, for example, Nguyen's museum curator (discussed in §5.5) who fills their collection with beautiful objects chosen entirely on the basis of testimony. I have already argued that there is good reason to accept Nguyen's conclusion that their behaviour is unproblematic, and this judgement also extends to their asserting *in appropriate contexts* that these works are beautiful. In particular, it would be perfectly legitimate to do so in those cases—such as producing publicity for the exhibition, writing descriptions of the works for public display—where they are speaking in their professional capacity. It seems clear that, in these specific cases, they are not really speaking on their own behalf but, rather, playing the part of a Jane Fairfax by reporting what they take to be the general judgement on this issue (or, perhaps, the aggregate judgements of the experts they have consulted).

---

[9] Similarly, as Franzén (2018: 5) highlights, it appears entirely felicitous for someone to assert that 'I am sure that the novel is wonderful, but I haven't read it'. My discussion of the role of such qualified statements in §6.5 explains, once again, why this is precisely what ASA would predict.

Could we say something similar with respect to the examples I have discussed? I think not. Consider, for example, a pessimist who claims that what a jury member in obscenity cases is *really* asked to judge is whether the work in question is regarded by qualified critics as possessing great artistic merit. An explanation of this kind seems ill-fitted to the facts of how the cases under consideration are actually conducted. In the *Lady Chatterley* case, for example, there was frequent debate between the prosecuting counsel and the various experts called concerning the simple issue of whether the work in question was a 'good book, by a good writer' (Rolph 1961: 47). Further, the way in which these debates were conducted—often featuring lengthy discussions of the quality of particular passages in the work—would be entirely inexplicable if we took the relevant point of controversy to surround how the novel was generally regarded amongst any particular class of individuals. On the contrary, transcripts make it clear that these witnesses were regarded by all participants in the proceedings as offering, inter alia, testimony concerning the merits of the work itself. Similarly, while the jury were given lengthy instructions concerning the kinds of individual (and the kinds of ways) in which a book must have a 'tendency to deprave and corrupt' (ibid. 10–17) their instructions regarding what it meant for a work to have literary merit (ibid. 18, 33–4) didn't make even a passing mention to the standards of any particular group.

The pessimist's hand seems, if anything, to be even weaker when it comes to the other examples under consideration. I have already argued that it is implausible to regard apparent beliefs about lost works as self-effacing, and I can't see any reason why we shouldn't reach the same conclusion regarding the corresponding assertions. Similarly, I can't see any motivation, beyond a desire to save the pessimist's overall position, for endorsing the claim that all apparently future tensed aesthetic assertions are actually self-effacing.[10]

What happens if we consider an even wider range of cases though? Many of our (apparent) aesthetic judgements do not concern artworks (lost or otherwise). There are also judgements of natural beauty, of the aesthetic properties of mathematical and scientific theories, and of various other kinds. Which side of the debate do cases of these kinds favour? This question is not an easy one to answer, and I do not have a precise account of the stance we should take with respect to the legitimacy of *AF*-violating assertions in these areas.

The mathematical case is, perhaps, the easiest to deal with. While it may sometimes convey misleading signals to assert that one mathematical conjecture is more elegant than another on the basis of testimony, I suspect that—given the context in which such claims would typically be made—the misleading signals here will be primarily mathematical rather than aesthetic. Someone who makes

---

[10] I argue elsewhere (in Robson 2015b) that a consideration of an even wider class of cases provides a further challenge to the pessimist's position.

144 AESTHETIC TESTIMONY

such an assertion (sans qualification) is more likely to be trying to pass themselves off as a mathematician than an aesthetician.[11] Other cases are more difficult. I am, for example, not sure what to make of statements such as 'the sunset last night was beautiful' and 'the northern lights are sublime' in the mouth of someone who has only learned these things from testimony. They strike me as a little strange but not as problematic as parallel assertions with respect to presently existing artworks. And a claim such as 'I hope to finally be able to see the northern lights in person, they're far more beautiful than photographs can capture' strikes me as (very close to) unproblematic. One possible explanation for this ambivalence is that, although assertions of this kind don't typically signal anything especially valuable (it hardly takes a skilled appreciator to recognize the beauty of a sunset)—and, as such, there is no particular pressure to adopt a norm such as *AF* to weed out fakers—our tendency to apply *AF* in closely parallel cases concerning artworks exerts some psychological pressure to apply it in these cases also.[12] Such an explanation is, however, highly speculative and I do not wish to commit myself to the truth of this account. I will argue in §7.5, though, that the very 'messiness' of cases like this ultimately ends up favouring pragmatic explanations such as *AF*.

7.4. A Gustatory Analogy

Let's turn now to the second kind of example, non-aesthetic cases where a norm parallel to *AF* appears to be active. It might initially seem unclear why examples of this kind favour optimism. After all, the pessimists aren't committed to adopting any specific position regarding these non-aesthetic cases. In this section, I will explain—via an extended examination of assertions involving gustatory taste—why I believe examples of this kind can lend support to a pragmatic explanation such as ASA. I will begin by briefly exploring this case and then explain why I take it to support my account regarding aesthetic assertion.

It seems problematic to make certain assertions with respect to food which we haven't ourselves tasted. While it would be perfectly unremarkable, for example, to make the descriptive claim that a cheese we haven't tasted is made from goat's milk or produced primarily in Azeitão, it would appear very odd to claim that it tastes beautiful, that it is delicious, or that it is exquisite. Of course, as with the aesthetic case, this oversimplifies things somewhat since there are clearly various exceptions here. It would, for example, be unproblematic to make claims of this

---

[11] This is, perhaps, what has led some, e.g. Williams (1972), to question the value of testimony in mathematics.
[12] Especially since, in contrast to the lost works case, there is genuine potential for our conversational partners to arrive at mistaken views concerning the source of the relevant beliefs.

kind about some item of food on the basis of tasting an exact duplicate, tasting some matching artificial flavouring, or perhaps—as David Lewis (1990: 500) suggests—on the basis of an artificial experience which 'could in principle be produced in you by precise neurosurgery, very far beyond the limits of present-day technique'. I will, however, largely ignore such complications in what follows and focus on the simplified claim that these assertions are problematic when found in a mouth which hasn't also contained the relevant items.[13] What explains this fact?

One obvious explanation would be that the assertions in question are aesthetic assertions and are, therefore, problematic for whatever reason we end up appealing to in the aesthetic case. Despite its immediate attractions, though, this explanation quickly encounters difficulties. First, we would need to accept the claim that judgements concerning the tastes of various items of food and drink *can* be genuinely aesthetic judgements, a claim which some philosophers have been keen to reject. Scruton (1979: 114), for example, famously claimed that the so-called 'lower senses', such as taste, aren't aesthetic.[14] I will not, however, pursue this worry here for two reasons. First, my own view is—for reasons highlighted in, for example, Baker (2016) and Korsmeyer (2002)—that this position is mistaken. Second, there is a deeper difficulty which renders this debate irrelevant for present purposes.

While (some of) the problematic examples of assertions I mentioned above are (plausibly) aesthetic in nature, other assertions of this kind clearly aren't. Consider, for example, the claim that a particular cheese 'has a strong fruity aftertaste', 'is subtly creamier than the cheese produced in the neighbouring valley', or 'has a slightly sweet nutty taste'. These claims, once again, appear problematic to assert in the absence of a tasting experience but they also appear—regardless of our general view regarding the relationship between the sense of taste and the aesthetic—to be plainly non-aesthetic. Given this, their impermissibility cannot be subsumed under any general rule concerning the impermissibility of particular aesthetic assertions. It is also important to note that no such restriction applies to the deliverances of our other senses. We do not, for example, need to see an object for ourselves in order to assert complex claims about its colour or listen to a tune ourselves to assert detailed claims about its pitch.[15]

My own suggestion in the gustatory case would be to adopt a pragmatic explanation very much in the mode of ASA. This explanation, once again, appeals to the propensity of the relevant assertions to send misleading signals concerning

---

[13] Though, I suspect, a detailed analysis of such counterexamples will provide further support for a norm paralleling *AF*.

[14] Beardsley (1981: 111) provides a useful overview of some of the most influential arguments for this view.

[15] As with the claims in the previous chapter about aesthetic and mundane assertions, these are only meant to serve as default positions. I do not mean to deny that it is *sometimes* problematic to make assertions of this kind regarding other sensory modalities.

the abilities of those who make them. If I say, for example, that a cheese 'has a slightly sweet nutty taste' then I signal that I have been able to discern this subtle flavour myself when tasting the item in question, something which requires a rather discriminating palate. As such, were I to assert this claim without having discerned this matter for myself—and without suitable qualifications—I would be sending a problematically misleading signal.

As with ASA, two immediate worries arise here. First, we need to consider why such a signalling system—without which no misleading signals could be sent—arose in the first place. Second, we need to explain why it is that parallel signalling systems don't (typically) arise with respect to other sensory modalities. Comprehensively responding to either of these questions would require an extremely lengthy digression, but a quick comparison with my response in the aesthetic case should give some indication of how an appropriate response would proceed. In both domains we can observe that there is a widespread practice of individuals competing, whether formally or otherwise, to demonstrate their superior skills. In the gustatory case this would include, for example, their ability to taste the subtle differences between coffee beans which are indistinguishable to most consumers or to discern hidden elements in a favourite vintage which others have overlooked. And, again, there is a long-standing tradition of criticism and learned discourse which tie into these practices. These factors clearly differentiate our gustatory practice from those concerning, for example, vision and audition.[16] Further, it's worth noting that the gustatory realm provides the only real challenger to the aesthetic for the domain where the risk of snobbery is most ubiquitous. Finally, we can see that, as with the aesthetic realm, our discussions of food are regularly ones in which our interest in merely transmitting accurate information typically takes a backseat to other considerations.

With some indication of how the gustatory equivalent of ASA would proceed in place, we can now turn to consider why we should accept an account of this kind. Once again, the motivations here very closely mirror those which I have proffered in the aesthetic case. There are, for example, parallels to the lost work case since there would often be no oddity in some (appropriately informed) individual making assertions about the taste of dodo meat. Such assertions have no potential to mislead since it will typically be obvious to all concerned that they are not reporting the results of their own first-hand judgements. Similarly, it will often be unproblematic to make various assertions about how food *will* taste or *must* taste on the basis of testimony. All of these exceptions are, again, easy to explain on the basis of the kind of pragmatic account I am proposing but remain mysterious for those who endorse an epistemic explanation.[17]

---

[16] By this I do not, of course, mean that such competitive displays are completely absent in these areas but merely that they do not enjoy anything approaching the same level of prevalence.

[17] For some additional arguments against an epistemic approach here see Meskin and Robson 2015.

The above is, admittedly, rather brief, and there is much more that could be said to explain and motivate a pragmatic explanation for the (im)permissibility of various gustatory assertions. This is, however, a task for another time. For the time being, my main concern is to highlight why I take such an explanation to lend support to ASA. Accepting a gustatory signalling account would, I propose, give you at least two reasons for being sympathetic to ASA.

First, the curiously atypical behaviour of assertions in both domains is so strikingly parallel that it would be surprising in the extreme to find that the explanation for this in one domain was of a radically different kind from that in the other (a claim which is shared by those, such as (Ninan 2014), who explicitly reject the species of explanation I am proposing here). Accepting a pragmatic account in the gustatory case would, therefore, provide a strong presumption in favour of pragmatic accounts in the aesthetic domain.

Second, return to the main objection to ASA I am considering in this chapter; that the implicatures I have proposed in the aesthetic case behave very differently to any extant species of implicature. It's clear, though, that this unusual behaviour would be shared by the relevant implicatures in the gustatory case as well. Once again, the implicatures don't seem to be cancellable by the standard means applied to other conversational implicatures ('it has a slightly sweet nutty taste but I've never tasted it'), nor do they 'project out' in some of the ways we would expect from conventional implicatures ('if the cheese has a smooth subtle flavour then I'll order some more for the party'). Those who already accept the kind of account I have proposed in the gustatory case would, therefore, be committed to rejecting the contention that there are no extant examples of implicatures which operate in the way ASA suggests.

It might be objected, though, that this second benefit only applies if we accept that the implicature I am proposing in the gustatory case is parallel to, yet still distinct from, that which I am proposing in the aesthetic case. If, however, we merely treat the two cases—as e.g. Ninan (2014: 290) does—as two aspects of the same phenomenon then this will do nothing to show that there is an example of implicature *distinct from that which I have proposed in the aesthetic case* which shares its non-standard features. Fortunately, though, there is good reason to hold that there are two different pragmatic norms in play here. While there are, as I hope to have illustrated, clear analogies between the aesthetic and the gustatory cases, the norms of assertion in the two domains are not entirely parallel.

Consider, for example, another kind of exception in the gustatory case; cases where the pronouncement in question seems too obvious to require any real skill in judging. The most obvious gustatory examples of this kind involve negative evaluations. For example, there would be nothing misleading about someone claiming, on the basis of widespread press coverage to this effect, that 'Nintendo Switch cartridges are coated in a chemical which tastes revolting' even if they have (wisely) never tried licking these cartridges.[18] However, exceptions of this kind also arise in descriptive cases. For example, asserting that peppers with a Scoville rating of over a million are extremely spicy wouldn't, so far as I can see, carry any implicature that you've tasted any of these for yourself. However, it is interesting to note that parallel exceptions do not tend to arise in the aesthetic case. For example, while I've suggested in previous chapters that I can clearly come to know a piece of aesthetic common knowledge (such *Guernica*'s being harrowing) on the basis of testimony, it would still be misleading for me to assert this fact (sans qualification).

Disanalogies of this kind provide us with reason to doubt that we are dealing with a single unified phenomenon—whether pragmatic or otherwise—in both the aesthetic and the gustatory case. However, given the various important parallels between the two domains that I have highlighted, this in no way undermines my general line of argument. I am merely trying to convince you that the same general kind of pragmatic norm is active in both cases, not that the norms involved are strictly parallel.

7.5. Summing up

I have argued above, then, that there is good reason to accept pragmatic explanations for *AF* and, in particular, to accept an explanation along the lines of ASA. We must now weigh these benefits against the costs I highlighted in §7.2. That is, the cost of claiming either (i) that the implicatures involved are non-standard examples of some existing kind of implicature or (ii) that they are examples of some entirely novel species of implicature. I noted that neither of these costs would be insignificant, but I hope to have shown that they are worth bearing.

First, I have demonstrated that the linguistic data cannot easily be captured by epistemic explanations of *AF*. Second, I have argued that pragmatic explanations are better placed to account for various neglected cases than the epistemic alternative. Third, I have marshalled additional support by appealing to an analogy between aesthetic assertions and assertions of gustatory taste, arguing that the contours of the gustatory case are best explained by appealing to an account which parallels ASA. One final factor is also worthy of brief consideration. That is, that merely reflecting on how 'messy' the phenomena under discussion are lends additional credence to certain kinds of pragmatic explanation. Let me explain.

---

[18] For an example of such coverage see <http://www.telegraph.co.uk/technology/2017/03/02/nintendo-switch-game-cartridges-taste-revolting>.

The very fact that consideration of a full range of aesthetic assertions unearths some complicated and difficult to classify cases provides reason for favouring an account broadly in the spirit of the one I have offered. On my account, *AF* is non-constitutive, meaning that something can literally be an aesthetic assertion without being governed by (or even tending to be governed by) such a norm. The fact that our aesthetic assertions concerning presently existing artworks are typically governed by *AF* is the result of many fragile and contingent factors. By contrast, the norms of belief appealed to by pessimistic accounts are typically taken to be constitutive norms (see e.g. Goldman 2006: 333 and Hopkins 2011: 139). Given this, most pessimists will maintain that for something to be an aesthetic judgement it must be governed (or at least tend to be governed) by their norms of belief. So, if the pessimist's account were correct, we would have good reason to expect there to be a clear gulf between cases where the relevant beliefs, and so the corresponding assertions, are problematic and those in which they are not. The situation we actually find ourselves in is, however, far more complicated than this. Further, these complications would only deepen if we were to widen the range of cases under consideration still more (to include e.g. the beauty of human beings and their characters).[19] This full picture would, I suggest, present us with a patchwork landscape featuring many complex and difficult to classify cases. This is exactly the sort of situation one would expect to arise given that, as ASA claims, it is a highly contingent matter whether (and with what force) *AF* applies in a given case.

Given all of this, and despite the costs already noted, we have a clear motivation to accept pragmatic accounts such as ASA. Before moving on, though, I want to briefly consider another candidate explanation for *AF*, an explanation which doesn't belong to either of the rival camps I have discussed.

7.6. A Third Contender

So far in this chapter I have been considering the debate between epistemic and pragmatic explanations for *AF*. There is, however, a third contender which needs to be considered. According to this third view, it is part of the *meaning* of aesthetic assertions such as 'the Trevi Fountain is beautiful' that the person making these assertions has experienced the object for themselves. As such, they are straightforwardly false in the absence of such experience. What is being suggested here is not merely that there is some implicature (or presupposition, etc.) that the

---

[19] An interesting literary example occurs in chapter 4 of *Don Quixote* where the titular hero demands that some Toledo traders acknowledge the surpassing beauty of Dulcinea but refuses to allow them to see her (or even a picture of her). However, various features of this particular case mean that it should be uncontroversially problematic (thanks to Greg Currie for bringing this example to my attention).

individual has had the relevant experience. Rather, the claim is that reference to this experience is part of the *semantics* of such judgements.[20]

As it stands this account is rather underspecified and there are evidently many different ways in which it could be cashed out. For now, though, let's focus on a simple version according to which an aesthetic claim such as 'this is beautiful' asserts something like 'I experienced this object as being beautiful'. Explanations of this kind present us with a straightforward explanation for the problematic nature of the assertions we are focusing on. The reason I cannot legitimately claim that 'the Trevi fountain is beautiful' in the absence of first-hand experience is that such an assertion would be false. Further, they do a much better job than the standard pessimistic explanation in accommodating some of the cases I have considered. It would, for example, be a simple matter to adapt this account to fit future tense cases. If 'this will be beautiful' really means 'I *will* experience this as being beautiful' then there is no obvious reason to think that we couldn't know this on the basis of testimony.[21] It isn't all good news for proponents of semantic explanations though and they appear no better placed than proponents of the epistemic explanation to account for some of the cases we've been discussing. Consider, again, the *Lady Chatterley* case or, with reference to the gustatory analogy, the felicity of asserting 'I've never tried their food because it's too spicy'. The ability (or not) of this account to handle various cases is, however, moot since the account itself is based on an implausible semantics of aesthetic assertion.

One concern with the proposed semantics is that it undermines some important distinctions between aesthetic claims and claims concerning so-called 'predicates of personal taste'. It might seem plausible to claim that an assertion of 'x is fun' should be interpreted as meaning something like 'I found x fun' but there are important disanalogies between predicates of personal taste (such as 'fun') and aesthetic terms (such as 'beautiful').[22] First, the old Kantian saw that the latter, but not the former, seems to involve some kind of demand for universal agreement. This is something which—as noted in e.g. Baker and Robson (2017: 439)—has important consequence for, amongst other things, debates concerning disagreement in the relevant domains. It doesn't seem unreasonable to allow that all (or virtually all) putative disagreements about which activities are fun either fail to be

---

[20] Franzén (2018) proposes a rival semantic account which differs in some important respects from the one I will discuss in this chapter. While I believe that some (though by no means all) of the considerations I raise will tell against Franzén's account also, there is no need for me to attempt a rebuttal of his view since Franzén (2018: 13) explicitly takes his account to be committed to optimism.

[21] A pattern that transfers to various predicates of personal taste. It would e.g. be illegitimate to assert that something was enjoyable on the basis of testimony but unproblematic to assert that you will enjoy it.

[22] I do not mean to endorse the semantics for 'fun' suggested here but merely to indicate that it seems (prima facie) more plausible than its aesthetic analogue.

genuine disagreements or else constitute so called 'faultless disagreements'.[23] Yet, the same result seems much less plausible in aesthetic cases. While it may well be that certain aesthetic disagreements *are* faultless (such as those concerning which of Bach's pieces is the most beautiful or whether Rembrandt's works are superior to van Gogh's), others clearly aren't. It would, for example, strike me as absurd to suggest that there could be a faultless disagreement over whether Thomas Kinkade's paintings are superior to Rembrandt's. Similarly, the proposed semantics for aesthetic judgements would be difficult to square with the existence of aesthetic expertise and the role of argumentation within aesthetic discourse.

A further worry for this proposal is that it would render some perfectly ordinary claims paradoxical. Consider someone who asserts of a work that 'it may well be beautiful, but I just can't see it myself'. This would be an entirely unremarkable assertion for someone to make when, for example, first presented with an instance of an unfamiliar art form which is widely regarded as beautiful.[24] On the semantics under discussion, though, this assertion would be equivalent to claiming that 'I may have found it beautiful, but I didn't find it beautiful'. Similarly, this semantics would have to reject any claim to the effect that 'there are many beautiful objects which I've never perceived for myself'. Finally, someone who laments their previous poor taste in the aesthetic realm may well assert 'I found the painting very beautiful when I first saw it but later realized that it wasn't beautiful'. Again, such an assertion would be paradoxical if we accept the experiential semantics.

It might be objected, though, that these difficulties only arise because of the particular, and particularly crude, version of the semantic account which I have chosen to focus on. There are, after all, many kinds of broadly experiential semantics which could be adopted. We might, for example, endorse an assertoric version of the kind of appreciative account discussed in §2.7 such that 'x is beautiful' is equivalent to something like 'I have (veridically) perceived the value of the beautiful making properties as realized in x'. Or a counterfactual account such that 'x is beautiful' means 'I would find x beautiful were I to experience it under appropriate conditions'. I contend, though, that each of these approaches—and, more generally, any version of the semantic approach—is liable to be impaled on one horn of the following dilemma. They will either fall victim to close variants of (some of) the worries I have raised for the simple view above or they will no longer offer any kind of explanation for *AF*.

We can see that the assertoric version of the appreciative account falls foul of the first of these worries. While the requirement that the experience in question

---

[23] For discussion of the nature and consequences of such views see e.g. Kölbel (2004), Baker (2014), and Palmira (2015).
[24] Indeed, given their lack of familiarity with the art form in question, denying that the work was beautiful would exhibit a deeply problematic lack of intellectual humility.

be veridical allows this view to avoid some of the difficulties outlined above (such as that of the individual repudiating the judgements of their earlier self) it still falls victim to others. It would, for example, still render it contradictory to assert that 'there are many beautiful objects which I've never experienced for myself' or that 'it may well be beautiful, but I just couldn't see it myself'. A properly formulated counterfactual view, by contrast, would be able to avoid all such difficulties but at the cost of no longer being able to justify accepting a norm such as *AF*. If the claim that '*x* is beautiful' means at root something like 'I would find *x* beautiful were I to experience it under appropriate conditions', then this is something which we will often be able to truly assert in violation of *AF*. If, therefore, there is something problematic about such assertions we must look beyond their truth value to find it. This concession would, once again, leave us with the choice between epistemic and semantic explanations.

A possible response here would be to argue that the relevant question isn't whether semantic explanations are true but whether they are influential. Perhaps the folk are (presumably tacitly) in the grip of a false theory about the nature of aesthetic assertions, a theory which leads them to judge that the assertions in question are problematic. There are, however, two importantly different ways in which such a response could be spelled out. First, someone might claim that the assertions in question are widely, but falsely, believed to be illicit owing to the widespread acceptance of a false theory. Second, they could maintain that the assertions in question are *genuinely* problematic since—given the widespread acceptance of this mistaken semantic theory—there is a perennial danger of misleading our interlocutors when we make aesthetic assertion in violation of *AF*.

My own view is that there is good reason to reject both of these stories but there is no need for me to argue for this claim here. My main purpose in these last two chapters has been to rebut the pessimist's argument from assertion and either of these views would, if successful, allow the optimist to do just that. If the assertions in question really aren't problematic—or are only problematic because of the widespread acceptance of some false theory—then it looks as if it is the pessimist, rather than the optimist, who has some explaining to do. In particular, they would need to explain why the beliefs in question being illegitimate doesn't also render the corresponding assertions illicit.

7.7. Where to Now?

In this chapter I have argued that there is good reason to prefer a pragmatic explanation such as ASA to the kind of epistemic explanation which the pessimist offers. Given this, consideration of the peculiarities of aesthetic assertion not only fails to support pessimism but, on the contrary, provides additional motivation for embracing optimism. With this, my defence of optimism is now complete. In a sense, though, the work is just beginning. To return to a point raised in the introduction, recent decades have seen an explosion of interest relating to various question within social epistemology. Asking, for example, about the epistemic significance of so-called 'peer disagreement', about whether groups can know things which their members do not, about the best ways to structure social institutions so as to promote epistemic goods, and much more besides.[25] These topics have, however, been almost entirely neglected within aesthetics.[26] This neglect, I suspect, has more than a little to do with the widespread acceptance of pessimism concerning aesthetic testimony. To close, then, I would like to suggest that those of us concerned with the epistemology of the aesthetic should begin to move beyond the narrow confines of the debate concerning the legitimacy of aesthetic testimony and into these wide, and relatively unexplored, pastures.

---

[25] For some representative discussions see Goldman (1999) and the essays in Lackey (2014).
[26] Thi Nguyen (2020a, 2020b) has recently gone some way towards addressing this neglect.

Bibliography

Adler, J. (2003). *Belief's Own Ethics*. Cambridge, MA: MIT Press.
Adler, J., and Hicks, M. (2013). 'Non-Evidential Reasons to Believe.' In *The Aim of Belief*, ed. T. Chan. Oxford: Oxford University Press, 140–66.
Alcaraz Leon, M. J. (2008). 'The Rational Justification of Aesthetic Judgments.' *Journal of Aesthetics and Art Criticism*, 66: 291–300.
Alison, A. (1790/2019). *Essays on the Nature and Principles of Taste*. London: Forgotten Books.
Allen, K. (2019). 'Should we Believe Philosophical Claims on Testimony?' *Proceedings of the Aristotelian Society*, 119: 105–25.
Alston, W. P. (1991). *Perceiving God: The Epistemology of Religious Experience*. Ithaca, NY: Cornell University Press.
Alter, T. (2007). 'The Knowledge Argument.' In *The Blackwell Companion to Consciousness*, ed. M. Velmans and S. Schneider. Oxford: Blackwell, 396–405.
Andow, J. (2014). 'A Semantic Solution to the Problem with Aesthetic Testimony.' *Acta Analytica*, 30: 211–18.
Andow, J. (2018). 'Aesthetic Testimony and Experimental Philosophy.' In *Advances in Experimental Philosophy of Aesthetics*, ed. F. Cova and S. Réhault. London: Bloomsbury, 33–58.
Aristotle (1997). *Poetics*. New York: Dover.
Augustine (2010). *Revisions*. New York: New City Press.
Auvray, M and Spence, C. (2008). 'The Multisensory Perception of Flavor.' *Consciousness and Cognition*, 17: 1016–31.
Ayer, A. J. (1936). *Language, Truth, and Logic*. London: Gollancz.
Baker, C. (2014). 'The Role of Disagreement in Semantic Theory.' *Australasian Journal of Philosophy*, 92: 37–54.
Baker, C., and Robson, J. (2017). 'An Absolutist Theory of Faultless Disagreement in Aesthetics.' *Pacific Philosophical Quarterly*, 98: 429–48.
Baker, T. (2016). 'Transparency, Olfaction and Aesthetics.' *Analysis*, 76: 121–30.
Beardsley, M. C. (1962). 'On the Generality of Critical Reasons.' *Journal of Philosophy*, 59: 477–86.
Beardsley, M. C. (1969). 'Aesthetic Experience Regained.' *Journal of Aesthetics and Art Criticism*, 28: 3–11.
Beardsley, M. C. (1981). *Aesthetics: Problems in the Philosophy of Criticism*. Indianapolis, IN: Hackett.
Bergqvist, A. (2010). 'Why Sibley is Not a Generalist After All.' *British Journal of Aesthetics*, 50: 1–14.
Bird, A. (2007). 'Justified Judging.' *Philosophy and Phenomenological Research*, 74: 81–110.
Blackburn, S. (1980). 'Truth, Realism, and the Regulation of Theory.' *Midwest Studies in Philosophy*, 5: 353–72.
Blackburn, S. (1988). 'Attitudes and contents.' *Ethics*, 98: 501–17.
Blackburn, S. (1998). *Ruling Passions*. Oxford: Oxford University Press.
Blackburn, S. (2010). 'Truth, Beauty and Goodness.' In *Oxford Studies in Metaethics*, vol. 5, ed. Russ Shafer-Landau. Oxford: Oxford University Press, 295–314.

Blome-Tillmann, M. (2008). 'Conversational Implicature and the Cancellability Test.' *Analysis,* 68: 156–60.
Booth, A. R., and Rowbottom, D. P. (eds). (2014). *Intuitions.* Oxford: Oxford University Press.
Brady, E., and Levinson, J. (eds). (2001). *Aesthetic Concepts: Essays After Sibley.* Oxford: Oxford University Press.
Breitenbach, A. (2015). 'Beauty in Proofs: Kant on Aesthetics in Mathematics.' *European Journal of Philosophy,* 23: 955–77.
Brown, J. (2006). 'Contextualism and Warranted Assertibility Manoeuvres.' *Philosophical Studies,* 130: 407–35.
Budd, M. (2003). 'The Acquaintance Principle.' *British Journal of Aesthetics,* 43: 386–92.
Burge, T. (1993). 'Content Preservation.' *Philosophical Review,* 102: 457–88.
Bykvist, K., and Hattiangadi, A. (2007). 'Does Thought Imply Ought?' *Analysis,* 67: 277–85.
Cappelen, H. (2012). *Philosophy Without Intuitions.* Oxford: Oxford University Press.
Cappelen, H., and Hawthorne, J. (2009). *Relativism and Monadic Truth.* Oxford: Oxford University Press.
Carlson, A. (2000). *Aesthetics and the Environment: The Appreciation of Nature, Art and Architecture.* New York: Routledge.
Carroll, N. (2009). *On Criticism.* New York: Routledge.
Chignell, A. (2010). 'The Ethics of Belief.' In *Stanford Encyclopedia of Philosophy,* ed. E. Zalta. https://plato.stanford.edu/entries/ethics-belief/
Chrisman, M. (2010). 'Constructivism, Expressivism and Ethical Knowledge.' *International Journal of Philosophical Studies,* 18: 331–53.
Christensen, D. (2009). 'Disagreement as Evidence: The Epistemology of Controversy.' *Philosophy Compass,* 4: 756–67.
Chudnoff, E. (2013). *Intuition.* Oxford: Oxford University Press.
Coady, C. A. J. (1992). *Testimony: A Philosophical Study.* Oxford: Clarendon Press.
Cohen, S. (1988). 'How to be a Fallibilist.' *Philosophical Perspectives,* 2, 91–123.
Cohen, S. (1999). 'Contextualism, Skepticism, and the Structure of Reasons.' *Noûs,* 33: 57–89.
Cohen, S. (2001). 'Contextualism Defended: Comments on Richard Feldman's "Skeptical Problems, Contextualist Solutions".' *Philosophical Studies,* 103: 87–98.
Costello, D. (2007). 'Kant After Lewitt: Towards an Aesthetics of Conceptual Art.' In *Philosophy and Conceptual Art,* ed. P. Goldie and E. Schellekens. Oxford: Oxford University Press, 92–116.
Cowan, R. (2020). 'The Puzzle of Moral Memory.' *Journal of Moral Philosophy,* 17: 202–28.
Crisp, R. (2014). 'Moral Testimony. Pessimism: A Defence.' *Aristotelian Society Supplementary Volume,* 88: 129–43.
Crowther, P. (2010). *The Kantian Aesthetic: From Knowledge to the Avant-Garde.* Oxford: Oxford University Press.
Currie, G. (1998). 'Realism in Character and the Value of Fiction.' In *Aesthetics and Ethics,* ed. J. Levinson. Cambridge: Cambridge University Press, 161–81.
Currie, G. (2011). 'The Master of the Masek Beds: Handaxes, Art, and the Minds of Early Humans.' In *The Aesthetic Mind: Philosophy and Psychology,* ed. E. Schellekens and P. Goldie. Oxford: Oxford University Press, 9–31.
Currie, G., and Ichino, A. (2012). 'Aliefs don't Exist, Though Some of their Relatives Do.' *Analysis,* 72: 788–98.
Cutting, J. E. (2003). 'Gustave Caillebotte, French Impressionism, and Mere Exposure.' *Psychonomic Bulletin and Review,* 10: 319–43.
Cutting, J. E. (2006). 'The Mere Exposure Effect and Aesthetic Preference.' In *New Directions in Aesthetics, Creativity and the Arts,* ed. P. Locher, C. Martindale, and L. Dorfman. Amityville, NY: Baywood Publishing Co., 33–46.

Davies, S. (2010). 'Why Art is Not a Spandrel.' *British Journal of Aesthetics*, 50: 333–41.
De Bruin, W. B. (2005). 'Save the Last Dance for Me: Unwanted Serial Position Effects in Jury Evaluations.' *Acta Psychologica*, 118: 245–60.
DeRose, K. (1992). 'Contextualism and Knowledge Attributions.' *Philosophy and Phenomenological Research*, 52: 913–29.
DeRose, K. (2009). *The Case for Contextualism: Knowledge, Skepticism, and Context*. Oxford: Oxford University Press.
DeRose, K. (2018). *The Appearance of Ignorance*. Oxford: Oxford University Press.
Deutsch, M. E. (2015). *The Myth of the Intuitive: Experimental Philosophy and Philosophical Method*. Cambridge, MA: MIT Press.
Dickie, G. (1962). 'Is Psychology Relevant to Aesthetics?'. *The Philosophical Review*, 71: 285–302.
Dickie, G. (1974). *Art and the Aesthetic: An Institutional Analysis*. Ithaca, NY: Cornell University Press.
Dickie, G. (1987). 'Beardsley, Sibley, and Critical Principles.' *Journal of Aesthetics and Art Criticism*, 46: 229–37.
Dissanayake, E. (2001). *Homo Aestheticus: Where Art Comes from and Why*. Seattle: University of Washington Press.
Dixon, P., Bortolussi, M., and Sopčák, P. (2015). 'Extratextual Effects on the Evaluation of Narrative Texts.' *Poetics*, 48: 42–54.
Dowling, C. (2010). 'The Aesthetics of Daily Life.' *British Journal of Aesthetics*, 50: 225–42.
Dretske, F. I. (1970). 'Epistemic Operators.' *Journal of Philosophy*, 67: 1007–23.
Dunning, D., Heath, C., and Suls, J. (2004). 'Flawed Self-Assessment.' *Psychological Sciences in the Public Interest*, 5: 69–106.
Dutton, D. (1983). 'The Forger's Art.' In *The Forger's Art: Forgery and the Philosophy of Art*, ed. D. Dutton. Berkeley, CA: University of California Press, 1–57.
Dutton, D. (2009). *The Art Instinct*. New York: Oxford University Press.
Eaton, A. W. (2008). 'Feminist Philosophy of Art.' *Philosophy Compass*, 3: 873–93.
Eaton, M. M. (1994). 'The Intrinsic, Non-Supervenient Nature of Aesthetic Properties.' *Journal of Aesthetics and Art Criticism*, 52: 383–97.
Faulkner, P. (2011). *Knowledge on Trust*. Oxford: Oxford University Press.
Feldman, R., and Conee, E. (1985). 'Evidentialism.' *Philosophical Studies*, 48: 15–34.
Fletcher, G. (2016). 'Moral Testimony: Once More with Feeling.' In *Oxford Studies in Metaethics 11*, ed. R. Shafer-Landau. Oxford: Oxford University Press, 45–73.
Focosi, F. (2019). 'Aesthetic Properties, the Acquaintance Principle, and the Problem of Nonperceptual Arts.' *Journal of Aesthetic Education*, 53: 61–77.
Franzén, N. (2018). 'Aesthetic Evaluation and First-Hand Experience.' *Australasian Journal of Philosophy*, 96: 669–82.
Freeland, C. (2003). *Art Theory: A Very Short Introduction*. Oxford: Oxford University Press.
Fricker, E. (1994). 'Against Gullibility.' In *Knowing from Words*, ed. B. K. Matilal and A. Chakrabarti. Dordrecht: Kluwer Academic Publishers, 125–61.
Fricker, E. (1995). 'Telling and Trusting: Reductionism and Anti-Reductionism in the Epistemology of Testimony.' *Mind*, 104: 393–411.
Fricker, E. (2006). 'Testimony and Epistemic Autonomy.' In *The Epistemology of Testimony*, ed. J. Lackey and E. Sosa. Oxford: Oxford University Press, 225–50.
Friend, S. (2008). 'Imagining Fact and Fiction.' In *New Waves in Aesthetics*, ed. K. Stock and K. Thomson-Jones. Basingstoke: Palgrave Macmillan UK, 150–69.
Gaut, B. (1998). 'The Ethical Criticism of Art.' In *Aesthetics and Ethics: Essays at the Intersection*, ed. J. Levinson. Cambridge: Cambridge University Press, 182–203.
Geach, P. T. (1965). 'Assertion.' *Philosophical Review*, 74: 449–65.

Gelfert, A. (2006). 'Kant on Testimony.' *British Journal for the History of Philosophy*, 14: 627–52.
Gibbard, A. (1990). *Wise Choices, Apt Feelings: A Theory of Normative Judgment*. Cambridge, MA: Harvard University Press.
Gibbard, A. (2003). *Thinking How to Live*. Cambridge, MA: Harvard University Press.
Ginsburgh, V., and van Ours, J. (2003). 'Expert Opinion and Compensation: Evidence from a Musical Competition.' *American Economic Review*, 93: 289–96.
Gluer, K., and Wikforss, A. (2009). 'Against Content Normativity.' *Mind*, 118: 31–70.
Goldie, P. (2007). 'Towards a Virtue Theory of Art.' *British Journal of Aesthetics*, 47: 372–87.
Goldman, A. H. (1995). *Aesthetic Value*. Boulder, CO: Westview Press.
Goldman, A. H. (2006). 'The Experiential Account of Aesthetic Value.' *Journal of Aesthetics and Art Criticism*, 64: 333–42.
Goldman, A. H. (2010). 'Why Social Epistemology is Real Epistemology.' In *Social Epistemology*, ed. A. Haddock, A. Millar, and D. Pritchard. Oxford: Oxford University Press, 1–28.
Goldman, A. I. (1999). *Knowledge in a Social World*. Oxford: Oxford University Press.
Gorodeisky, K. (2010). 'A New Look at Kant's View of Aesthetic Testimony.' *British Journal of Aesthetics*, 50: 53–70.
Gorodeisky, K., and Marcus, E. (2018). 'Aesthetic Rationality.' *Journal of Philosophy*, 115: 113–40.
Graham, P. J. (1997). 'What is Testimony?' *Philosophical Quarterly*, 47: 227–32.
Graham, P. J. (2006). 'Can Testimony Generate Knowledge?' *Philosophica*, 78: 105–27.
Grice, H. P. (1989). *Studies in the Way of Words*. Cambridge, MA: Harvard University Press.
Grimm, S. (2012). 'The Value of Understanding.' *Philosophy Compass*, 7: 103–17.
Groll, D., and Decker, J. (2014). 'Moral Testimony: One of These Things is Just Like the Others.' *Analytic Philosophy*, 55: 54–74.
Hanson, L. (2013). 'The Reality of (Non-Aesthetic) Artistic Value.' *Philosophical Quarterly*, 63: 492–508.
Hanson, L. (2015). 'Conceptual Art and the Acquaintance Principle.' *Journal of Aesthetics and Art Criticism*, 73: 247–58.
Hauser, M. (1992). 'Costs of Deception: Cheaters are Punished in Rhesus Monkeys (Macaca Mulatta).' *Proceedings of the National Academy of Sciences*, 89: 12137–9.
Hawthorne, J. (2004). *Knowledge and Lotteries*. Oxford: Oxford University Press.
Hazlett, A. (2015). 'Towards Social Accounts of Testimonial Asymmetries.' *Noûs*, 51: 49–73.
Hess, E. H. (1965). 'Attitude and Pupil Size.' *Scientific American*, 212: 46–54.
Hills, A. (2009). 'Moral Testimony and Moral Epistemology.' *Ethics*, 120: 94–127.
Hills, A. (2010). *The Beloved Self: Morality and the Challenge from Egoism*. Oxford: Oxford University Press.
Hills, A. (2015). 'Cognitivism about Moral Judgement.' In *Oxford Studies in Metaethics*, volume 10, ed. R. Shafer-Landau. Oxford: Oxford University Press, 1–25.
Hills, A. (2017). 'Aesthetic Understanding.' In *Making Sense of the World: New Essays on the Philosophy of Understanding*, ed. S. Grimm. New York: Oxford University Press, 159–65.
Hills, A. (2022). 'Aesthetic Testimony, Understanding and Virtue.' *Noûs*, 56: 21–39.
Hindriks, F. (2007). 'The Status of the Knowledge Account of Assertion.' *Linguistics and Philosophy*, 30: 393–406.
Hopkins, R. (2000). 'Beauty and Testimony.' In *Philosophy, the Good, the True and the Beautiful*, ed. A. O'Hear. Cambridge: Cambridge University Press. 209–36.
Hopkins, R. (2001). 'Kant, Quasi-Realism, and the Autonomy of Aesthetic Judgement.' *European Journal of Philosophy*, 9: 166–89.

Hopkins, R. (2006). 'How to Form Aesthetic Belief: Interpreting the Acquaintance Principle.' *Postgraduate Journal of Aesthetics*, 3: 85–99.
Hopkins, R. (2007). 'What is Wrong with Moral Testimony?' *Philosophy and Phenomenological Research*, 74: 1–24.
Hopkins, R. (2011). 'How to be a Pessimist about Aesthetic Testimony.' *Journal of Philosophy*, 108: 138–57.
Hopkins, R. (n.d.). 'Norms of Use.' Manuscript.
Horowitz, S. (2014). 'Epistemic Akrasia.' *Noûs*, 48: 718–44.
Hume, D. (1738/2007). *A Treatise of Human Nature*. Oxford: Oxford University Press.
Hume, D. (1757/1875). 'Of the Standard of Taste.' In *Essays Moral, Literary and Political*. London: Grant Richards.
Hungerland, I. C. (1968). 'Once Again, Aesthetic and Non-Aesthetic.' *Journal of Aesthetics and Art Criticism*, 26: 285–95.
Hutcheson, F. (1726/2004). *An Inquiry into the Original of Our Ideas of Beauty and Virtue*. Indianapolis: Liberty Fund.
Irvin, S. (2008). 'Scratching an Itch.' *Journal of Aesthetics and Art Criticism*, 66: 25–35.
Irvin, S. (2014). 'Is Aesthetic Experience Possible?' In *Aesthetics and the Sciences of Mind*, ed. G. Currie, M. Kieran, A. Meskin, and J. Robson. Oxford: Oxford University Press, 37–56.
Isenberg, A. (1949). 'Critical Communication.' *Philosophical Review*, 58: 330–44.
Iseminger, G. (1981). 'Aesthetic Appreciation.' *Journal of Aesthetics and Art Criticism*, 39: 389–97.
Jay, C. (2016). 'Testimony, Belief, and Non-Doxastic Faith: The Humean Argument for Religious Fictionalism.' *Religious Studies*, 52: 247–61.
Kant, I. (1790/2005). *Critique of Judgement*, tr. J. H. Bernard. New York: Dover.
Kennick, W. E. (1958). 'Does Traditional Aesthetics Rest on a Mistake?' *Mind*, 67: 317–34.
Kidd, I. J. (2015). 'Beauty, Virtue, and Religious Exemplars.' *Religious Studies*, 53: 171–81.
Kieran, M. (2010). 'The Vice of Snobbery: Aesthetic Knowledge, Justification and Virtue in Art Appreciation.' *Philosophical Quarterly*, 60: 243–63.
Kieran, M. (2011). 'The Fragility of Aesthetic Knowledge: Aesthetic Psychology and Appreciative Virtues.' In *The Aesthetic Mind: Philosophy and Psychology*, ed. P. Goldie and E. Schellekens. Oxford: Oxford University Press, 32–43.
Kirchin, S. (ed.). (2013). *Thick Concepts*. Oxford: Oxford University Press.
Kirwin, C. (2011). 'Why Sibley is (Probably) Not a Particularist After All.' *British Journal of Aesthetics*, 51: 201–12.
Kivy, P. (1980). 'A Failure of Aesthetic Emotivism.' *Philosophical Studies*, 38: 351–65.
Knight, R. P. (1805/2018). *An Analytical Inquiry into the Principles of Taste*. London: Forgotten Books.
Köhler, S. (2017). 'Expressivism, Belief, and All That.' *Journal of Philosophy*, 114: 189–207.
Kölbel, M. (2004). 'Faultless Disagreement.' *Proceedings of the Aristotelian Society*, 104: 53–73.
Konigsberg, A. (2012). 'The Acquaintance Principle, Aesthetic Autonomy, and Aesthetic Appreciation.' *British Journal of Aesthetics*, 52: 153–68.
Korsmeyer, C. (2002). *Making Sense of Taste: Food and Philosophy*. Ithaca, NY: Cornell University Press.
Korsmeyer, C. (2013). 'Taste.' In *The Routledge Companion to Aesthetics*, 3rd ed., ed. B. Gaut and D. M. Lopes. New York: Routledge, 257–66.
Kruger, J., and Dunning, J. (1999). 'Unskilled and Unaware of it: How Difficulties in Recognizing one's own Incompetence Lead to Inflated Self-Assessments.' *Journal of Personality and Social Psychology*, 77: 1121–34.

Lackey, J. (2005). 'Memory as a Generative Epistemic Source.' *Philosophy and Phenomenological Research*, 70: 636–58.
Lackey, J. (2006a). 'Knowing from Testimony.' *Philosophy Compass*, 1: 432–48.
Lackey, J. (2006b). 'The Nature of Testimony.' *Pacific Philosophical Quarterly*, 87: 177–97.
Lackey, J. (2008). *Learning from Words: Testimony as a Source of Knowledge*. Oxford: Oxford University Press.
Lackey, J. (2011). 'Assertion and Isolated Second-Hand Knowledge.' In *Assertion: New Philosophical Essays*, ed. J. Brown and H. Cappelen. Oxford: Oxford University Press, 251–76.
Lackey, J. (2013). 'Deficient Testimonial Knowledge.' In *Knowledge, Virtue, and Action: Putting Epistemic Virtues to Work*, ed. T. Henning and D. Schweikard. New York: Routledge, 30–52.
Lackey, J. (ed.). (2014). *Essays in Collective Epistemology*. New York: Oxford University Press.
Laetz, B. (2008). 'A Modest Defense of Aesthetic Testimony.' *Journal of Aesthetics and Art Criticism*, 66: 355–63.
Le Morvan, P. (2017). 'Knowledge Before Gettier.' *British Journal for the History of Philosophy*, 25: 1216–38.
Lenain, T. (2012). *Art Forgery: The History of a Modern Obsession*. London: Reaktion Books.
Levinson, J. (1994). 'Being Realistic about Aesthetic Properties.' *Journal of Aesthetics and Art Criticism*, 52: 351–4.
Levinson, J. (2001). 'Aesthetic Properties, Evaluative Force, and Differences of Sensibility.' In *Aesthetic Concepts: Essays After Sibley*, ed. E. Brady and J. Levinson. Oxford: Oxford University Press, 61–80.
Levinson, J. (2005). 'Aesthetic Properties.' *Proceedings of the Aristotelian Society*, 79: 191–227.
Levinson, J. (2009). 'The Aesthetic Appreciation of Music.' *British Journal of Aesthetics*, 49: 415–25.
Lewis, D. (1990). 'What Experience Teaches.' In *Mind and Cognition: A Reader*, ed. William Lycan. Oxford: Basil Blackwell, 499–519.
Lewis, D. (1996). 'Elusive Knowledge.' *Australasian Journal of Philosophy*, 74: 549–67.
Lillehammer, H. (2002). 'Moral Cognitivism.' *Philosophical Papers*, 31: 1–25.
Livingston, P. (2003). 'On an Apparent Truism in Aesthetics.' *British Journal of Aesthetics*, 43: 260–78.
Locke, J. (1689/1849). *An Essay Concerning Human Understanding*. London: William Tegg.
Lopes, D. M. (2009). *A Philosophy of Computer Art*. New York: Routledge.
Lopes, D. M. (2011). 'The Myth of (Non-Aesthetic) Artistic Value.' *Philosophical Quarterly*, 61(244): 518–36.
Lopes, D. M. (2014a). 'Feckless Reason.' In *Philosophical Aesthetics and the Sciences of Mind*, ed. G. Currie, M. Kieran, A. Meskin, and J. Robson. Oxford: Oxford University Press, 21–36.
Lopes, D. M. (2014b). *Beyond Art*. Oxford: Oxford University Press.
López de Sa, D. (2011). 'The Many Relativisms: Index, Content, and Beyond.' In S. Hales (ed.), *The Blackwell Companion to Relativism*. Oxford: Blackwell, 102–17.
Lord, E. (2016). 'On the Rational Power of Aesthetic Testimony.' *British Journal of Aesthetics*, 56: 1–13.
Lord, E. (2018). 'How to Learn about Aesthetics and Morality through Acquaintance and Testimony.' In R. Shafer-Landau (ed.), *Oxford Studies in Metaethics*, vol. 13. Oxford: Oxford University Press, 71–97.
Ludlow, P., Nagasawa, Y., and Stoljar, D. (eds). (2004). *There's Something about Mary: Essays on Phenomenal Consciousness and Frank Jackson's Knowledge Argument*. Cambridge, MA: MIT Press.

McAllister, J. W. (2005). 'Mathematical Beauty and the Evolution of the Standards of Mathematical Proof.' In *The Visual Mind II*, ed. M. Emmer. Cambridge, MA: MIT Press, 15–34.
MacFarlane, J. (2009). 'Nonindexical Contextualism.' *Synthese*, 166: 231–50.
McGonigal, A. (2006). 'The Autonomy of Aesthetic Judgement.' *British Journal of Aesthetics*, 46(4): 331–48.
McGrath, S. (2009). 'The Puzzle of Pure Moral Deference.' *Philosophical Perspectives*, 23: 321–44.
McGrath, S. (2011). 'Skepticism about Moral Expertise as a Puzzle for Moral Realism.' *Journal of Philosophy*, 108: 111–37.
McHugh, C. (2011). 'What do we Aim at When we Believe?' *Dialectica*, 65: 369–92.
McKinnon, R. (2017). 'How to be an Optimist about Aesthetic Testimony.' *Episteme*, 14: 177–96.
McShane, P. J. (2018). 'The Non-Remedial Value of Dependence on Moral Testimony.' *Philosophical Studies*, 175(3): 629–47.
Maddy, P. (1980). 'Perception and Mathematical Intuition.' *Philosophical Review*, 89: 163–96.
Matravers, D. (2005). 'Aesthetic Properties I.' *Proceedings of the Aristotelian Society, Supplementary Volumes*, 79: 191–210.
Meskin, A. (2004). 'Aesthetic Testimony: What can we Learn from Others about Beauty and Art?' *Philosophy and Phenomenological Research*, 69: 65–91.
Meskin, A. (2006). 'Solving the Puzzle of Aesthetic Testimony.' In *Knowing Art*, ed. M. Kieran and D. McIver Lopes. Dordrecht: Springer, 109–24.
Meskin, A. (n.d.). 'Aesthetic Unreliability.' Manuscript.
Meskin, A., and Robson, J. (2015). 'Taste and Acquaintance.' *Journal of Aesthetics and Art Criticism*, 73: 127–39.
Meskin, A., and Robson, J. (n.d.). 'Comments on "Aesthetic Rationality".' Manuscript.
Meskin, A., Liao, S., and Andow, J. (n.d.). 'Aesthetic Testimony: Some Empirical Evidence.' Manuscript.
Meskin, A., Phelan, M., Moore, M., and Kieran, M. (2013). 'Mere Exposure to Bad Art.' *British Journal of Aesthetics*, 53: 139–64.
Miller, G. (2000). *The Mating Mind*. London: William Heinemann.
Millikan, R. G. (1984). *Language, Thought and Other Biological Categories*. Cambridge, MA: MIT Press.
Mogensen, A. L. (2017). 'Moral Testimony Pessimism and the Uncertain Value of Authenticity.' *Philosophy and Phenomenological Research*, 95: 261–84.
Montero, B. (2006). 'Proprioception as an Aesthetic Sense.' *Journal of Aesthetics and Art Criticism*, 64: 231–42.
Moore, G. E. (1942). 'A Reply to my Critics.' In *The Philosophy of G. E. Moore*, ed. P. A. Schlipp. New York: Tudor Publishing Co, 533–677.
Morgan, A. (2017). 'Solving the Puzzle of Aesthetic Assertion.' *Southwest Philosophy Review*, 33(1): 95–103.
Mothersill, M. (1961). 'Critical Reasons.' *Philosophical Quarterly*, 2: 74–8.
Mothersill, M. (1994). *Beauty Restored*. Oxford: Oxford University Press.
Neilson, J. (n.d.). 'Artistic Expression and the Law.' Manuscript.
Neta, R., and Rohrbaugh, G. (2004). 'Luminosity and the Safety of Knowledge.' *Pacific Philosophical Quarterly*, 85: 396–406.
Ninan, D. (2014). 'Taste Predicates and the Acquaintance Inference.' *Semantics and Linguistic Theory*, 24: 290–309.
Nguyen, C. T. (2017). 'The Uses of Aesthetic Testimony.' *British Journal of Aesthetics*, 57: 19–36.

Nguyen, C. T. (2020a). 'Autonomy and Aesthetic Engagement.' *Mind*, 129: 1127–56.
Nguyen, C. T. (2020b). 'Echo Chambers and Epistemic Bubbles.' *Episteme*, 17: 141–61.
Nickel, P. (2001). 'Moral Testimony and Its Authority.' *Ethical Theory and Moral Practice*, 4: 253–66.
Novitz, D. (1991). 'Love, Friendship, and the Aesthetics of Character.' *American Philosophical Quarterly*, 28: 207–16.
Owens, D. J. (2003). 'Does Belief have an Aim?' *Philosophical Studies*, 115: 283–305.
Palmira, M. (2015). 'The Semantic Significance of Faultless Disagreement.' *Pacific Philosophical Quarterly*, 96: 349–71.
Pettit, P. (1983). 'The Possibility of Aesthetic Realism.' In *Pleasure, Preference and Value*, ed. E. Schaper. Cambridge: Cambridge University Press, 17–38.
Plassmann, H., O'Doherty, J., Shiv, B., and Rangel, A. (2008). 'Marketing Actions can Modulate Neural Representations of Experienced Pleasantness.' *Proceedings of the National Academy of Sciences*, 105: 1050–4.
Pollock, J. (forthcoming). 'Content Internalism and Testimonial Knowledge.' *Inquiry*.
Potts, C. (2005). *The Logic of Conventional Implicatures*. Oxford: Oxford University Press.
Price, C. (n.d.) 'Belief and Truth: Aim or Function?' Manuscript.
Ranalli, C. (2020). 'The Puzzle of Philosophical Testimony.' *European Journal of Philosophy*, 28: 142–63.
Ransom, M. (2019). 'Frauds, Posers and Sheep: A Virtue Theoretic Solution to the Acquaintance Debate.' *Philosophy and Phenomenological Research*, 98: 417–34.
Reid, T. (1983). *Inquiry and Essays*. Indianapolis: Hackett.
Ridge, M. (2009). 'Moral Assertion for Expressivists.' *Philosophical Issues*, 19: 182–204.
Robson, J. (2012). 'Aesthetic Testimony.' *Philosophy Compass*, 7: 1–10.
Robson, J. (2013). 'Appreciating the Acquaintance Principle: A Reply to Konigsberg.' *British Journal of Aesthetics*, 53: 237–45.
Robson, J. (2014a). 'A Social Epistemology of Aesthetics.' *Synthese*, 191: 2513–28.
Robson, J. (2014b). 'Aesthetic Autonomy and Self-Aggrandisement.' *Royal Institute of Philosophy Supplement*, 75: 3–28.
Robson, J. (2015a). 'Aesthetic Testimony and the Norms of Belief Formation.' *European Journal of Philosophy*. 23: 750–63.
Robson, J. (2015b). 'Norms of Belief and Norms of Assertion in Aesthetics.' *Philosophers' Imprint*, 15: 1–19.
Robson, J. (2017). 'Against Aesthetic Exceptionalism.' In *Art and Belief*, eds. E. Sullivan-Bissett, H. Bradley, and P. Noordhof. Oxford: Oxford University Press, 213–29.
Robson, J. (2018). 'Is Perception the Canonical Route to Aesthetic Judgement.' *Australasian Journal of Philosophy*, 96: 657–68.
Robson, J. (2019). 'Aesthetic Testimony and the Test of Time.' *Philosophy and Phenomenological Research*, 96: 729–48.
Robson, M. I. T. (2011). 'Possible Worlds and the Beauty of God.' *Religious Studies*, 47: 479–92.
Rolph, C. (ed.). (1961). *The Trial of Lady Chatterley*. Baltimore, MD: Penguin.
Rysiew, P. (2007). 'Epistemic Contextualism.' *Stanford Encyclopaedia of Philosophy*, ed. E. Zalta. https://plato.stanford.edu/entries/contextualism-epistemology/.
Saito, Y. (1998). 'The Aesthetics of Unscenic Nature.' *Journal of Aesthetics and Art Criticism*, 56: 101–11.
Salganik, M., and Watts, D. (2008). 'Leading the Herd Astray: An Experimental Study of Self-Fulfilling Prophecies in an Artificial Cultural Market.' *Social Psychology Quarterly*, 71: 338–55.
Savile, A. (1977). 'On Passing the Test of Time.' *British Journal of Aesthetics*, 17: 195–209.

Savile, A. (1982). *The Test of Time*. Oxford: Oxford University Press.
Schaffer, J. (2006). 'The Irrelevance of the Subject: Against Subject-Sensitive Invariantism.' *Philosophical Studies*, 127: 87–107.
Schaffer, J. (2011). 'Perspective in Taste Predicates and Epistemic Modals.' In *Epistemic Modality*, ed. A. Egan and B. Weatherson. Oxford: Oxford University Press, 179–226.
Schlichter, A. (1986). 'The Origins and Deictic Nature of Wintu Evidentials.' *Evidentiality: The Linguistic Coding of Epistemology*, ed. W. Chafe and J. Nichols. Norwood, NJ: Ablex Publishing Corporation, 46–59.
Scruton, R. (1976). *Art and Imagination*. London: Methuen.
Scruton, R. (1979). *The Aesthetics of Architecture*. Princeton: Princeton University Press.
Shaffer, M. (2007). 'Taste, Gastronomic Expertise, and Objectivity.' In *Food and Philosophy: Eat, Think, and Be Merry*, eds. F. Allhoff and D. Monroe. Malden, MA: Blackwell, 73–87.
Shah, N., and Velleman, V. (2005). 'Doxastic Deliberation.' *Philosophical Review*, 114: 497–534.
Shelley, J. R. (1998). 'Hume and the Nature of Taste.' *Journal of Aesthetics and Art Criticism*, 56: 29–38.
Shieber, J. (2009). 'Locke on Testimony: A Reexamination.' *History of Philosophy Quarterly*, 26: 21–41.
Sibley, F. (1959). 'Aesthetic Concepts.' *Philosophical Review*, 68: 421–50.
Sibley, F. (1965). 'Aesthetic and Nonaesthetic.' *Philosophical Review*, 74: 135–59.
Sibley, F. (1968). 'Objectivity and Aesthetics.' *Proceedings of the Aristotelian Society*, 42: 31–72.
Sibley, F. (1974). 'Particularity, Art and Evaluation.' *Proceedings of the Aristotelian Society*, 48: 1–21.
Sinclair, N. (2006). 'The Moral Belief Problem.' *Ratio*, 19: 249–60.
Sinclair, N. (2007). 'Propositional Clothing and Belief.' *Philosophical Quarterly*, 57: 342–62.
Sinclair, N., and Robson, J. (forthcoming). 'Speculative Aesthetic Expressivism.' *British Journal of Aesthetics*.
Sliwa, P. (2012). 'In Defense of Moral Testimony.' *Philosophical Studies*, 158: 175–95.
Smith, B., Smith, T., Taylor, L., and Hobby, M. (2005). 'Relationship between Intelligence and Vocabulary.' *Perceptual and Motor Skills*, 100: 101–8.
Smith, B.C. (2007). 'The Objectivity of Tastes and Tastings.' In *Questions of Taste: The Philosophy of Wine*, ed. B. Smith. Oxford: Signal Books, 41–78.
Smith, M. J. (1994). 'Must Reliable Signals Always be Costly?' *Animal Behaviour*, 47: 1115–20.
Sorensen, R. (2007). 'Bald-Faced Lies! Lying without the Intent to Deceive.' *Pacific Philosophical Quarterly*, 88: 251–64.
Sosa, E. (1991). *Knowledge in Perspective: Selected Essays in Epistemology*. Cambridge: Cambridge University Press.
Sosa, E. (2006). 'Scepticism about Intuition.' *Philosophy*, 81: 633–48.
Soucek, B. (2009). 'Resisting the Itch to Redefine Aesthetics: A Response to Sherri Irvin.' *Journal of Aesthetics and Art Criticism*, 67: 223–6.
Stanley, J. (2005). *Knowledge and Practical Interests*. Oxford: Clarendon Press.
Steglich-Petersen, A. (2006). 'No Norm Needed: On the Aim of Belief.' *Philosophical Quarterly*, 56: 499–516.
Stevenson, C. L. (1963). *Facts and Values: Studies in Ethical Analysis*. New Haven: Yale University Press.
Sweeney, K. W. (2007). 'Can Soup be Beautiful? The Rise of Gastronomy and the Aesthetics of Food.' In *Food and Philosophy: Eat, Think, and be Merry*, ed. F. Allhoff and D. Monroe. Malden, MA: Wiley-Blackwell, 117–32.

Tanner, M. (2003). 'Ethics and Aesthetics are —?' In *Art and Morality*, ed. J. Bermudez and S. Gardner. New York: Routledge, 19–36.
Tobia, K., Buckwalter, W., and Stich, S. (2013). 'Moral Intuitions: Are Philosophers Experts?' *Philosophical Psychology*, 26(5): 629–38.
Todd, C. S. (2004). 'Quasi-Realism, Acquaintance and the Normative Claims of Aesthetic Judgement.' *British Journal of Aesthetics,* 44: 277–96.
Tormey, A. (1973). 'Critical Judgments.' *Theoria*, 39: 35–49.
Vrij, A., Fisher, R., Mann, S., and Leal, S. (2008). 'A Cognitive Load Approach to Lie Detection.' *Journal of Investigative Psychology and Offender Profiling*, 5: 39–43.
Wallbank, R., and Robson, J. (2022). 'Over-Appreciating Appreciation.' In *Perspectives on Taste*, ed. J. Wyatt, J. Zakkou, and D. Zeman. Abingdon, Oxon: Routledge, 40–57.
Warner, M. (2016). *The Aesthetics of Argument*. Oxford: Oxford University Press.
Weinberg, J. M. (2007). 'How to Challenge Intuitions Empirically Without Risking Skepticism.' *Midwest Studies in Philosophy,* 31: 318–43.
Weinberg, J. M., Gonnerman, C., Buckner, C., and Alexander, J. (2010). 'Are Philosophers Expert Intuiters?' *Philosophical Psychology*, 23(3): 331–55.
Weiner, M. (2003). 'Accepting Testimony.' *Philosophical Quarterly*, 53(211): 256–64.
Weiner, M. (2007). 'Norms of Assertion.' *Philosophy Compass*, 2: 187–95.
Weiner, M. (2006). 'Are All Conversational Implicatures Cancellable?' *Analysis*, 66: 127–30.
Welbourne, M. (1981). 'The Community of Knowledge.' *Philosophical Quarterly*, 31: 302–14.
Welbourne, M. (1994). 'Testimony, Knowledge and Belief.' In *Knowing from Words*, ed. B. K. Matilal and A. Chakrabarti. Dordrecht: Springer. 297–313.
Welbourne, M. (1986). *The Community of Knowledge*. Aberdeen: Aberdeen University Press.
Whiting, D. (2013a). 'Nothing But the Truth: On the Norms and Aims of Belief.' In *The Aim of Belief*, ed. T. Chan. Oxford: Oxford University Press, 184–203.
Whiting, D. (2013b). 'Truth: The Aim and Norm of Belief.' *Teorema*, 32: 121–35.
Whiting, D. (2015). 'The Glass is Half Empty: A New Argument for Pessimism about Aesthetic Testimony.' *British Journal of Aesthetics,* 55: 91–107.
Williams, B. (1972). 'Knowledge and Reasons.' In *Problems in the Theory of Knowledge*, ed. G. H. Von Wright. The Hague: Martinus Nijhoff, 1–14.
Williams, B. (1995). *Making Sense of Humanity and Other Philosophical Papers 1982–1993*. Cambridge: Cambridge University Press.
Williamson, T. (1996). 'Knowing and Asserting.' *Philosophical Review,* 105: 489–523.
Williamson, T. (2000). *Knowledge and Its Limits*. Oxford: Oxford University Press.
Williamson, T. (2005). 'Knowledge, Context and Agent's Point of View.' In *Contextualism in Philosophy*, ed. G. Preyer and G. Peter. Oxford: Oxford University Press, 91–114.
Wittgenstein, L. (1967). *Lectures and Conversations on Aesthetics, Psychology and Religious Belief*. Berkeley, CA: University of California Press.
Wollheim, R. (1980). *Art and its Objects*, 2nd ed. Cambridge: Cambridge University Press.
Young, J. O. (2017). 'Introduction.' In *Semantics of Aesthetic Judgements*, ed. J. Young. Oxford: Oxford University Press, 1–16.
Zangwill, N. (1990). 'Two Dogmas of Kantian Aesthetics.' *Proceedings of XIth International Congress in Aesthetics*. Nottingham: Nottingham Polytechnic Press, 1–12.
Zangwill, N. (1995). 'The Beautiful, the Dainty and the Dumpy.' *British Journal of Aesthetics*, 35(4): 317–30.
Zangwill, N. (2002). 'Are There Counterexamples to Aesthetic Theories of Art?' *Journal of Aesthetics and Art Criticism*, 60: 111–18.

Index

For the benefit of digital users, indexed terms that span two pages (e.g., 52-53) may, on occasion, appear on only one of those pages.

Acquaintance Principle, the 8-9, 46-50, 63-8, 71-2, 121-4
aesthetic common knowledge 99-101, 110-13, 115-18, 147-8
aesthetic practices 12, 29, 58, 99, 105-8, 112-13, 134
aesthetics
  of character 14, 149
  of God 14
  of mathematics 14-15, 143-4
  of nature 14, 99-101, 109, 112-13, 116-18, 143
  scope of 10, 13-16
Andow, J 19-20, 26, 47, 81-4, 96
Appreciative Signalling Account 126-8, 130-2, 134-8, 140-2, 144-9, 152-3
appreciation 10-11, 29, 32-3, 40, 45-53, 56-7, 65, 74, 83, 85, 98, 101-2, 126, 128, 130, 143-4, 151
argument from assertion 40-1, 57-8, 96, 119-53
asymmetry theses 20-7, 29-30, 84-5, 94-6, 104-5, 112
Augustine 1

Baker, T 145
bank cases 88-91, 93, 114-16
Beardsley, MC 7, 14
Blackburn, S 18, 30, 39-40, 76-7, 119
Brown, J 37-8, 93
Budd, M 7-9, 37, 42-3, 45-6, 48-9, 63

Cappelen, H 56
Carroll, N 136
Coady, CAJ 1-3, 135-6
conventional implicature 139-40, 147
conversational implicature 139-40, 147
Creative Signalling Account 125-6
Currie, G 75, 124-5
Cutting, JE 59

Davies, S 124-6
DeRose, K 88-91, 94-5, 114-16
Dickie, G 48-9, 52, 61
disagreement 9-10, 16, 41, 103-5, 117-18, 150-3
disguised mules 91-2
Don Quixote 149n19
Dretske, FI 91
Dutton, D 124-7

Eaton, A 115n23
Emma 102-3

emotivism 39-40, 83
epistemic contextualism 11-12, 30, 79, 87-96, 98-100, 111, 113-16, 118
epistemic norms 28, 71, 86-8, 93, 123n12
evolution 125-6
expressivism 10-11, 18, 38-46, 51, 75-8

folk belief 55-7, 83
folk practice 54-5, 57-60, 62
Franzén, N 30, 138-9
Freeland, C 141n6
Frege-Geach problem 51
Fricker, E 41
Friend, S 80
friendly recommendations 105-6, 111-12

Gaut, B 14-15
Gibbard, A 40, 44-6, 51-2, 76-7
Ginsburgh, V 60-1
Goldman, AH 56, 65-6, 149
Goldman, AI 9-10
Gorodeisky, K 28, 30, 33-4, 36-7, 50-1, 96, 105-6
Graham, PJ 3
Grice, HP 124
Gricean maxims 72-3, 120-1, 124, 128
gustatory taste 1-2, 21-2, 65-6, 138, 144-8

Hanson, L 15n4, 35n4
Hawthorne, J 56, 93
Hazlett, A 19-20, 26, 47, 66-7, 80-2, 86, 114
Hills, A 1-2, 21-2, 64-7, 74-5, 80, 130n25
Hopkins, R 1, 7, 16-17, 19-22, 24-8, 33-4, 47, 51, 63, 66-7, 73-4, 80, 86-8, 91-3, 105-6, 108-11, 120-1, 124, 134, 149
Hume, D 4-5, 14, 84-5, 115-16
Hutcheson, F 6

Ichino, A 75
invariantism 93, 112-13
intuitions 11, 56-7, 79-86, 96, 99-105, 108-9, 111-15, 141
Irvin, S 14, 19
Iseminger, G 49

judgement
  accounts of 16-18, 68-9
  aesthetic 13-18
  colour 20-2, 37-8, 48, 85, 119, 145

judgement (*cont.*)
  gustatory–*see* gustatory taste
  mundane 21–6, 29, 35, 37, 56, 58, 61–3, 65–6, 68, 70–2, 74–5, 80–2, 95–6, 104–5, 117–19

Kant, I 5–7, 14, 33–4, 58, 64, 150–1
Kieran, M 85, 126–9
Konigsberg, A 49–50
Korsmeyer, C 14, 65, 145

Lackey, J 1–4, 119, 122–3
Lady Chatterley case 106n11, 135–6, 141, 143, 150
Laetz, B 8–9, 20, 33, 36–7, 39–40, 100, 106–7, 141
Levinson, J 49, 101
Lewis, D 116–17, 144–5
Liao, S 81, 83–4
Lillehammer, H 17
Livingston, P 36
Locke, J 1
Lopes, DM 19, 46–9
Lord, E 19–20, 96n35
lost works 11–12, 100, 103–4, 109, 111–12, 143, 144n12

McGonigal, A 34
McGrath, S 64–5
McKinnon, R 19–20
Marcus, E 50–1
Matravers, D 39–40
Meskin, A 7–9, 15–16, 19, 24–5, 33, 36, 39–40, 47, 50, 56–8, 81–5, 122–3
meta-aesthetics 18, 75–6
Miller, G 124–5
Millikan, RG 69n22
minimal belief 76
moral testimony 2n3, 9n27, 20–2, 40–1, 64–8, 74–5
Mothersill, M 6–7, 30, 119

Neilson, J 106–7, 135–6
Nguyen, CT 19–20, 26, 29, 97–8, 106–7, 109–10, 142
Ninan, D 122–3, 138–9, 147
non-reductionism 4–5, 25–6
Norms
  Epistemic 71, 86–7, 93
  non-epistemic 28, 86–8, 108, 112
  of assertion 14, 96, 119–49
  of belief 19–20, 68–73, 137–8, 149

optimism concerning aesthetic testimony
  constitutive 11, 30, 54–5, 68, 78
  contextualist 11, 30, 79, 94–6, 98–100, 111, 113–15, 118
  descriptive 58, 61–2
  extreme 26–7, 30–1, 81–2, 94, 114–15
  moderate 30, 81–2, 112
Ours, J 60–1

pessimism concerning aesthetic testimony
  constitutive 10–11, 28, 32–53
  descriptive 58–62, 69
  extreme 19–20, 26, 103–4, 111–12
  moderate 81–2, 103–4
  unavailability 10–12, 28–9, 33, 69–72, 86, 95, 101–6, 108, 111–12
  unusability 10–12, 28–9, 33–4, 69–70, 86–8, 99, 103–4, 106–12
Pettit, P 8–9, 28, 37, 47–8
principles of taste 7, 63, 122
private display 97
public display 106–7, 109–10

Ransom, M 47n23
reductionism 4–5, 25–6
Reid, T 1, 4–5
relativism 56, 83, 117
relevant alternatives 30, 90–2, 94, 113

Saito, Y 14
Salganik, M 60
sceptical alternatives 94–6, 115–18
scepticism
  global 19
  about intuitions 82–3
  about testimony 19, 21–3, 56, 73–4, 101–2
  about the aesthetic 19, 23, 56, 69, 73–4, 104–5
Scruton, R 18, 37, 40–5, 75–6, 145
Sibley, F 7, 14–16, 32–3, 36–8, 80, 115–16
signaling 85, 120, 125–30, 132–4, 137, 146–7
Sinclair, N 17, 39, 76
Sliwa, P 41, 67
social epistemology 9–10, 152–3
Sorensen, R 3–4
Sosa, E 3–4
Stanley, J 93

Todd, CS 16–18, 34, 37–42, 45–6, 50–1, 75–6
Tormey, A 7–8, 16–17

uliefs 74–5, 78
Understanding 29, 45, 66–7, 66n20, 74–5

Watts, D 60
Weiner, M 120, 140
Whiting, D 28, 47, 72, 79–80
Williams, B 1–2, 21–2, 64–7
Williamson, T 71, 120
Wittgenstein, L 61
Wollheim, R 8, 19–20, 46–9, 63, 65–6